PRINCE2® for Beginners

Thinking about using PRINCE2 to manage your projects or preparing for PRINCE2 training? Need a rounded introduction to help you get to grips with the basics?

PRINCE2® for Beginners: from introduction to passing your Foundation exam is the perfect start. This readable end-to-end explanation is simple enough to introduce you to the basics, yet includes everything you need to know to get through the Foundation exam. This new concise edition starts from a more accessible level than other detailed manuals or brief refreshers and will help ease you into the topic and put the method into a real-world context.

This new concise edition now includes more support for the Foundation exam, including a student guide to the exam itself, sample answers and explanations. Whether you are looking for a reliable introduction or a quick reference to prepare you for PRINCE2 training and study, *PRINCE2® for Beginners* will give you the grounding to take your knowledge and application to the next level.

Colin Bentley has been a project manager since 1966, working as a consultant to many international firms such as the London Stock Exchange, Microsoft Europe, Tesco Stores and the BBC. Bentley has been working with PRINCE2, PRINCE and its predecessor, PROMPT II, since 1975. He wrote the original PRINCE2 manual and was the author of all revisions to the manual until 2009. He was the Chief Examiner for all examination papers in PRINCE2 until his retirement in 2010.

'PRINCE2 is the most widely used and highly respected project management method in the world. With his inimitable clear and direct style, Colin makes it crystal-clear what PRINCE2 is all about. The method is presented in a way that makes all elements simple to understand. Colin has turned decades of experience into a well-structured narrative that will pay dividends to any reader for many years to come, on their journey from taking the Foundation examination to becoming an experienced practitioner.'

John Howarth, Chairman,
Tanner James Management Consultants,
Australia

'Colin has done an excellent job in summarising the PRINCE2 manual and I have no hesitation is recommending this book to anyone with an interest in PRINCE2 who would like an understanding of the method, and for those studying for their Foundation Qualification it will be invaluable.'

David W. Atkinson FAPM

PRINCE2® for Beginners

From introduction to passing your Foundation exam

Fourth edition

Colin Bentley

LONDON AND NEW YORK

First published in 1997 as Prince2™ A Practical Handbook
Second edition 2002
Third edition 2010
By Butterworth-Heinemann, an imprint of Elsevier

Fourth edition 2015
By Routledge
2 Park Square, Milton Park, Abingdon, Oxon OX14 4RN

and by Routledge
711 Third Avenue, New York, NY 10017

Routledge is an imprint of the Taylor & Francis Group, an informa business

British Library Cataloguing in Publication Data
A catalogue record for this book is available from the British Library

Library of Congress Cataloging in Publication Data
Bentley, Colin.
[Prince 2]
PRINCE 2 for beginners: from introduction to passing your foundation exam / Colin Bentley. -- Fourth edition.
pages cm
"First published 1997 as Prince 2: A Practical Handbook"--Title page verso.
Includes bibliographical references and index.
1. Project management--Great Britain. I. Title. II. Title: PRINCE2 for beginners.
HD69.P75B463 2015
658.4'040941--dc23
2014030742

ISBN: 978-1-138-82412-6 (hbk)
ISBN: 978-1-138-82413-3 (pbk)
ISBN: 978-1-315-74091-1 (ebk)

Typeset in Bembo and Optima
by GreenGate Publishing Services, Tonbridge, Kent

Contents

Chapter 1

Introduction

This book is intended for those who require a basic understanding of the PRINCE2® method and/or are looking to pass the PRINCE2 Foundation exam. For those with a basic understanding of PRINCE2 and a wish to go further, I would strongly recommend the companion book, *The PRINCE2 Practitioner.*

'Project management is just common sense.' Of course it is. So why do so many of us get it wrong? Even if we get one project right, we probably make a mess of the next. And why do we keep getting it wrong time after time? You need to be armed with a little more than common sense when diving into a project such as constructing a pyramid. It is no good getting half way through, then remembering you forgot to put in the damp course!

Why do so many professionals say they are project managing, when what they are actually doing is firefighting?

The answer is that, where project management is concerned, most of us do not learn from our mistakes. We do not think about the process, document it, structure it, repeat it and use past experience to improve the model. Problems are likely to arise in every project we tackle, but many of these problems could have been avoided by planning ahead and controlling how things happen against that plan.

Those who are starting a project for the first time should not have to re-invent the wheel. They should be able to build on the experience of previous project managers. By the time we are doing our tenth project we should have a method that helps us avoid mistakes we made in the previous nine.

PRINCE2 is a structured project management method based on the experience of many other project managers – some who have contributed from their mistakes or omissions, others from their success. It can be applied to any kind or size of project, i.e. the basic philosophy is always the same. The method should be tailored to suit the size, importance and environment of the project. Common sense says, 'Don't use a sledgehammer to crack a walnut', but equally do not agree important things informally where there is any chance of a disagreement later over what was agreed.

1.1 TYPICAL PROJECT PROBLEMS

So let's have a look at some typical problems from several different points of view.

Many years ago I was asked to implement PRINCE2 in the computer department of a large international company. They had drawn up a list of six typical complaints from their customers.

1. The end product was not what we originally asked for.
2. The system and the project changed direction without our realizing it.
3. The costs escalated without our realizing it, but by then it was too late to stop.
4. We were told the system would be delivered late, but by this time, it was too late for us or the computer department to supply extra effort.
5. We were not kept informed during most of the development, and even now we do not really understand how to make the system work.
6. The programs are not reliable, hence maintenance costs are more than we expected.

This was an embarrassing list for them, showing that the customers were ignored during most of the project. This was apart from poor planning and control problems during the project from their own perspective.

Speaking of control, the now-defunct Hoskyns Group did a survey of projects some years ago and listed symptoms that they found to indicate projects that were out of control. You might recognize some of the symptoms:

- Unclear direction.
- Over- or under-worked staff.
- People and equipment not available when needed.
- Examples of rework or wasted effort.
- The final tasks were rushed.
- Poor quality work.
- Projects late and overspent.
- Small problems had a big impact.

But why do these problems occur? Their causes show the reasons why a formal project management method is needed:

- Lack of customer involvement.
- Lack of coordination.
- Lack of communication.
- Inadequate planning.
- Lack of progress control.
- Lack of quality control.
- Insufficient measurables.

So there we have it. Without good project management projects will:

- take more time than expected;
- cost more than expected;
- deliver a product that is not exactly what the customer wants;
- deliver a product of inadequate quality;
- not reveal their exact status until they finish (if they ever do!).

These experiences show us why a good project management method, such as PRINCE2, is needed if our projects are to be well managed and controlled.

1.2 BENEFITS OF A PROJECT MANAGEMENT METHOD

- The method is repeatable and therefore teachable.
- It builds on experience.
- Everyone knows what to expect.
- If a project is handed over in the middle, it is useful to know what documents to look for and where to find them.
- There is early warning of problems.
- It is proactive, not reactive (but has to be prepared to be reactive to unexpected events – illness, pregnancy, accident, external event).

Organizations are becoming increasingly aware of the opportunities for adopting a 'project' approach to the way in which they address the creation and delivery of new business products or implement any change. They are also increasingly aware of the benefits which a single, common, structured approach to project management can bring – as is provided through PRINCE2.

Chapter 2

An Overview of PRINCE2

2.1 INTRODUCTION

All organizations need to change and move on in order to survive. Standing still often means going backwards, but 'business as usual' has to continue. Therefore, an organization has to do two things:

1. Carry on with everyday 'business as usual' operations.
2. Change and upgrade those 'business as usual' operations to match the direction and strategies needed for the future.

The changing and upgrading is done by projects.

PRINCE2 is a scalable, flexible project management method, suitable for use on any type of project. It has been derived from the experiences of professional project managers, and refined over years of use in a wide variety of contexts. It is owned by Axelos and is available free of charge for users. Axelos has an ongoing commitment to maintaining the currency of the method, together with the manual.

PRINCE2 provides:

1. controlled management of change by the business in terms of its investment and return on investment;
2. active involvement of the users of the final product throughout its development to ensure the business product will meet the functional, environmental, service and management requirements of the users;
3. more efficient control of development resources.

A key approach of the method is that it firmly distinguishes the *management* of the development process from the *techniques* involved in the development process itself.

2.2 PROJECT CHARACTERISTICS

PRINCE2 defines five characteristics of project work that make a project different from regular business operations:

1. **Change:** We use projects to introduce change to a business.
2. **Uncertainty:** A project changes one or more things or develops something new. These are steps into the unknown, and introduce uncertainty in what will be ahead of us in the project.
3. **Temporary:** A project team comes together, does a job and is then disbanded.
4. **Unique:** In some major or minor ways each project is unique. It may be completely unlike anything we have done before, or we may have repeated the same job several times, but at a different location or with different people.
5. **Cross-functional:** A project needs different people with different skills; some to define what is required, others to develop the required products. These people may work for several different line managers, maybe even different companies. So managing these resources is a potential problem for the Project Manager.

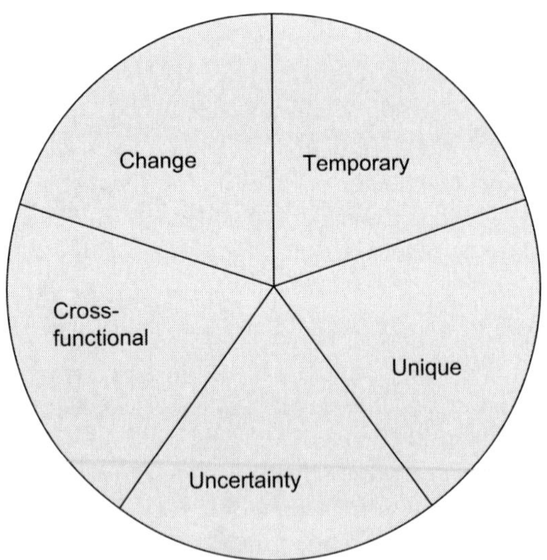

FIGURE 2.1 Project characteristics

2.3 PROJECT PERFORMANCE VARIABLES

If a project is to be successful, there are six project performance variables to control:

1. Cost.
2. Time.
3. Quality.
4. Scope.
5. Benefits.
6. Risk.

2.4 KEY PRINCIPLES

There are seven principles on which PRINCE2 is founded (Figure 2.2). This set of principles is unique to the PRINCE2 method. As you read this book, you will see how they are interwoven with the processes and themes to form a tremendously strong structure.

The seven PRINCE2 principles are:

1. Continued business justification.
2. Learn from experience.
3. Defined roles and responsibilities.
4. Manage by stages.
5. Manage by exception.
6. Focus on products.
7. Tailor to suit the project environment.

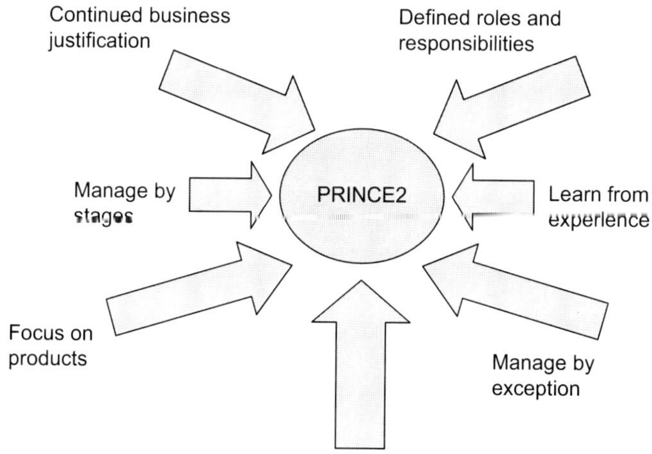

FIGURE 2.2 The seven PRINCE2 principles

The seven principles are expanded below.

2.4.1 Continued Business Justification

PRINCE2 states that a project should be driven by its Business Case. Even projects to meet compulsory requirements should be justified. The existence of a viable Business Case should be proved before the project is allowed to start, and its continued justification should be confirmed at all major decision points during the project. This principle can be summarized in the following points:

- Do not start a project unless there is a sound Business Case for it.
- Check that the project is still viable at regular intervals in the project.
- Stop the project if the justification has disappeared.
- The Business Case should be:
  - documented and approved;
  - the basis for all decision-making.
- Ensure the project remains aligned to its business objectives and the expected benefits.

Justification for the project may change, but it must remain valid.

2.4.2 Learn from Experience

Project management should never be 'reinventing the wheel'. Those involved in the project may have previous experience, there will be earlier projects in the company from which lessons can be learned and there are other sources (for example, the internet, suppliers, sister companies) of valuable lessons that can be used by the project.

Lessons learned should be sought at the beginning of a project (in the process *Starting up a Project*) and as the project progresses, and any new lessons learned during the project passed on to other projects at the close.

2.4.3 Defined Roles and Responsibilities

Project management is different from line management.

Projects require a temporary organization for a finite timescale and a specific business purpose. Managing the project staff can be a headache for a Project Manager. A project is temporary and may include staff who report to different line managers or even work for other organizations. The project may require a mixture of full-time and part-time resources. So how do we ensure that everyone knows who is responsible for what?

An explicit project management team structure is required. Project staff must know not only their own roles and responsibilities, but also those of others. Good communication depends on this.

The roles and responsibilities are divided into three groups, the interests of which must be represented in any project (Figure 2.3). These are:

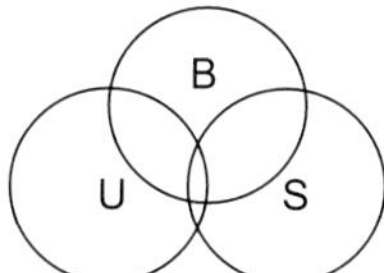

FIGURE 2.3 Business, user and supplier interests

- Business.
- User.
- Supplier.

PRINCE2 provides an organization structure that engages everyone involved: the business, user and supplier stakeholder interests. Within the structure there are defined roles and responsibilities for every member of the project management team. Those appointed agree to a role description and sign their acceptance of that role. (Depending on the size of the project, roles can be split or combined.)

2.4.4 Manage by Stages

This comes from two different thoughts:

1. In PRINCE2, the business, user and supplier interests combine to provide a management team in overall control of the project. This is called the Project Board. The members still have their own work responsibilities. The Project Manager has the day-to-day control of the project, but the Project Board is ultimately accountable for the project. PRINCE2 doesn't like the idea of regular progress meetings, but there must be some key points in a project when the Project Board needs to review progress and decide if it wants to continue with the project. A project is therefore broken down into stages, based on delivery of the project's products, to form these key points.
2. Very often a project will last longer and contain more detail than can be planned with any accuracy at the outset.

Based on these thoughts, PRINCE2 divides a project into management stages. PRINCE2 has a Project Plan, an overview of the whole project, which is often a 'best guess', but the Project Manager plans only the next stage in detail – only as much as can be accurately judged – and the Project Board keeps control by approving only one stage at a time, reviewing the status at stage end and deciding whether to continue or not.

The number of stages depends on the size, complexity and risk content of the project.

At the end of each stage, a plan is presented for the next stage, together with an updated view of the Business Case, Project Plan, the risks and suggested tolerances for the next stage. Thus senior management can review progress so far and decide from the information presented to them whether to authorize the next stage or not.

2.4.5 Manage by Exception

PRINCE2 recognizes four levels of authority in a project. Authority is delegated from one management level to the next. Each management level is allocated tolerances within which they can continue without the need to refer to the next higher level of management. There are six tolerance limits:

1. **Time:** +/− amounts of time on the target completion dates.
2. **Cost:** +/− amounts of planned budget.
3. **Quality:** +/− degrees off a quality target (for example, a product that weighs a target 10kg with an allowed −50g to +10g tolerance).
4. **Scope:** permissible variation of the plan's products (for example, mandatory requirements +/− desirable requirements).
5. **Risk:** limits on the plan's exposure to threats (for example, the risk of not meeting the target date against the risk of overspending).
6. **Benefit:** +/− degrees off an improvement goal (for example, 30% to 40% staff saving).

To cut down on unnecessary meetings or problem referrals, PRINCE2 has the principle of allowing a management level to continue its work as long as there is no forecast that a tolerance will be exceeded. Only when there is a forecast of a tolerance being exceeded does the next higher level of authority need to be consulted.

FIGURE 2.4 Four levels of authority

2.4.6 Focus on Products

A PRINCE2 project focuses on the definition and delivery of products, in particular their quality requirements. Planning, controls and quality needs are all product-based. (See Appendix C – Product-based Planning.)

2.4.7 Tailor to Suit the Project Environment

PRINCE2 is tailored to suit the project's environment, size, risk, complexity, importance, and capability of the people involved. Tailoring is considered before the project begins; roles may be split or combined, processes and documents may be combined, it may be agreed that some reports can be oral, and some decisions made by phone or email, rather than at meetings.

2.5 STRUCTURE OF THE PRINCE2 METHOD

There are three parts to the structure of the method itself:

- Processes.
- Themes.
- Techniques.

It offers a set of *processes* that provide a controlled start, controlled progress and a controlled close to a project. The processes explain what should happen and when it should be done.

It has a number of *themes* to explain its philosophy about various project aspects, why they are needed and how they can be used. This philosophy is implemented through the processes.

It offers only a few *techniques*. The use of most of them is optional. You may already have a technique that is covering that need satisfactorily. The exception is the Product-based Planning technique. This is a very important part of the PRINCE2 method. Its understanding and use bring major benefits, and every effort should be made to use it.

PRINCE2 has a process-based approach to project management. The processes define the management activities to be carried out during the project. In addition, PRINCE2 describes a number of themes that are applied within the appropriate processes. Figure 2.5 shows the themes positioned around the central process model.

2.5.1 The Themes

The PRINCE2 themes are the following.

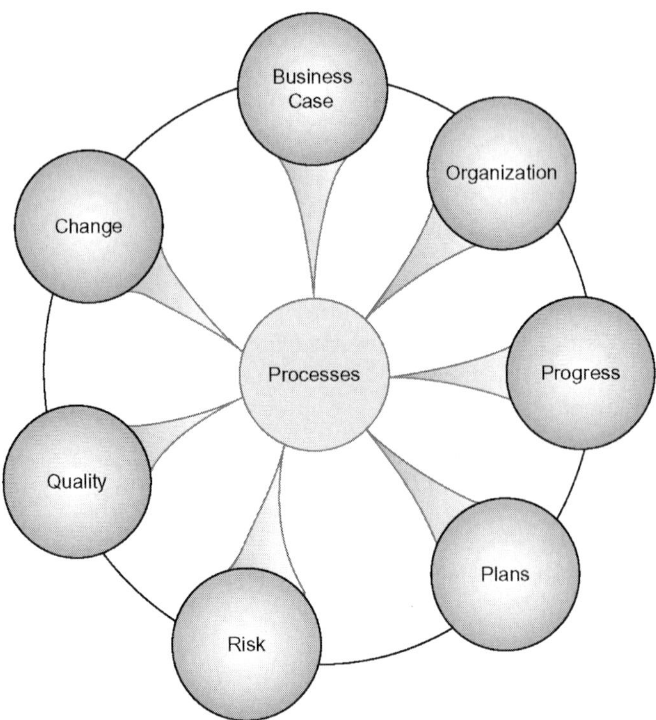

FIGURE 2.5 The PRINCE2 themes

2.5.1.1 Business Case

Every project should be driven by a business need. If it has no justification in terms of the business, it should not be undertaken. The Project Board should check the existence of a valid Business Case before the project begins and at every end stage assessment.

2.5.1.2 Organization

PRINCE2 provides the structure of a project management team, plus a definition of the roles, responsibilities and relationships of all staff involved in the project. PRINCE2 describes *roles*. According to the size and complexity of a project, these roles can be combined or shared.

2.5.1.3 Plans

PRINCE2 offers a series of plan levels that can be tailored to the size and needs of a project, and an approach to planning based on products rather than activities.

2.5.1.4 Progress

PRINCE2 has a set of controls which facilitate the provision of key decision-making information, allowing the organization to pre-empt problems and make decisions on problem resolution. For senior management these controls are based on the concept of 'management by exception', i.e. if we agree a plan, let the Project Manager get on with it unless something is forecast to go wrong.

A project is split into stages as a way of defining the review and commitment points of a project in order to promote sound management control of risk and investment.

2.5.1.5 Quality

PRINCE2 recognizes the importance of quality and incorporates a quality approach to the management and technical processes. It begins by establishing the customer's quality expectations and follows these up by laying down standards and quality inspection methods to be used, and checking that these are being used correctly throughout the project life cycle.

2.5.1.6 Risk

Risk is a major factor to be considered during the life of a project. PRINCE2 defines the key moments when risks should be reviewed, outlines an approach to the analysis and management of risk and tracks these through all the processes.

2.5.1.7 Change

The Change theme covers change control and configuration management – two tasks that go hand in hand.

PRINCE2 emphasizes the need for change control, and this is enforced by a change control technique plus identification of the processes that apply the change control.

Tracking the components of a final product and their versions for release is called 'configuration management'. There are many methods of configuration management available. PRINCE2 does not attempt to invent a new one, but defines the essential facilities and information requirements for a configuration management method and how it should link with other PRINCE2 themes and techniques.

2.5.2 The Processes

The steps of project management are described in seven processes, which are summarized in Figure 2.6.

Any project run under PRINCE2 will need to address each of these processes *in some form*. However, the key to successful use of the process model

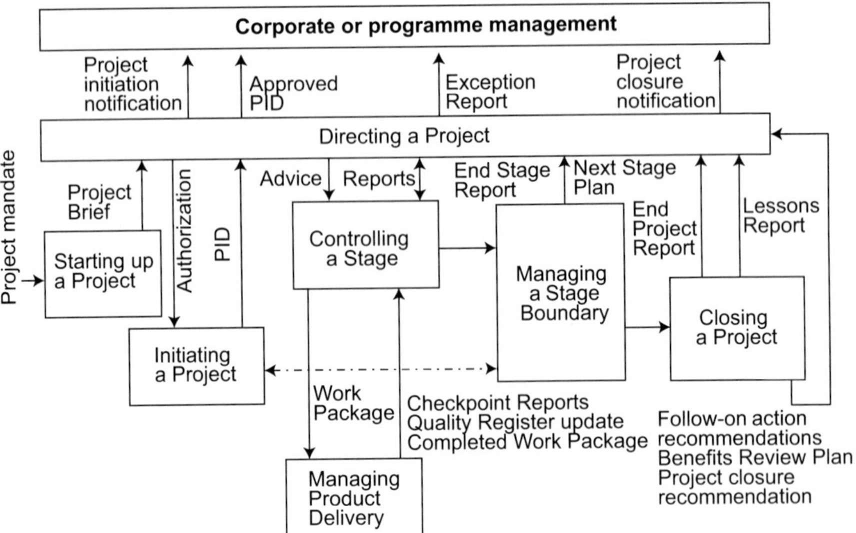

FIGURE 2.6 The seven PRINCE2 processes

is in tailoring it to the needs of the individual project. Each process should be approached with the question: 'How extensively should this process be applied on this project?'

2.5.2.1 Starting up a Project

This process is intended to be a very short, pre-project process with six objectives:

1. Design and appoint the project management team.
2. Ensure that the objectives of the project are known.
3. Decide on the approach which will be taken by the project to provide a solution.
4. Identify the customer's quality expectations.
5. Identify the project tolerances set by senior management.
6. Plan the work needed to draw up the PRINCE2 'contract' between customer and supplier.

2.5.2.2 Initiating a Project

This process identifies how the required quality will be achieved, creates a Project Plan to give a guide on how long the project will take and what the cost is likely to be. It then prepares the information on whether there is sufficient justification to proceed with the project, establishes a sound management basis for the project and creates a detailed plan for the next stage – as much of the project as management wish to authorize. The management product created is the Project Initiation Documentation, the baseline against which progress and success will be measured.

2.5.2.3 Directing a Project

This process is aimed at the Project Board, the management team representing the sponsor, the users of the final product and the suppliers of the product. These roles are responsible for the project, and are the key decision-makers. They are usually very busy people and should be involved only in the decision-making process of a project. PRINCE2 helps them achieve this by adopting the philosophy of 'management by exception'. The *Directing a Project* process covers the steps to be taken by the Project Board throughout the project from start-up to project closure and has five major steps:

1. Authorizing the preparation of a Project Plan and Business Case for the project.
2. Approving the project go-ahead.
3. Checking that the project remains justifiable at key points in the project life cycle.
4. Monitoring progress and giving advice as required.
5. Ensuring that the project comes to a controlled close.

2.5.2.4 Controlling a Stage

This process describes the Project Manager's monitoring and control activities in ensuring that a stage stays on course and reacting to unexpected events. The process forms the core of the Project Manager's effort on the project, and is the process that handles day-to-day management of the project development activity.

Throughout a stage there will be many cycles of:

- Authorizing work to be done.
- Gathering progress information about that work.
- Watching for changes to requirements.
- Watching for changes in risks.
- Reviewing the stage status.
- Reporting.
- Taking any necessary corrective action.

The process covers these cycles, together with the ongoing work of the management of risk and change control.

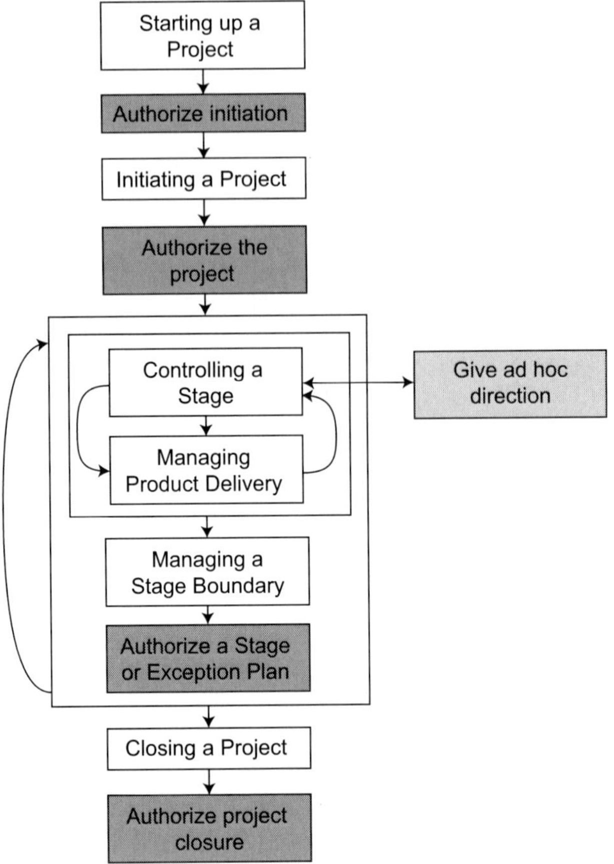

FIGURE 2.7 Stage work cycle

2.5.2.5 Managing Product Delivery

This process provides a control mechanism so that the Project Manager and specialist teams can agree details of the work required. This is particularly important where one or more teams are from third party suppliers and may not be using PRINCE2. The work agreed between the Project Manager and Team Manager, including target dates, quality and reporting requirements, is called a Work Package.

The process covers:

- making sure that work allocated to the team is authorized and agreed;
- planning the team work;
- ensuring that the work is done;
- ensuring that products meet the agreed quality criteria;

- reporting any new risks or changes to the Project Manager;
- reporting on progress and quality to the Project Manager;
- obtaining acceptance of the finished products.

2.5.2.6 Managing a Stage Boundary

The objectives of this process are to:

- check that all work from the current stage is finished;
- plan the next stage;
- update the Project Plan;
- update the Business Case;
- update the risk assessment;
- report on the outcome and performance of the stage which has just ended;
- obtain Project Board approval to move into the next stage.

If the Project Board requests the Project Manager to produce an Exception Plan (see '8.7 Produce an Exception Plan' for an explanation), this process also covers the steps needed for that.

2.5.2.7 Closing a Project

This process covers the Project Manager's work to request Project Board permission to close the project either at its natural end or at a premature close decided by the Project Board. The objectives are to:

- note the extent to which the objectives set out at the start of the project have been met;
- confirm the user acceptance of the final products;
- confirm that maintenance and support arrangements are in place (where appropriate);
- make any recommendations for follow-on actions;
- ensure that all lessons learned during the project are annotated for the benefit of future projects;
- report on whether the project management activity itself has been a success or not;
- prepare a plan to check on achievement of the product's claimed benefits.

2.6 STRUCTURE OF THIS BOOK

Having gone through an introduction and overview of the PRINCE2 method of project management, this book will explore the processes and themes. This will provide a project skeleton and a general project timeframe, and where appropriate there will be links from processes to the themes. It also includes sample descriptions of the PRINCE2 roles and standard Product Descriptions.

Chapter 3

Starting up a Project (SU)

3.1 WHAT DOES THE PROCESS DO?

How does a project start? A 'project mandate' is the term used in PRINCE2 to describe the trigger for a project. The project mandate handed down to the Project Manager may be a full specification of a problem, a brief written request to 'look into' something or 'do something about …', or even a verbal request (Figure 3.1). This process will turn this request (over whose format there may have been no control by the Project Manager) into a Project Brief, which is a complete set of terms of reference (Cartoon 3.1).

What the process does:

- Appoints (at least most of) the project management team.
- Completes (or confirms the existence of) terms of reference for the project (Project Brief).
- Ascertains the customer's quality expectations.
- Checks for lessons from earlier projects from which the project can learn.
- Checks that there is sufficient justification for requesting the resources to initiate a project (outline Business Case).

CARTOON 3.1 Project mandate

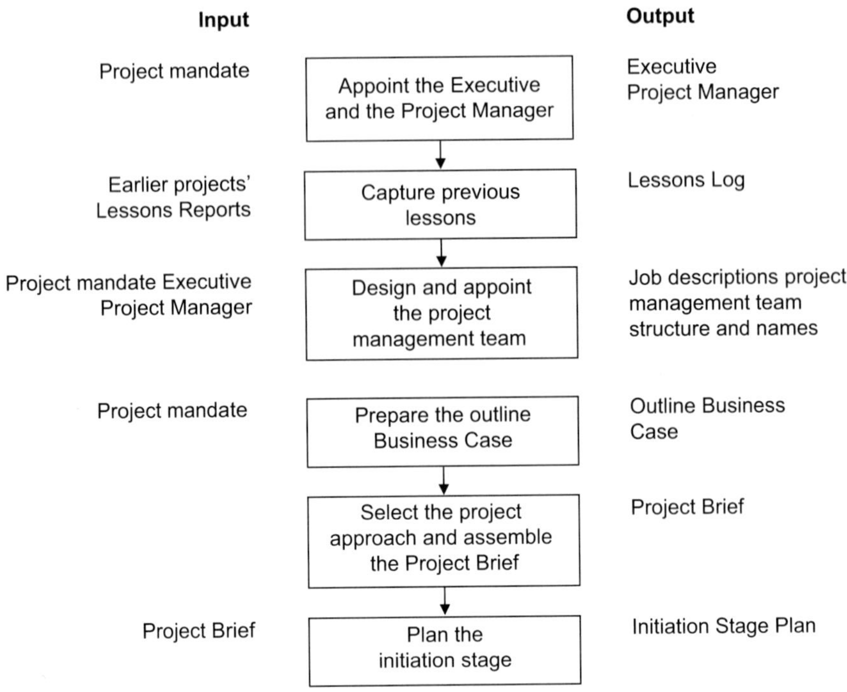

FIGURE 3.1 Starting up a project

- Defines the acceptance criteria.
- Identifies the type of solution to be provided (the project approach).
- Plans the initiation stage.

3.2 WHY?

The purpose of this process is to gather basic information about what the project's scope is, what level of quality is required from the final product, what the approach to providing a solution will be and what measurements the customer will apply to check that the final product is acceptable. At least one decision-maker (the Executive) must be appointed in order to look at the information gathered and decide if it justifies proceeding to initiating a project. All of this work must be managed, so we also need a Project Manager to be appointed.

The process has to establish:

- what is to be done;
- who will make the decisions;

- who is funding the project;
- who will say what is needed;
- what quality is required;
- who will provide the resources to do the work.

3.3 APPOINT THE EXECUTIVE AND PROJECT MANAGER

3.3.1 What Does the Activity Do?

- Corporate or programme management appoint the Executive and Project Manager, and prepare their job descriptions (Figure 3.2).

3.3.2 Why?

Every project needs a sponsor and key decision-maker, but usually this person is too busy to manage the project on a day-to-day basis. Therefore, we also need a Project Manager to do the planning and control, and both roles need to be resourced before anything can happen (in a controlled manner) in a project.

3.3.3 Responsibility

Corporate or programme management should appoint these two roles.

3.3.4 How?

This is achieved by taking the following actions:	Links to other parts of the book
Corporate or programme management identify the Executive to be responsible for the project.	Organization theme and B.2
Either corporate or programme management or the Executive or both identify a suitable Project Manager.	Organization theme and B.5
The standard PRINCE2 role descriptions are tailored by discussion between corporate or programme management and the Executive and Project Manager.	Appendix B
The tailored roles are documented, and both sign two copies of their job descriptions. The individual keeps one, and the other is kept in the project filing once the project filing system has been set up.	
The Project Manager sets up a Daily Log for the project.	13.7.3.9

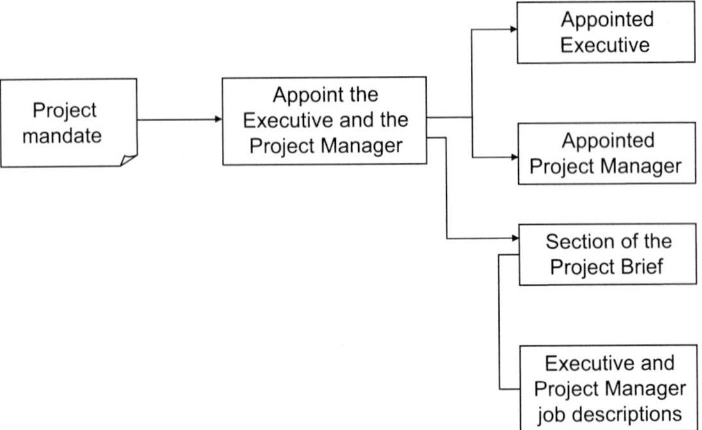

FIGURE 3.2 Appoint the Executive and the Project Manager

3.4 CAPTURE PREVIOUS LESSONS

3.4.1 What Does the Activity Do?

- Looks at Lessons Reports from other projects to see if any lessons can be learned and applied to the current project (Figure 3.3).

3.4.2 Why?

It would be foolish to repeat the mistakes of earlier projects, or fail to benefit from things they tried that were successful.

3.4.3 Responsibility

The Project Manager is responsible for this activity. He or she may use Project Support to find the documentation.

3.4.4 How?

This is achieved by taking the following actions:	Links to other parts of the book
Create a Lessons Log for the project.	A.14
Review Lessons Reports from earlier projects, especially ones with similarities to the current one.	A.15
Talk to those with previous experience on similar projects.	
Document any useful lessons learned in this project's Lessons Log.	

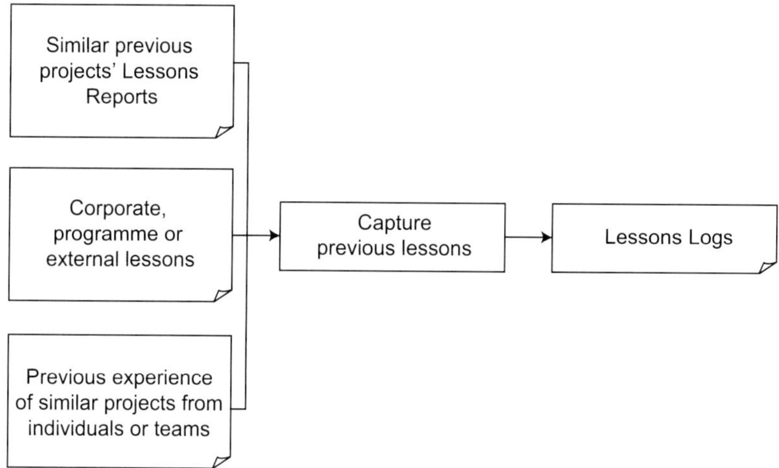

FIGURE 3.3 Capture previous lessons

3.5 DESIGN AND APPOINT THE PROJECT MANAGEMENT TEAM

3.5.1 What Does the Activity Do?

- Proposes the other Project Board members.
- Discusses with the Project Board members whether they will need help to carry out their Project Assurance responsibility.
- Designs any separate Project Assurance roles.
- Identifies candidates for any separate Project Assurance roles.
- Identifies any required Team Managers.
- Appoints the other Project Board members and any required Project Assurance and Project Support roles. There may also be Team Managers to be appointed, particularly for the early stages.
- Identifies any Project Support requirements (Figure 3.4).

3.5.2 Why?

This needs to be done, because you need to know, for example:

- Who will the users of the final product be, and who makes decisions for them?
- Who controls the resources?
- Who will create the required products?
- Is the project big enough to need Team Managers?
- Is there a central service that will supply Configuration Librarian support?

A job description for each member of the project management team needs to be agreed with the individual.

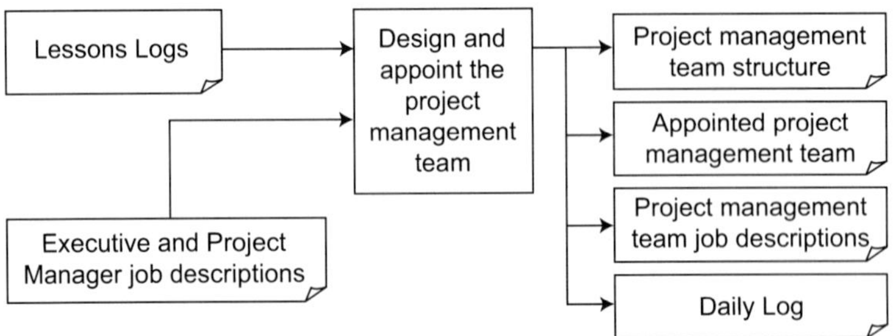

FIGURE 3.4 Design and appoint the project management team

The complete project management team needs to reflect the interests and have the approval of:

- corporate/programme management;
- the users of the final product, i.e. those who will specify details of the required product;
- the supplier(s) of that product.

After the project management team has been designed, the appointments need to be confirmed by corporate/programme management.

Project Board members must decide whether they want independent checks on their particular interests in the project as the project progresses (the Project Assurance part of the role), or whether they can do this verification themselves.

The Project Manager has to decide if any administrative support is needed, such as planning and control tool expertise, configuration management, filing or help with specialist techniques.

3.5.3 Responsibility

The Executive is responsible for the work of the process, but is likely to delegate much of the work to the Project Manager.

3.5.4 How?

This is achieved by taking the following actions:	Links to other parts of the book
Check for any lessons about setting up a project management team to be learned from previous Lessons Reports.	A.15
Identify customer areas that will use or control the end product, the commitment required and the level of authority and decision-making which is suitable for the criticality and size of the project (Senior User).	Organization theme

Continued

This is achieved by taking the following actions:	Links to other parts of the book
Identify who will provide the end product(s) (Supplier) and the level of commitment and authority required from them.	B.4
Identify candidates for the roles.	
Check out their availability and provisional agreement.	
Check whether the Project Board members will carry out their own Project Assurance responsibility.	B.1 and B.7
Try to find out what volume of change requests might come in during the project. If it is high, discuss with the proposed Project Board if it wants to appoint a Change Authority to handle change request decisions.	Change theme
Identify candidates for any Project Assurance functions which are to be delegated.	B.7
Check out their availability.	
Decide if any Project Support will be required.	B.8
Identify resources for any required support.	
The project management team design is presented to corporate/ programme management for approval.	
The Executive informs each project management team member of their appointment.	
The Project Manager discusses and agrees each member's job description with them.	Appendix B
Capture any identified risks in the Daily Log.	A.7

3.6 PREPARE THE OUTLINE BUSINESS CASE

3.6.1 What Does the Activity Do?

- Prepares a high-level view of the justification for the project – at least enough to justify the expenditure needed to initiate the project. At this point it may only be a set of reasons why the project is needed. The project mandate may contain a suitable outline; otherwise it has to be developed. The outline will be expanded into a full Business Case in the *Initiating a Project* process (Figure 3.5).

3.6.2 Why?

It is very easy to spend too much time in a project on the design and creation of products. This is the interesting work, and there is often a lot of senior

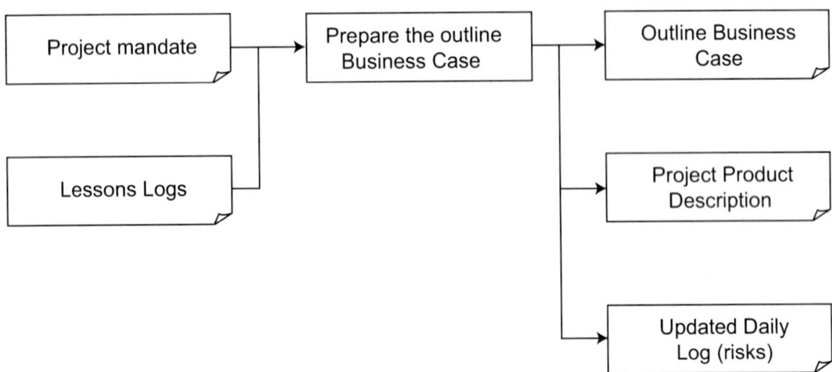

FIGURE 3.5 Prepare the outline Business Case

management pressure to 'just get it done'. With this attitude it is easy to overlook *why* the project is being done and whether the *benefits* will outweigh the *cost* of the project.

3.6.3 Responsibility

The responsibility lies with the Executive, but often the Project Manager will be asked to do a lot of the research and presentation.

3.6.4 How?

This is achieved by taking the following actions:	Links to other parts of the book
The Executive prepares the outline Business Case, based on the following: • Understand the background of the project request. • Understand the objectives of, and the reasons for, the project as, hopefully, defined in the project mandate. Otherwise obtain this information from interviews, any feasibility study or other documents. • Check the objectives against corporate or programme objectives and strategies. • Identify the source of the funding. • Review the Lessons Log for any lessons that might affect the business justification.	B.2
• Ensure that corporate or programme management agree with the prepared outline Business Case.	

Continued

This is achieved by taking the following actions:	Links to other parts of the book
• The Project Manager creates the Project Product Description. • Identify the customer's quality expectations. • Identify and agree the final product's acceptance criteria. • Check the feasibility of achieving any mentioned timescale for the project. • Add any new risks to the Daily Log.	Quality theme and A.25
• Summarize any key risks to viability in the outline Business Case.	B.2

3.7 SELECT THE PROJECT APPROACH AND ASSEMBLE THE PROJECT BRIEF

3.7.1 What Does the Activity Do?

- Decides on what kind of a solution (project approach) will be provided and the general method of providing that solution.
- Identifies the skills required by the project approach (Figure 3.6).
- Identifies any timing implications of the project approach.
- Fills in any gaps in the project mandate handed down.

The main project approaches to be considered are:

- Build a solution from scratch.
- Take an existing product and modify it.
- Give the job to another organization to do it for you.
- Buy a ready-made solution off the shelf.

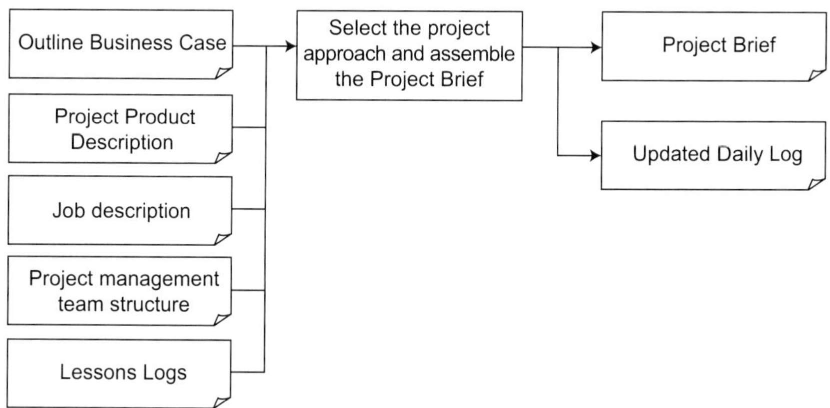

FIGURE 3.6 Select the project approach and assemble the Project Brief

3.7.2 Why?

The project approach will affect the timescale and costs of the project, plus possibly its scope and quality. This information should be made available to the Project Board in deciding whether to initiate the project.

A check should be made that the proposed project approach is in line with the customer's (or programme's) strategy.

The Project Brief is to ensure that sufficient information is available for the Project Board to make a decision on whether it wishes to proceed into initiation.

3.7.3 Responsibility

The Project Manager is responsible for examining the project mandate and collecting any missing details, and also for preparing the project approach. The outline Business Case is the responsibility of the Executive.

3.7.4 How?

This is achieved by taking the following actions:	Links to other parts of the book
Identify any time, money, resource, support or extension constraints.	
Check for any direction or guidance on the project approach from earlier documents, such as the project mandate or corporate/ programme strategies.	A.24
Check the Lessons Log, current industry thinking and any new techniques or tools available for help with the project approach.	A.14
Identify any security constraints.	
Check for any corporate/programme statement of direction which might constrain the choice of project approach.	
Produce a range of alternative project approaches.	
Compare the alternative approaches against the gathered information and constraints.	
Prepare a recommendation for the approach to be taken.	
Assemble the Project Brief.	A.22
Add to the Daily Log any risks shown up in the Project Brief.	A.7

3.8 PLAN THE INITIATION STAGE

3.8.1 What Does the Activity Do?

- Produces a plan for the initiation stage of the project (Figure 3.7).

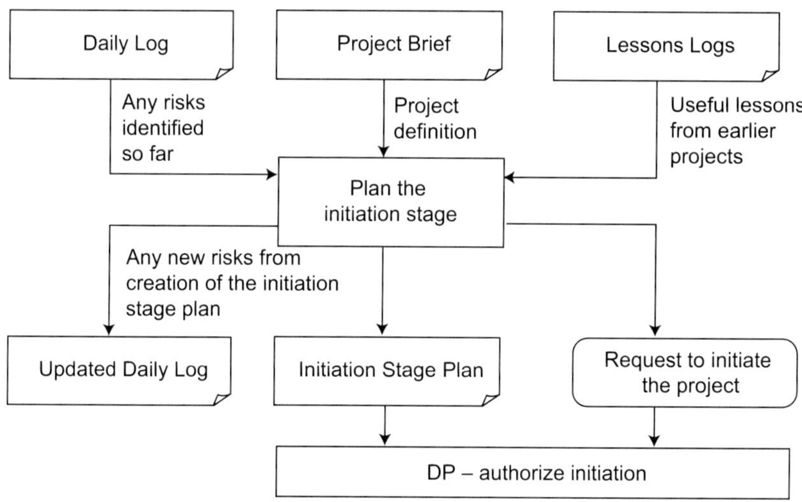

FIGURE 3.7 Plan the initiation stage

3.8.2 Why?

Preparing a document to get approval to start the project is an important task. That needs planning, and since initiation will consume some resources, the Project Board should approve the plan for it.

3.8.3 Responsibility

The Project Manager is responsible for this work.

3.8.4 How?

This is achieved by taking the following actions:	Links to other parts of the book
Examine the Project Brief and decide how much work is needed in order to produce the Project Initiation Documentation.	A.23
Evaluate the time needed to create the Project Plan.	Plans theme
Evaluate the time needed to create the next Stage Plan.	Plans theme
Evaluate the time needed to create or refine the Business Case.	Business Case theme
Review risks in the Daily Log to see if any might affect the initiation stage. Evaluate the time needed to perform risk analysis.	A.7

Continued

This is achieved by taking the following actions:	Links to other parts of the book
Define the reporting and control arrangements for initiation.	Progress theme
Create a plan for the initiation stage.	Plans theme
Update the Daily Log with any changed or new risks.	
Obtain Project Board approval for the plan.	Directing a Project process

Chapter 4

Initiating a Project (IP)

4.1 WHAT DOES THE PROCESS DO?

- Defines the quality standards, responsibilities, quality methods and tools to be used.
- Plans the whole project.
- Lays the foundation for a well-planned and controlled project.
- Confirms the existence of a viable Business Case.
- Re-assesses the risks facing the project.
- Ensures all the decision-makers are signed up to the project (Figure 4.1).

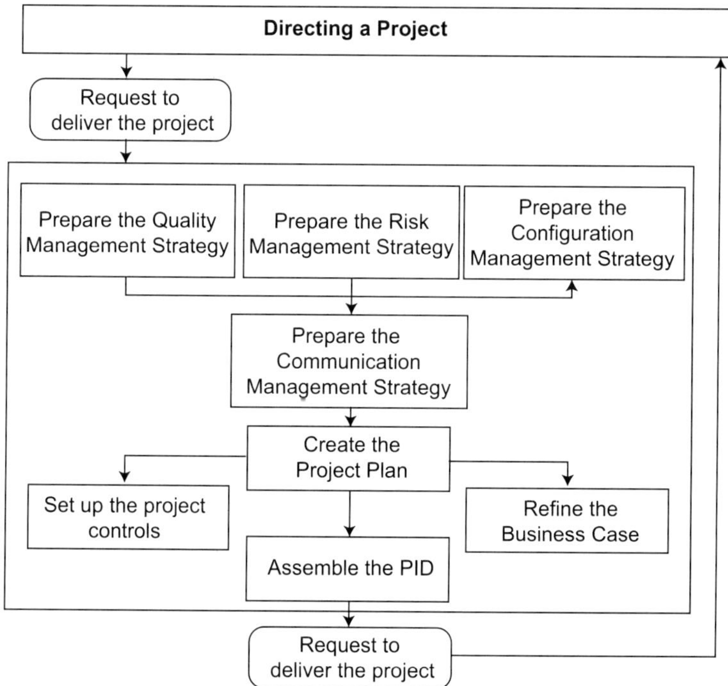

FIGURE 4.1 Initiating a Project

CARTOON 4.1 Project Board

4.2 WHY?

All stakeholders with an interest in the project should reach an agreement before any major expenditure starts on what, how, when and why it is being done, the expected benefits, and how the required quality will be achieved (Cartoon 4.1).

4.3 PREPARE THE QUALITY MANAGEMENT STRATEGY

4.3.1 What Does the Activity Do?

- Takes the customer's quality expectations, the customer and supplier's quality standards, and the project approach and defines how the customer's quality expectations will be achieved (Figure 4.2).

4.3.2 Why?

To be successful, the project must deliver a quality product, as well as meeting time and cost constraints. The means of achieving quality must be specified and agreed before work begins.

Quality work cannot be planned until the quality expectations of the customer are known.

The time and cost of the project will be affected by the amount of quality work that has to be done; therefore, quality planning must be done before a realistic Project Plan can be produced.

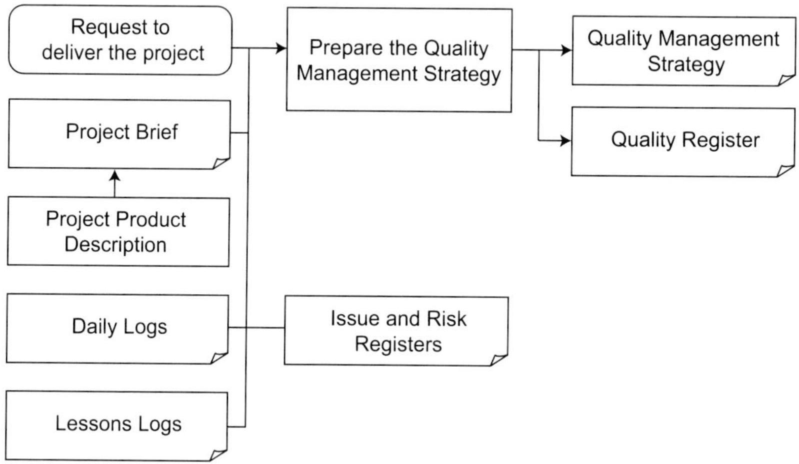

FIGURE 4.2 Prepare the Quality Management Strategy

4.3.3 Responsibility

The Project Manager and those with Project Assurance responsibilities are responsible for quality planning.

4.3.4 How?

This is achieved by taking the following actions:	Links to other parts of the book
Review the Project Product Description to understand the customer's quality expectations. • Establish links to any corporate/programme quality assurance function. • Establish the customer's quality standards. • Establish the supplier quality standards.	Quality theme and A.25
Review the Lessons Log for any lessons from earlier projects that might affect product quality.	Starting up a Project and A.14
Check the Daily Log for anything that affects product quality (unless the Risk and Issue Registers have been created already).	A.7
Decide if there is a need for an independent quality assurance function to have representation on the project management team.	
Identify quality responsibilities for project products of both the customer and supplier in their job descriptions.	Role Descriptions (Appendix B)

continued

This is achieved by taking the following actions:	Links to other parts of the book
Define the Quality Management Strategy, including: • Procedures to be used for quality planning, quality control and quality assurance. • Any tools and techniques to be used in achieving or checking quality. • Quality records to be kept. • Quality responsibilities (see the two entries above before 'Define the Quality Management Strategy').	A.26
Create a Quality Register.	

4.4 PREPARE THE RISK MANAGEMENT STRATEGY

4.4.1 What Does the Activity Do?

Describes the procedures to be used for risk identification and management, when these procedures should be carried out, and risk responsibilities (Figure 4.3).

4.4.2 Why?

As projects deal with change, the potential for risks will be ever-present; therefore, it needs to prepare in advance how it will deal with them.

4.4.3 Responsibility

The Project Manager will handle risk management. The Project Board has a responsibility to make the Project Manager aware of external risks. These may arise as a result of possible changes to corporate strategies or changes in the

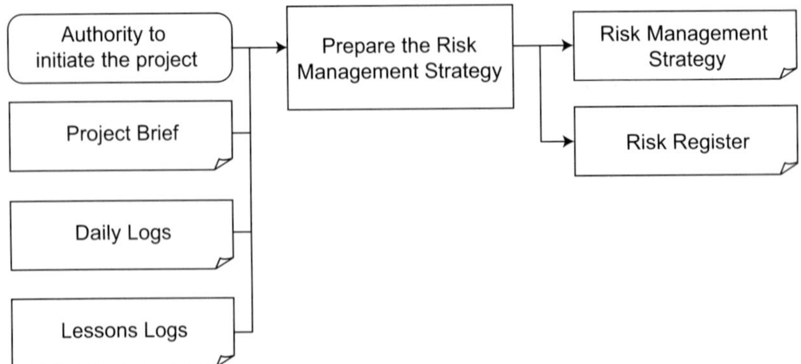

FIGURE 4.3 Prepare the Risk Management Strategy

composition of the Project Board. The Project Board is also required to make decisions on risk responses recommended by the Project Manager.

4.4.4 How?

This is achieved by taking the following actions:	Links to other parts of the book
Create a Risk Register.	A.29
Transfer any risks noted in the Daily Log.	A.7
Check for any corporate/programme risk strategies that should be used.	
Check the Lessons Log for any lessons on risk from earlier projects that might be useful.	A.14
Define the project's Risk Management Strategy, including: • procedures to identify and assess risks, plan and implement responses, and communicate actions; • any risk tools, software and techniques to be used; • records to be kept; • definition of risk categories; • guidance on grading probability, impact and proximity; • any early-warning indicators to be used; • risk tolerances for the project; • any risk budget to be used; • risk responsibilities.	A.28
Check the draft Risk Management Strategy with Project Assurance to determine that it satisfies the project's needs.	

4.5 PREPARE THE CONFIGURATION MANAGEMENT STRATEGY

4.5.1 What Does the Activity Do?

- Defines where and how project management and specialist products will be stored, how they will be identified, and how access to them will be controlled.
- Defines how changes will be controlled because of the close link between change control and configuration management (Figure 4.4).

4.5.2 Why?

Changes are inevitable in any project, and can destroy plans, the scope of the project, quality, benefits and the ability of one product to interface with another, etc., unless carefully controlled.

A project must maintain control over the management and specialist products created and used. There should only be one version of a product in circulation at any one time. All products should be protected against unauthorized changes. Time and money can be wasted if people work from old copies that should have been withdrawn.

4.5.3 Responsibility

The Project Manager is responsible for creation of the Configuration Management Strategy. Care must be taken to confirm the strategy with any Project Assurance, centre of expertise or company standards.

4.5.4 How?

This is achieved by taking the following actions:	Links to other parts of the book
Create an Issue Register and transfer to it any issues previously noted in the Daily Log.	A.12
Check for any existing strategies, standards or practices relating to configuration management at corporate/programme or supplier level.	
Check the Lessons Log for any lessons on the subject of change control and configuration management.	A.14
Review the Risk and Issue Registers for anything on the subject of change control or configuration management.	A.29 and A.12
Define the Configuration Management Strategy with: • the configuration management procedure to be used; • the issue and change control procedure to be used; • roles and responsibilities for both of these.	16. Change theme
Discuss with the Project Board whether a Change Authority and change budget should be set up.	16.2.1
Create Configuration Item Records for any management products already created or pre-existing, such as a feasibility study.	A.5
Check the proposed strategy with Project Assurance.	
Record any new risks or issues in the relevant register.	

4.6 PREPARE THE COMMUNICATION MANAGEMENT STRATEGY

4.6.1 What Does the Activity Do?

- Prepares a strategy of how the project management team will send and receive information to and from stakeholders, including media to be used and the frequency (Figure 4.5).

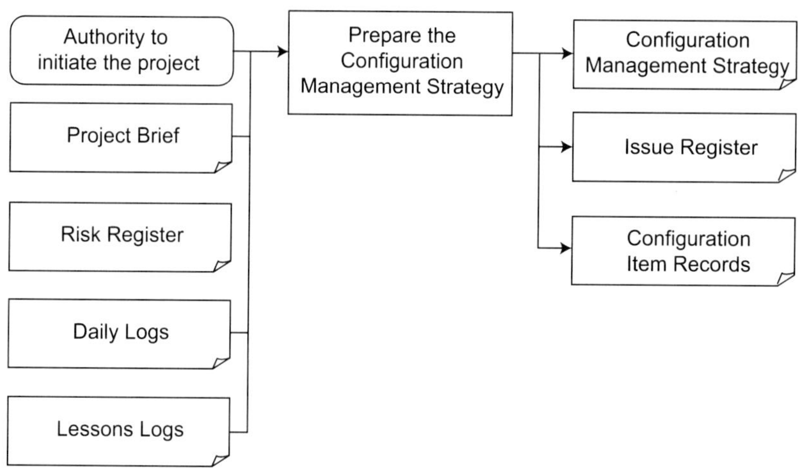

FIGURE 4.4 Prepare the Configuration Management Strategy

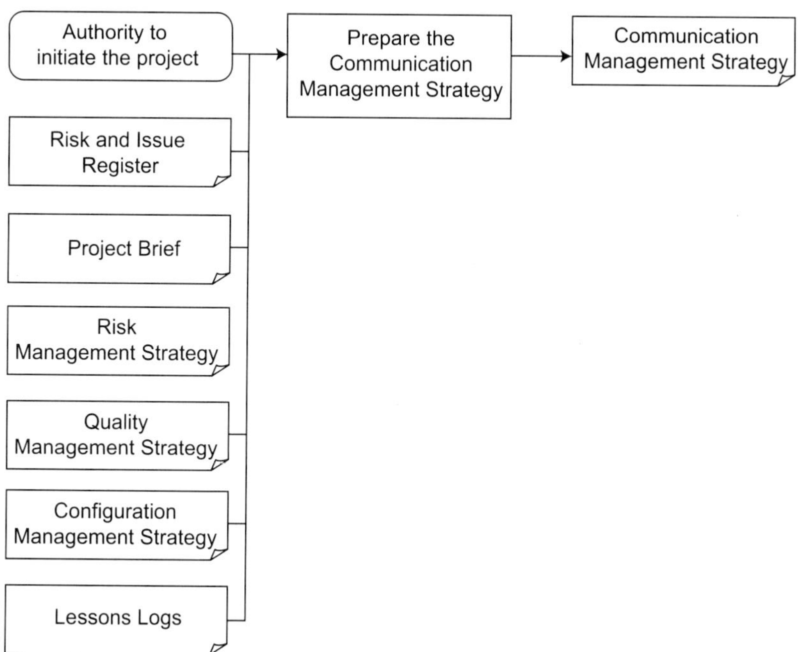

FIGURE 4.5 Prepare the Communication Management Strategy

4.6.2 Why?

It is important to keep stakeholders informed of project status, especially if the project is part of a programme. In this case the strategy must include details of all communications to and from the programme.

4.6.3 Responsibility

The Project Manager is responsible for creation of this strategy. Care must be taken to confirm the strategy with any Project Assurance, centre of expertise or company standards.

4.6.4 How?

This is achieved by taking the following actions:	Links to other parts of the book
Review the Project Brief to understand if any corporate/programme strategies, standards or practices relating to communication need to be used by the project.	A.22
Check the Lessons Log for any communications lessons.	A.14
Check the Risk and Issue Registers for any risks or issues concerning communications.	A.29 and A.12
Identify the information flow needed by the Quality, Risk and Configuration Management Strategies.	A.26, A.28, A.6
Identify with the help of the Project Board all stakeholders and find out their project information needs.	
Define the Communication Management Strategy, including: • Procedures. • Tools and techniques. • Stakeholder analysis. • Roles and responsibilities.	A.4
Review the strategy with Project Assurance.	
Record any new or changed risks or issues in the relevant register.	

4.7 CREATE THE PROJECT PLAN

4.7.1 What Does the Activity Do?

- Produces the Project Plan.
- Invokes the activity to produce the next Stage Plan (Figure 4.6).

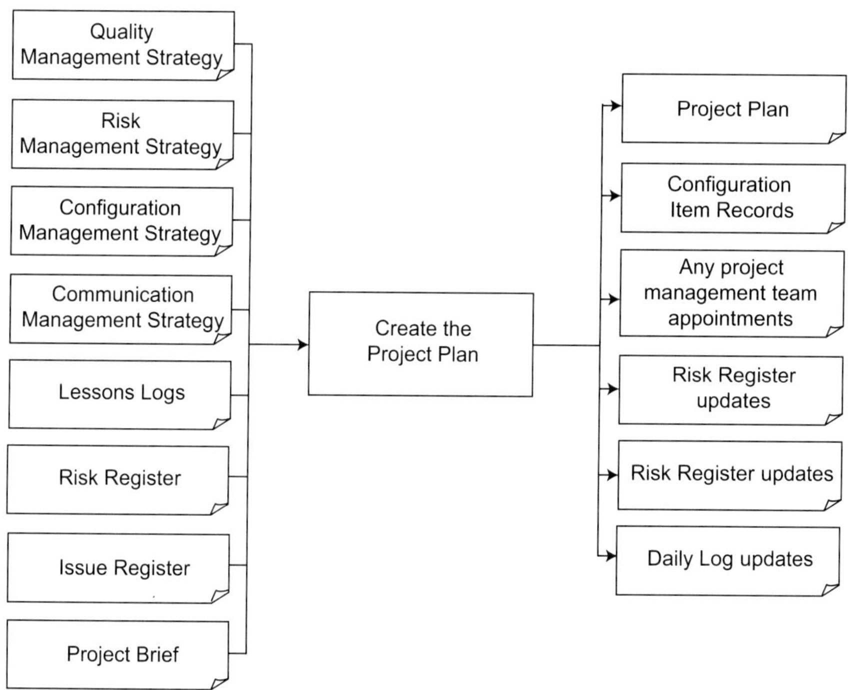

FIGURE 4.6 Create the Project Plan

4.7.2 Why?

As part of its decision on whether to proceed with the project, the Project Board needs to know how much it will cost and how long it will take. Details of the Project Plan also feed into the Business Case to indicate the viability of the project.

If the Project Board makes a general decision to proceed with the project, it needs to have more detailed information about the costs and time of the next stage before committing the required resources.

4.7.3 Responsibility

The Project Manager is responsible for the products of the activity. There may be help from any Project Support appointed, especially if any planning tool expertise is offered, and drafts of the plan should be checked with those carrying out Project Assurance functions, particularly in terms of the quality work.

4.7.4 How?

This is achieved by taking the following actions:	Links to other parts of the book
Review the Project Brief to understand what the project has to deliver and any prerequisites, constraints, external dependencies and assumptions.	A.22
Understand the selected project approach.	
Check the Lessons Log for any appropriate lessons.	A.14
Check the Risk and Issue Registers for anything that might affect the Project Plan.	A.29 and A.12
Identify any planning and control tools to be used.	
Decide on the method of estimating to be used.	
Review the four strategy documents to assess what allowances in planning should be made to meet the time and resources needed for their work.	
Use Product-based Planning to create the Project Plan.	Appendix C
Confirm the availability of the required resources.	
Create or update Configuration Item Records for the products in the plan.	A.5
Analyse project risks.	Risk theme
Modify the plan accordingly.	
Decide on a suitable breakdown of the project into stages.	Progress theme
Review the Project Product Description to see if it needs updating.	A.25
Invoke the *Plan the Next Stage* activity to produce the next Stage Plan.	
Check that both plans meet the requirements of the Quality Management Strategy.	Quality theme and A.26
Check the plans with Project Assurance.	

4.8 SET UP THE PROJECT CONTROLS

4.8.1 What Does the Activity Do?

- Establishes control points and reporting arrangements for the project, based on the project's size, criticality, risk situation, the customer's and supplier's control standards, and the diversity of interested parties (Figure 4.7).

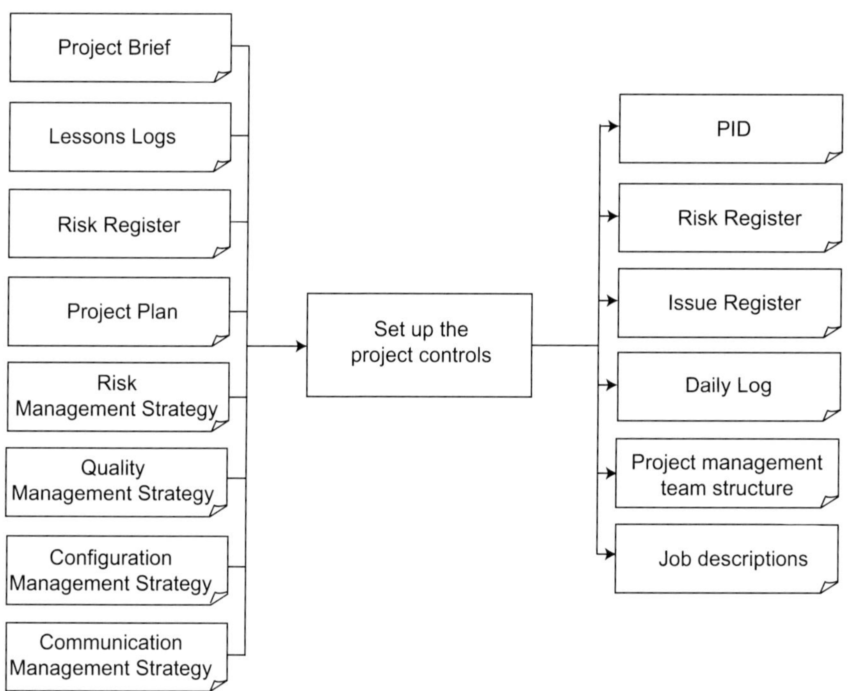

FIGURE 4.7 Set up the project controls

4.8.2 Why?

In order to keep the project under control it is important to ensure that:

- the right decisions are made by the right people at the right time;
- the right information is given to the right people at the right frequency and timing.

4.8.3 Responsibility

The Project Manager is responsible for establishing the monitoring and reporting necessary for day-to-day control, and agreeing the correct level of reporting and decision points for the Project Board to ensure management by exception.

4.8.4 How?

This is achieved by taking the following actions:	Links to other parts of the book
Read the Project Brief to understand if there are corporate or programme standards of controls to be used by the project.	A.22
Review the project's strategy documents to identify their control requirements.	
Check the Lessons Log for any lessons relating to project control.	
Check the Risk Register to see if the number and seriousness of risks identified so far should affect the timing and level of control activities.	A.29
Agree the stage breakdown with the Project Board.	13.2 Stages
Confirm project tolerances have been set by corporate/programme management.	
Ensure that escalation procedures across all project management levels are in place.	Configuration Management Strategy
Agree the format of reports to the Project Board.	A.11 and A.10
Agree the frequency of Project Board reports.	Progress theme
Summarize the controls in the Project Initiation Documentation.	A.23
Check the proposed controls with Project Assurance.	
Update the Risk and Issue Registers or Daily Log with any new or changed risks and issues.	

4.9 REFINE THE BUSINESS CASE

4.9.1 What Does the Activity Do?

- Takes whatever outline Business Case exists for the project, plus the Project Plan, and creates a full Business Case for inclusion in the Project Initiation Documentation.
- Creates a Benefits Review Plan (Figure 4.8).

4.9.2 Why?

Before commitment to the project it is important to ensure that there is sufficient justification for the resource expenditure. It is also important to plan in advance how and when measurement of the expected benefits can be done.

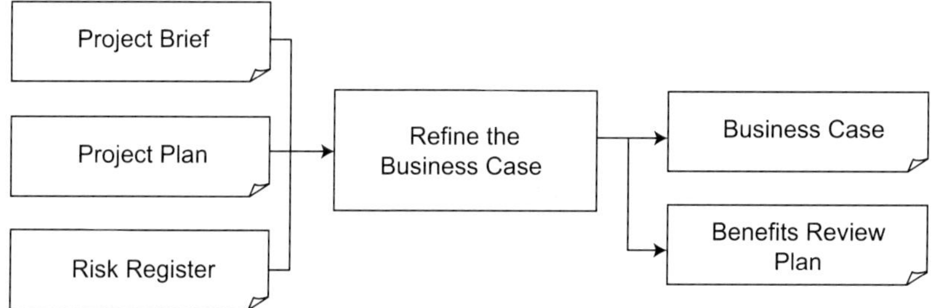

FIGURE 4.8 Refine the Business Case

4.9.3 Responsibility

The responsibility for the Business Case rests with the Executive, probably with input of reasons from the user(s). Much of the work will probably be delegated to the Project Manager.

4.9.4 How?

This is achieved by taking the following actions:	Links to other parts of the book
Check the Project Brief for any requirements from corporate/ programme management for the format and content of the Business Case.	A.22 and A.2
Check the Lessons Log for any lessons about Business Case preparation.	A.14
Take the outline Business Case and enhance it to be a complete Business Case with: • costs and timescale from the Project Plan; • any identified major risks; • expected benefits; • tolerance margins for each benefit.	A.2
Create the Benefits Review Plan, including: • how each benefit is to be measured; • a baseline measurement of the current situation for each benefit against which improvements or achievements can be measured; • when each benefit should be measured.	A.1
Update the Risk and Issue Registers (or Daily Log) with any new or changed risks and issues.	A.29 and A.12
Check the draft Business Case and Benefits Review Plan with Project Assurance, particularly the Executive's Project Assurance.	

CARTOON 4.2 Business benefits

4.10 ASSEMBLE THE PROJECT INITIATION DOCUMENTATION

4.10.1 What Does the Activity Do?

- Gathers together the information from the other *Initiating a Project* activities and assembles the Project Initiation Documentation (Figure 4.9).

4.10.2 Why?

The Project Initiation Documentation encapsulates all the information needed for the Project Board to make the decision on whether to go ahead with the project or not. It also forms a formal record of the information on which this decision was based, and can be used after the project finishes when judging how successful the project was.

4.10.3 Responsibility

The Project Manager is responsible for the assembly with the help of any appointed Project Support and the advice of those with Project Assurance responsibility.

CARTOON 4.3 (A) and (B) Project Initiation Documentation

4.10.4 How?

This is achieved by taking the following actions:	Links to other parts of the book
Transfer information from the Project Brief (background, objectives, constraints, project approach, etc.), checking if any of it needs expansion or change.	A.22
Incorporate into the Project Initiation Documentation all the information gathered during the *Initiating a Project* process.	A.23
Check for those who should receive a copy of the Project Initiation Documentation.	A.14
Distribute the Project Initiation Documentation to the Project Board and relevant stakeholders.	

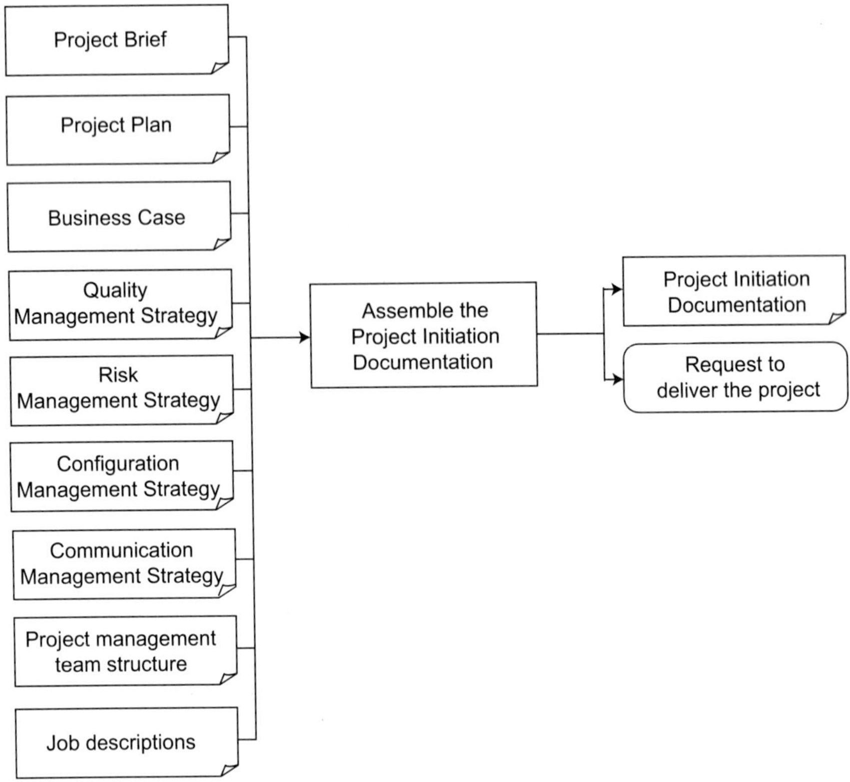

FIGURE 4.9 Assemble the Project Initiation Documentation

Chapter 5

Directing a Project (DP)

5.1 WHAT DOES THE PROCESS DO?

- Authorizes project initiation.
- Provides liaison with corporate/programme management.
- Advises the Project Manager of any external business events which might impact the project.
- Approves Stage Plans.
- Approves stage closure.
- Decides on any changes to approved products.
- Approves any Exception Plans.
- Gives ad hoc advice and direction throughout the project.
- Safeguards the interests of the customer and supplier.
- Approves project closure (Figure 5.1).

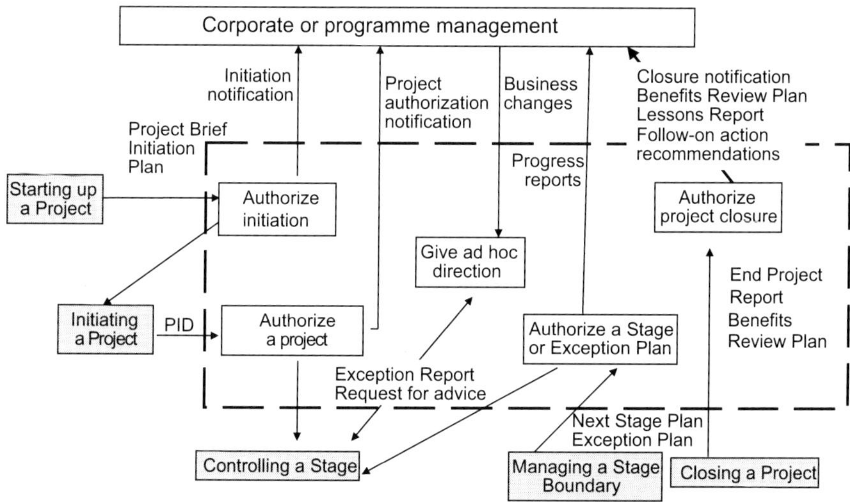

FIGURE 5.1 Directing a Project

5.2 WHY?

Day-to-day management is left to the Project Manager, but the Project Board must exercise overall control and take the key decisions.

5.3 AUTHORIZE INITIATION

5.3.1 What Does the Activity Do?

- Checks that adequate terms of reference exist.
- Checks and approves the initiation Stage Plan.
- Commits the resources required to carry out the initiation stage work (Figure 5.2).

5.3.2 Why?

The initiation stage confirms that a viable project exists and that everybody concerned agrees what is to be done. As with all project work, the effort required to do this needs the approval of the Project Board.

5.3.3 Responsibility

The Project Board is responsible, based on information provided by the Project Manager and those with Project Assurance responsibility.

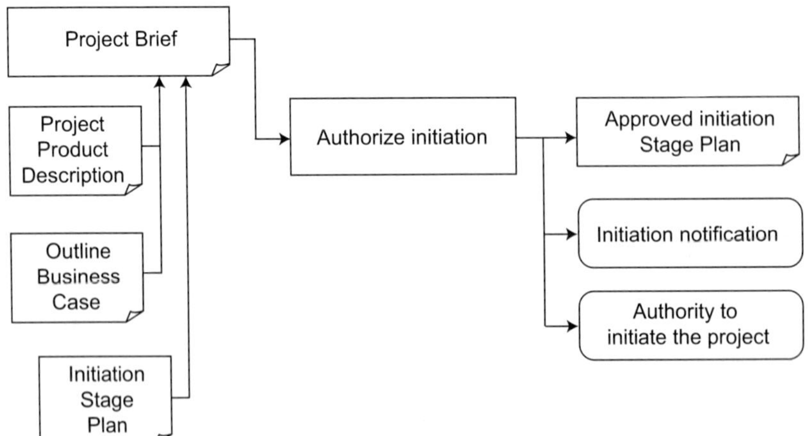

FIGURE 5.2 Authorize initiation

5.3.4 How?

This is achieved by taking the following actions:	Links to other parts of the book
Confirm the terms of reference in the Project Brief, checking if necessary with corporate/programme management.	A.22
Review and approve the Project Product Description.	A.25
Confirm the customer's quality expectations and acceptance criteria.	14.3.1
Check that the outline Business Case shows that there are valid reasons to authorize initiation at least.	
Confirm that the recommended project approach is suitable.	3.7
Formally approve appointments to the project management team and confirm that everyone has an agreed role description.	Appendix B
Check the initiation Stage Plan and approve it if satisfied.	
Agree tolerance margins for the initiation stage.	13.3
Agree control and reporting arrangements for the initiation stage.	
Inform all stakeholders that initiation has been authorized, and request any support required from them for initiation.	
Commit the resources required by the plan.	

5.4 AUTHORIZE A PROJECT

5.4.1 What Does the Activity Do?

- Decides whether to proceed with the project or not.
- Approves the next Stage Plan (Figure 5.3).

5.4.2 Why?

The activity allows the Project Board to check before major resource commitment that:

- a reasonable Business Case for the project exists;
- the project's objectives are in line with corporate or programme strategies and objectives;
- the project's estimated duration and cost are within acceptable limits;
- the risks facing the project are acceptable;
- adequate controls are in place.

5.4.3 Responsibility

The Project Board, with advice from those with Project Assurance responsibility.

5.4.4 How?

This is achieved by taking the following actions:	Links to other parts of the book
Confirm that the project's objectives and scope are clearly defined and understood by all.	
Confirm that the objectives are in line with corporate/programme objectives.	
Confirm that all authorities and responsibilities are agreed.	Organization theme
Confirm that the Business Case is adequate, clear and, wherever possible, measurable and confirms the viability of the project.	Business Case theme
Confirm that any useful lessons from previous projects have been incorporated.	
Confirm the existence of a credible Project Plan which is within the project constraints.	Plans theme
Check that the proposed project controls are prepared and are suitable for the type and size of the project.	Progress theme
Check that the plan for the next stage is reasonable and matches that portion of the Project Plan.	
Review and approve the Product Descriptions created so far.	
Have any desired changes made to the draft Project Initiation Documentation.	A.23
Confirm that the Quality, Risk, Configuration and Communication Management Strategies are prepared and that they provide adequate management and control over their areas.	A.26, A.28, A.6 and A.4
Check that the Benefits Review Plan is established, covers all the expected benefits and provides details of how and when each benefit will be measured.	Business Case theme
Confirm deviation limits for the project and the next stage.	Progress theme
Give written approval for the next stage (or not, if not satisfied with any of the details) and commit the necessary resources.	
Arrange a date for the next stage's end stage assessment.	Progress theme
Notify all stakeholders that the project has been authorized.	

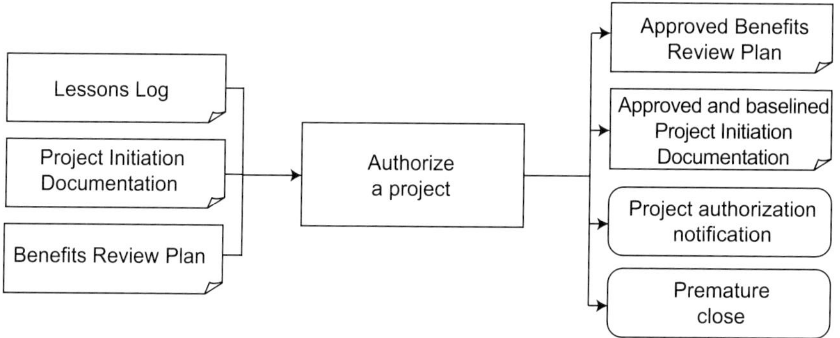

FIGURE 5.3 Authorize a project

5.5 AUTHORIZE A STAGE OR EXCEPTION PLAN

5.5.1 What Does the Activity Do?

- Authorizes each stage (except initiation) and any Exception Plans that are needed (Figure 5.4).

5.5.2 Why?

An important control for the Project Board is to approve only one stage at a time. At the end of one stage the Project Manager has to justify both progress so far and the plan for the next stage before being allowed to continue.

5.5.3 Responsibility

The Project Board carries responsibility for this process, based on information provided by the Project Manager and with advice from any separate Project Assurance responsibility.

5.5.4 How?

This is achieved by taking the following actions:	Links to other parts of the book
Review and approve the End Stage Report.	A.9
Compare the results of the current stage against the approved Stage Plan.	
Assess progress against the updated Project Plan.	
Ask the Project Manager to explain any deviations from the Stage and Project Plans that were approved before the start of the current stage.	

Continued

This is achieved by taking the following actions:	Links to other parts of the book
Assess the acceptability of the next Stage Plan against the Project Plan.	
Review and approve any new or revised Product Descriptions.	
Review the prospects of achieving the Business Case.	A.2
Review and approve any changes to the Benefits Review Plan.	A.1
Review the risks facing the project.	15 Risk theme
Get direction from corporate/programme management if the project is forecast to exceed tolerances or there is a change to the Business Case.	13.3 Progress theme
Review any Lessons Report that may have been created and direct it to the group that should take action on it.	A.15
Review tolerances and reporting arrangements for the next stage.	13.3
For any phased handover of products during the current stage: • Check that the handover was done in accordance with the procedures laid down in the Configuration Management Strategy. • Check that users and operational and maintenance staff were happy to accept the products.	
If any follow-on action recommendations were made in the End Stage Report, ensure that they are passed to the appropriate group for action.	A.9
Give approval to move into the next stage (if satisfied) and commit the required resources.	
If the Project Plan and/or Business Case show that the project is no longer viable, instruct the Project Manager to prematurely close the project.	
Communicate the decision to all interested parties as shown in the Communication Management Strategy.	A.4

5.6 GIVE AD HOC DIRECTION

5.6.1 What Does the Activity Do?

- Advises the Project Manager about any external events which impact the project.
- Gives direction to the Project Manager when asked for advice or a decision about an issue.
- Advises on or approves any changes to the project management team.
- Makes decisions on the actions to take on receipt of any Exception Reports (Figure 5.5).

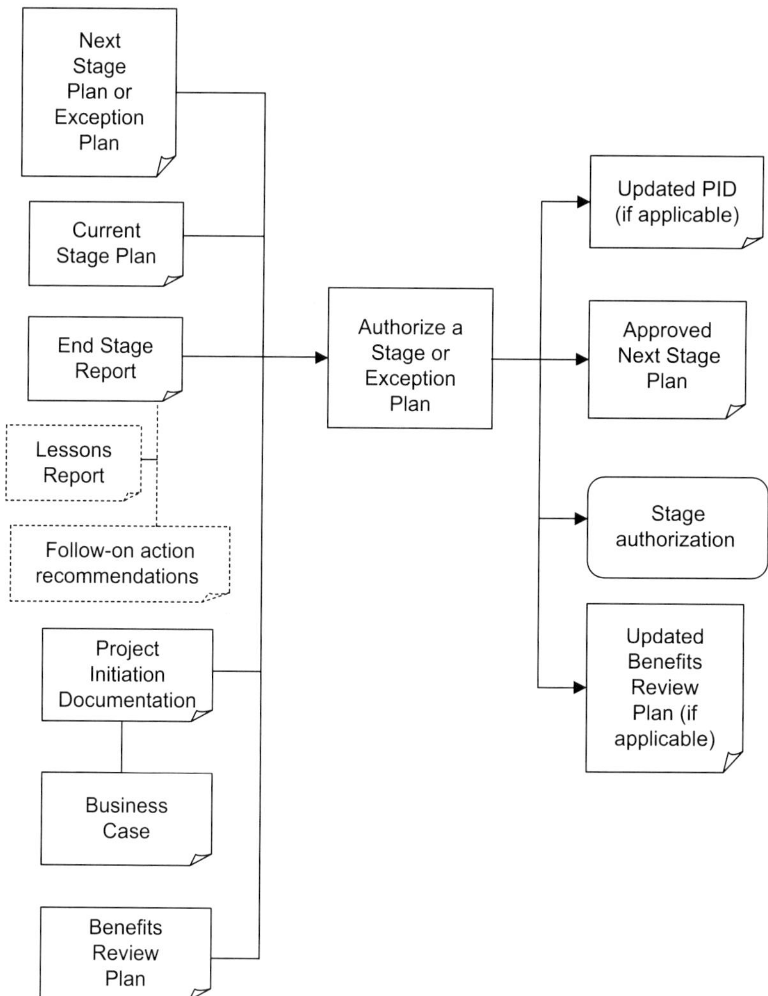

FIGURE 5.4 Authorize a Stage or Exception Plan

5.6.2 Why?

There may be a need for occasional Project Board direction outside end stage assessments.

5.6.3 Responsibility

The Project Board is responsible for this activity.

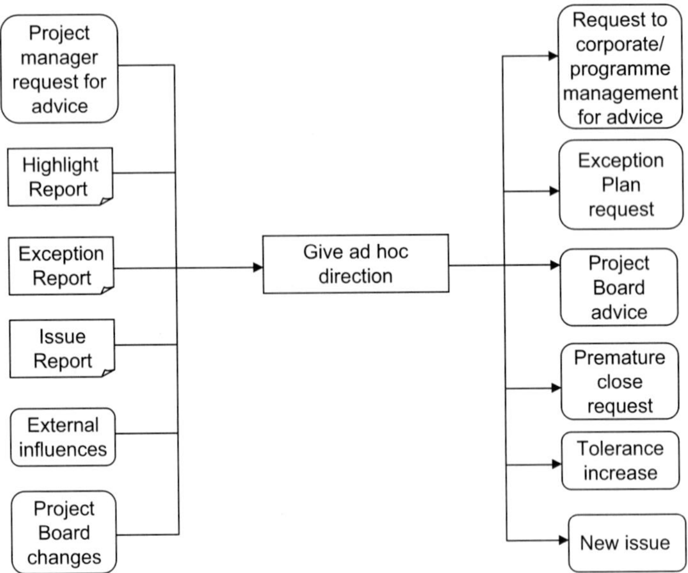

FIGURE 5.5 Give ad hoc direction

5.6.4 How?

This is achieved by taking the following actions:	Links to other parts of the book
Check for external events, such as business changes, which might affect the project's Business Case or risk exposure and inform the Project Manager.	
Monitor any allocated risk situations.	
Make decisions on any Exception Reports, such as: • Increase the threatened tolerance if this is possible within project tolerances. • Ask the Project Manager to produce an Exception Plan. • Instruct the Project Manager to bring about a premature close to the project. • Defer the decision on the situation until more information is available. • Defer the requested change until a subsequent update project. • Grant a concession for any off-specification.	A.10
Check for external events, such as business changes, which might affect the project's Business Case or risk exposure and inform the Project Manager.	
Monitor any allocated risk situations.	

Continued

This is achieved by taking the following actions:	Links to other parts of the book
Make decisions on any Exception Reports, such as: • Increase the threatened tolerance if this is possible within project tolerances. • Ask the Project Manager to produce an Exception Plan. • Instruct the Project Manager to bring about a premature close to the project. • Defer the decision on the situation until more information is available. • Defer the requested change until a subsequent update project. • Grant a concession for any off-specification.	A.10
Ensure that the project remains focused on its objectives and achievement of its Business Case.	A.2
Keep corporate/programme management advised of project progress.	
Make decisions about any necessary changes to the project management team.	11.4 Organization
Make decisions on informal requests for advice, seeking advice, where necessary, from corporate or programme management.	Change theme
Review Highlight Reports and respond to any action or advice requests in the report.	A.11

5.7 AUTHORIZE PROJECT CLOSURE

5.7.1 What Does the Activity Do?

- Checks that the objectives of the project have been met.
- Reviews any deviations of the project from its original aims and plans.
- Checks that there are no loose ends.
- Advises senior management of the project's termination.
- Recommends a plan for checking on achievement of the expected benefits (Figure 5.6).

5.7.2 Why?

There must be a defined end point in a project in order to judge its success. The Project Board must assure itself that the project's products have been handed over and are acceptable. Where contracts (and money) are involved, there must be agreement between customer and supplier that the work contracted has been completed.

5.7.3 Responsibility

The Project Board is responsible, advised by the Project Manager and any Project Assurance responsibility.

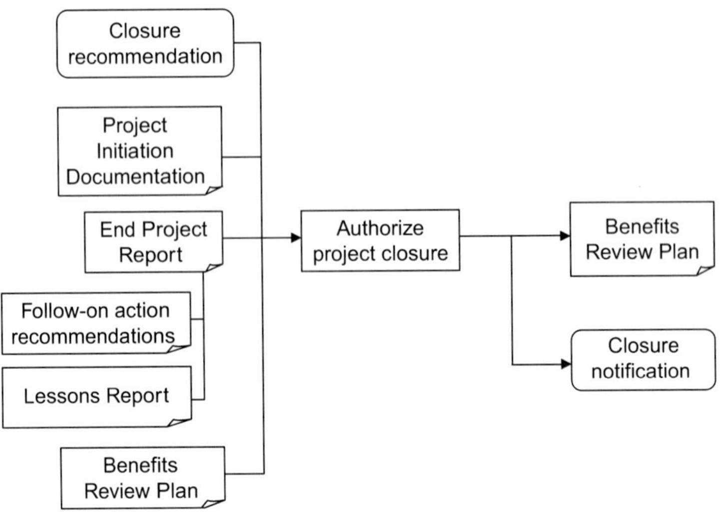

FIGURE 5.6 Authorize project closure

5.7.4 How?

This is achieved by taking the following actions:	Links to other parts of the book
Review the original and current versions of the Project Initiation Documentation to understand the project's original objectives and Business Case, any changes made to them during the project and the reasons for the changes.	A.23
Review the End Project Report against the Project Initiation Documentation and assess the performance of the project.	A.8
Check that the customer's acceptance criteria have been met and that all the required products have been delivered and accepted by the customer.	A.6
Check that there has been a satisfactory handover of the finished product(s) to those responsible for its use and support.	
Check that there are no outstanding issues.	
Approve the follow-on action recommendations and pass them to the appropriate group.	
Approve the Lessons Report and pass it to the appropriate body.	A.15
Release the resources allocated to the project.	
Advise corporate/programme management of the project's closure.	
Disband the project management team.	

Chapter 6

Controlling a Stage (CS)

6.1 WHAT DOES THE PROCESS DO?

- Manages the stage from stage approval to completion.
- Assigns work to be done.
- Monitors work progress and quality.
- Deals with issues and risks.
- Reports progress to the Project Board.
- Keeps the Business Case under review.
- Takes any corrective action to ensure that the stage stays within its tolerances (Figure 6.1).

6.2 WHY?

The production of the stage's products within budget, schedule and to the required quality must be driven by the Project Manager and also requires careful monitoring and control.

6.3 AUTHORIZE A WORK PACKAGE

6.3.1 What Does the Activity Do?

- Allocates work to be done to a team or individual, based on the needs of the current Stage Plan.
- Ensures that any work handed out is accompanied by measurements such as target dates, quality expectations, delivery and reporting dates.
- Ensures that agreement has been reached on the reasonableness of the work demands with the recipient (Figure 6.2).

6.3.2 Why?

No work in a stage should start without the permission and authority of the Project Manager; otherwise it would be very difficult to keep control. The Project Manager must control the sequence of at least the major activities of a stage and when they begin. This ensures that the Project Manager knows what those working on the project are doing and that the Stage Plan correctly reflects the work and progress. The Work Package is the means of authorizing work.

6.3.3 Responsibility

The Project Manager is responsible for the authorization of Work Packages. The recipient of the Work Package must agree with the targets and constraints before the authorization can be considered complete. The *Managing Product Delivery* process covers the steps of a Team Manager receiving a Work Package on behalf of a team.

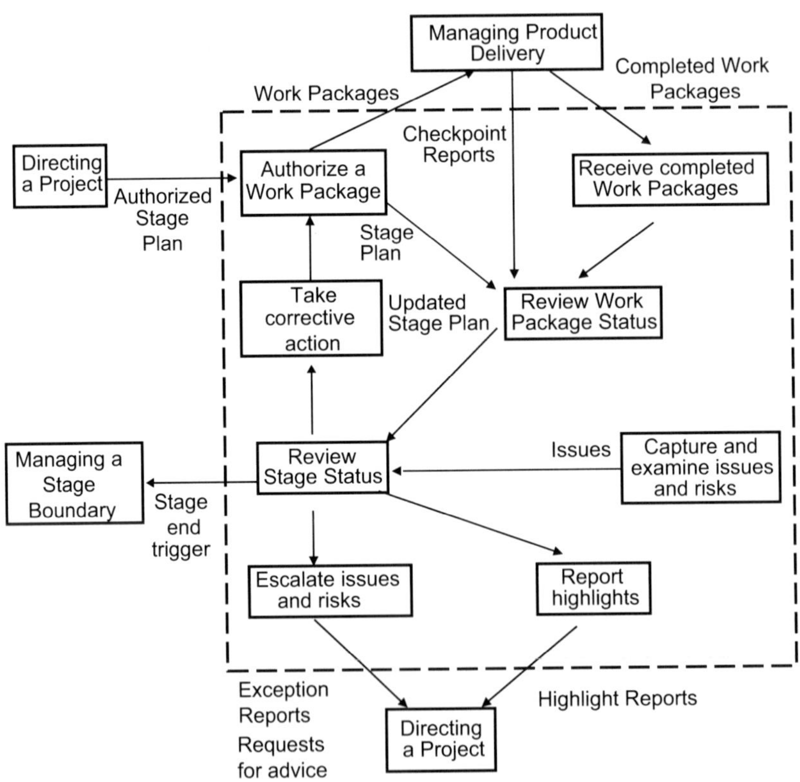

FIGURE 6.1 Controlling a Stage

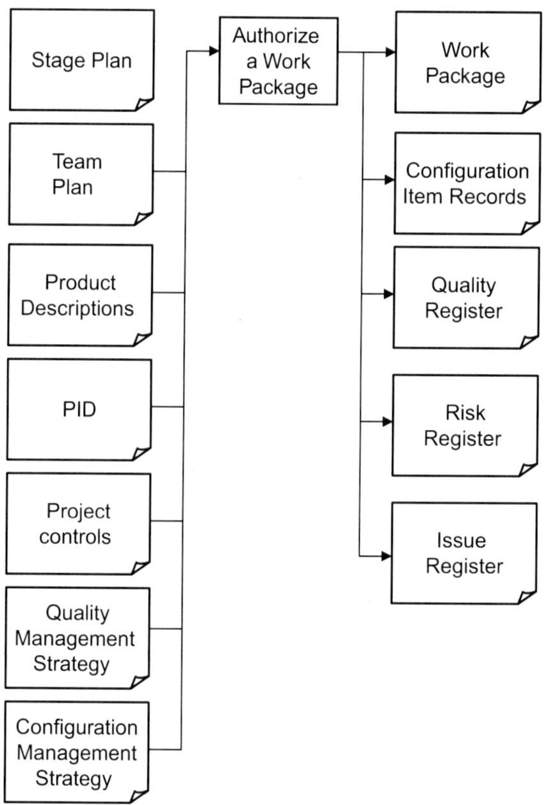

FIGURE 6.2 Authorize a Work Package

6.3.4 How?

This is achieved by taking the following actions:	Links to other parts of the book
Review the Stage Plan to understand the products required, the time, budget and tolerances available.	
Understand from the strategies in the Project Initiation Documentation the controls to be employed, the quality standards to be met and, if appropriate, how any products are to be handed over.	A.23
Ensure that there are Product Descriptions for the work to be done and that these are complete.	A.19
Identify specific quality checking needs.	

Continued

This is achieved by taking the following actions:	Links to other parts of the book
Create the Work Package.	Work Package Product Description
Discuss the Work Package with the Team Manager or team member (if an individual).	
Jointly assess any risks or problems and modify the Work Package and Risk Register as necessary.	A.29
Review the Team Plan for the work and ensure that sufficient resources and time have been allocated to it.	
Record the Team Manager's agreement for the work in the Work Package.	
Update the status of the relevant products' Configuration Item Records.	A.5
Update the Stage Plan with any adjustments made as part of the agreement.	
Update the Quality Register with details of any planned quality management activities.	A.27
Update the Risk and/or Issue Registers (if necessary).	A.29 and A.12

6.4 REVIEW WORK PACKAGE STATUS

6.4.1 What Does the Activity Do?

- Gathers information from Checkpoint Reports on the status of Work Packages to update the Stage Plan to reflect actual progress, effort expended and quality work carried out.
- Assesses the remaining effort and forecast completion dates of any incomplete work.
- Reviews the Team Plan with the Team Manager to see if work will be completed according to the plan.
- Reviews any Quality Register entries for the work to ascertain the quality status of products.
- Checks that Configuration Item Records reflect the correct status of their products (Figure 6.3).

6.4.2 Why?

In order to control the stage and make sensible decisions on what, if any, adjustments need to be made, it is necessary to gather information on what has actually happened and be able to compare this against what was planned.

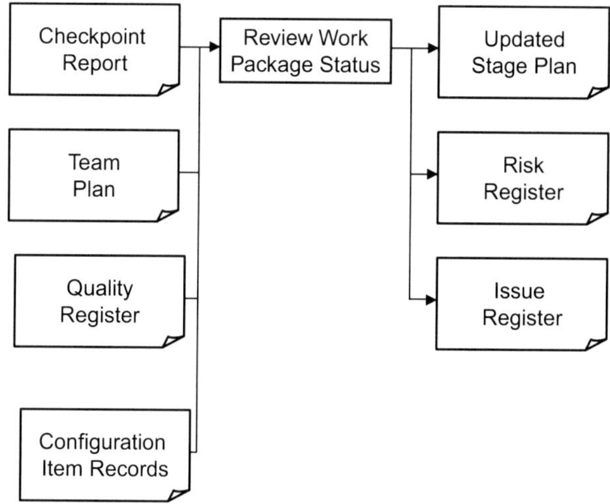

FIGURE 6.3 Review Work Package Status

6.4.3 Responsibility

The Project Manager is responsible, but may delegate the actual collection of data to Project Support.

6.4.4 How?

This is achieved by taking the following actions:	Links to other parts of the book
Collect Checkpoint Reports.	A.3
Update the Stage Plan with the information.	
Obtain estimates on time, cost and effort needed to complete work which is in progress or has not yet started.	
Check whether sufficient resources are available to complete the work as now estimated.	
Check the feedback on quality activities.	A.27
Note any potential or real problems.	

6.5 RECEIVE COMPLETED WORK PACKAGES

6.5.1 What Does the Activity Do?

- Balances with the activity *Deliver a Work Package* within the *Managing Product Delivery* process. It records the completion and return of approved Work Packages. The information is passed to the *Controlling a Stage* activity *Review the Work Package Status* (Figure 6.4).

6.5.2 Why?

Where work has been recorded as approved to a team or individual, there should be a matching process to record the return of the completed product(s) and its/their acceptance (or otherwise).

6.5.3 Responsibility

The Project Manager is responsible, assisted by any appointed Project Support staff

6.5.4 How?

This is achieved by taking the following actions:	Links to other parts of the book
Check the delivery against the requirements of the Work Package.	A.30
Obtain confirmation from the Quality Register that the planned quality checks have been carried out.	A.27
Check that the recipients have accepted the products.	
Ensure that the delivered products have been passed to the configuration library and baselined.	
Document any relevant team member appraisal information.	
Pass information about completion to update the Stage Plan.	

6.6 REVIEW STAGE STATUS

6.6.1 What Does the Activity Do?

- Provides a regular re-assessment of the status of the stage.
- Triggers new work.
- Triggers corrective action for any problems.
- Provides the information for progress reporting (Figure 6.5).

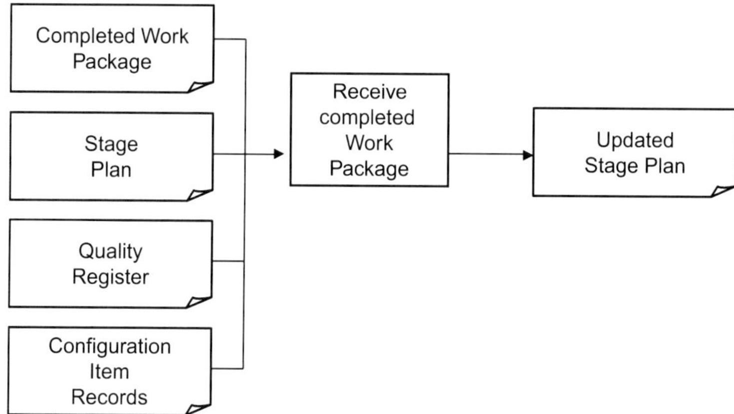

FIGURE 6.4 Receive completed Work Packages

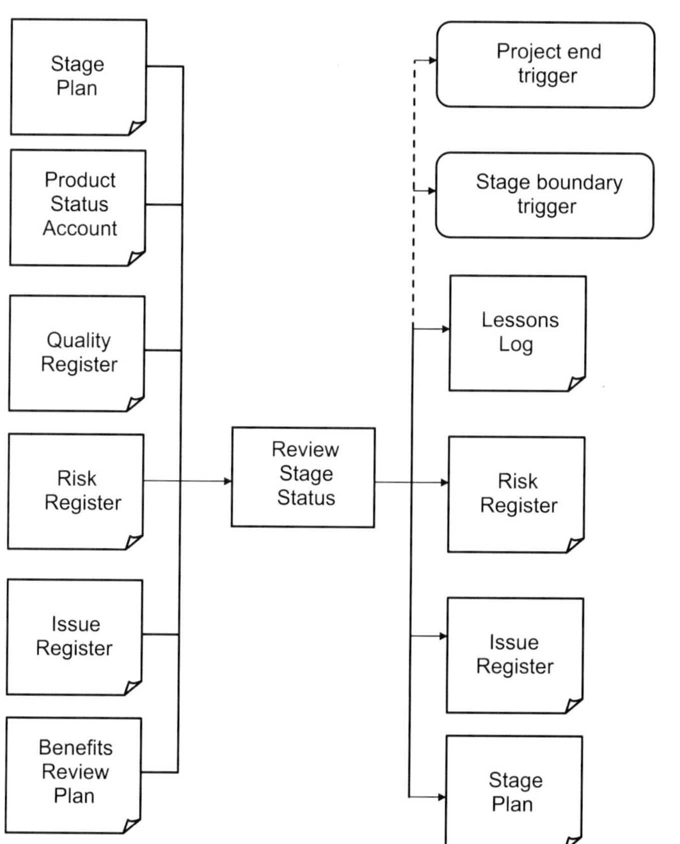

FIGURE 6.5 Review Stage Status

6.6.2 Why?

It is better to check the status of a stage on a regular basis and take action to avoid potential problems, rather than have problems occur as a surprise, and then have to react to them. The objective is therefore to maintain an accurate, up-to-date picture of the work and resource utilization within the stage.

6.6.3 Responsibility

This is the responsibility of the Project Manager, who may seek guidance from the Project Board (*Escalate Issues and Risks*) for any problems that appear to be beyond his/her authority.

6.6.4 How?

This is achieved by taking the following actions:	Links to other parts of the book
Review progress and forecasts against the Stage Plan.	
Review resource and money expenditure.	
Request, if appropriate, a Product Status Account to view the status of products planned in the stage.	A.21
Decide on and implement any actions in response to problems noted in the Quality Register.	A.27
Review the impact of any actions taken in response to issues in the Stage and Project Plans.	
Assess if the stage and project will remain within tolerances.	
Check the continuing validity of the Business Case.	A.2
Check for changes in the status of any risks.	
Check for any changes external to the project which may impact it.	
If any products are to be handed over at this point, ensure that the necessary procedures have been followed.	
Review the Lessons Log and decide whether a Lessons Report should be generated at this time.	A.14 and A.15
If the end of the stage is approaching, trigger production of the next Stage Plan.	Manage a Stage Boundary
If the end of the project is approaching, trigger the process *Closing a Project*.	Closing a Project

6.7 REPORT HIGHLIGHTS

6.7.1 What Does the Activity Do?

- Produces Highlight Reports for the Project Board (Figure 6.6).

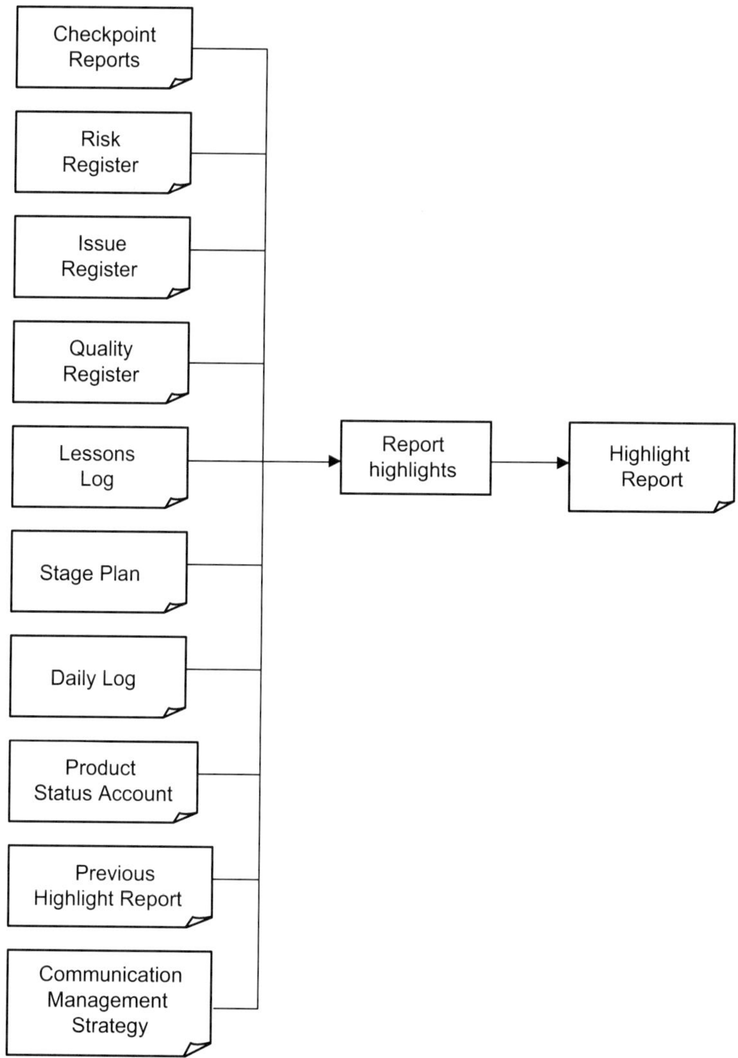

FIGURE 6.6 Report highlights

6.7.2 Why?

The Project Board needs to be kept informed of project progress if it is to exercise proper control over the project. Rather than have regular progress meetings, reports at regular intervals are recommended between end stage assessments. The Project Board decides the frequency of the reports at project initiation.

6.7.3 Responsibility

The Project Manager is responsible. This process covers the moments when the Project Manager has to stand back and take stock of the situation.

6.7.4 How?

This is achieved by taking the following actions:	Links to other parts of the book
Collate the information from any Checkpoint Reports made since the last Highlight Report.	7.4 'Execute a Work Package'
Review the previous Highlight Report for details of open concerns that were to be followed up and products that were to be completed in the period that has just finished.	A.11
Identify any significant Stage Plan revisions made since the last report.	6.4 'Review Work Package Status'
Identify current or potential risks to the Business Case.	
Assess the Issue Register for any potential problems which require Project Board attention.	A.12
Identify any change to other risks.	
Report a summary of this information to the Project Board.	A.11
Check the Communication Management Strategy for other recipients of the report.	A.4

6.8 CAPTURE AND EXAMINE ISSUES AND RISKS

6.8.1 What Does the Activity Do?

- Captures, logs and categorizes new issues (Figure 6.7).

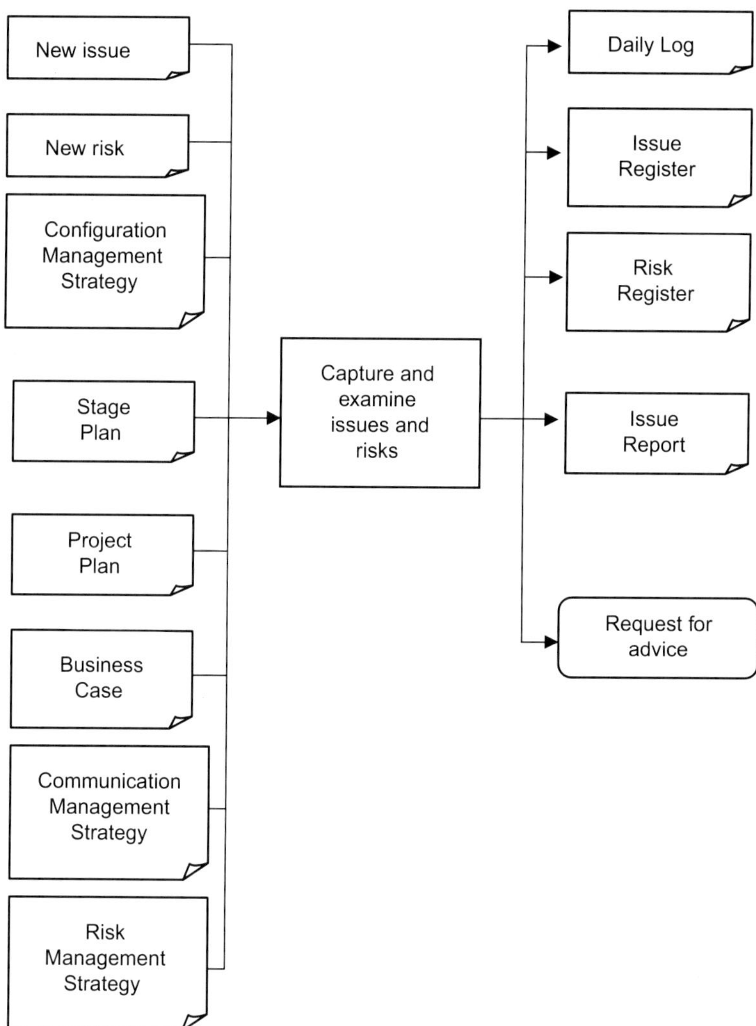

FIGURE 6.7 Capture and examine issues and risks

6.8.2 Why?

At any time during the project a problem may occur, a change may be requested or the answer to a question may be sought. If these are missed, it may mean that the project fails to deliver what is required. Alternatively, the project may run into some other trouble that could have been foreseen, had the issue been noted at the time it arose. There must be a process to capture these so that they can be presented for the appropriate decision and answer.

6.8.3 Responsibility

The Project Manager is responsible. If the project warrants it, help may be given by a Project Support function.

6.8.4 How?

This is achieved by taking the following actions:	Links to other parts of the book
The Project Manager ensures that all possible sources of issues and risks are being monitored.	Change theme
Issues that can be dealt with informally are noted in the Daily Log.	A.7
For issues that need to be managed formally: • Follow the issue and change control procedure in the Configuration Management Strategy. • Enter the issue in the Issue Register. • Raise an Issue Report. • Assess the category, severity and priority of the issue. • Assess the impact on the Stage Plan, Project Plan and Business Case.	A.13
For risks: • Follow the risk management procedure defined in the Risk Management Strategy. • Enter the risk event and cause in the Risk Register. • Assess the effect of the risk on the Stage Plan, Project Plan and Business Case. • Select the most suitable response and plan its implementation. • Check the Risk and Communication Management Strategies to see who should be informed of the risk.	Risk theme A.29 A.28 and A.4

6.9 ESCALATE ISSUES AND RISKS

6.9.1 What Does the Activity Do?

- Analyses each new issue and risk and recommends a course of action.
- Reviews each open issue and risk for any change to its circumstances or impact and potentially makes a new recommendation.
- Reviews all open issues for any impact on the project risks or the Business Case (Figure 6.8).

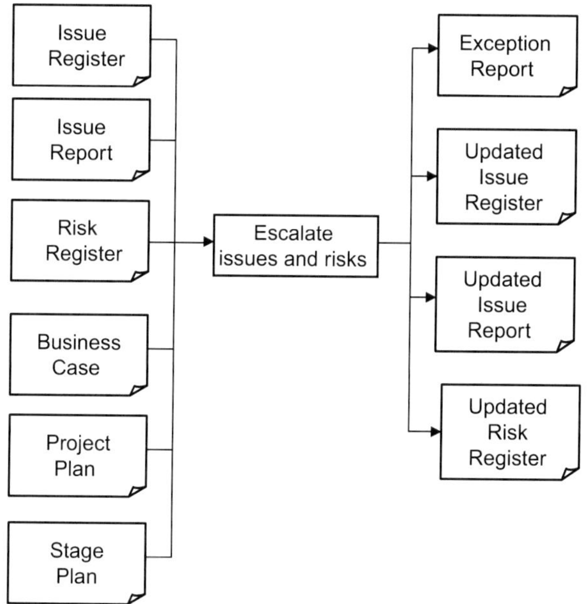

FIGURE 6.8 Escalate issues and risks

6.9.2 Why?

Part of the concept of management by exception is that the Project Manager will bring to the immediate attention of the Project Board anything that can be *forecast* to drive the plan beyond the tolerance limits agreed with the Project Board. This is part of the Project Board staying in overall control.

Where an issue threatens to go beyond tolerances and the Project Manager believes that corrective action cannot be taken within the authority limits imposed by the Project Board, then the situation must be brought to the attention of the Project Board for advice.

Having captured all issues in the *Controlling a Stage* activity *Capture and Examine Issues and Risks* (see 6.8), these should be examined for impact and the appropriate body for any extra information and decision identified.

Escalating issues and risks that threaten tolerances should not be seen as a failure. Project Boards welcome warnings of potential problems far more than advice of a situation when the event has already occurred.

6.9.3 Responsibility

The Project Manager, together with any staff allocated Project Assurance responsibility.

6.9.4 How?

This is achieved by taking the following actions:	Links to other parts of the book
Check the recommended response for its impact on the Stage and Project Plans and Business Case.	6.8 'Capture and Examine Issues and Risks'
Revise the recommendation if any problems are found in it.	
Describe the situation, options and recommendation to the Project Board in an Exception Report.	A.10
Check the Communication Management Strategy for any stakeholders who should also receive a copy of the report.	A.4
Direct the Project Board's decision to the relevant activity.	

6.10 TAKE CORRECTIVE ACTION

6.10.1 What Does the Activity Do?

- Takes action to remedy any problems that arise, within the limits of the tolerance margins established by the Project Board (Figure 6.9).

6.10.2 Why?

Failing to take action when the project is drifting away from the Stage Plan invites loss of control.

6.10.3 Responsibility

The Project Manager, assisted by any Project Support and Project Assurance staff appointed. If the corrective action is to issue a new Work Package or revise an existing one, then the relevant Team Manager will be involved (see activity *Authorize a Work Package* – 6.3).

6.10.4 How?

This is achieved by taking the following actions:	Links to other parts of the book
Ensure that all necessary information about the problem is available.	
Identify action options.	

Continued

This is achieved by taking the following actions:	Links to other parts of the book
Evaluate the effort and cost of the options and the impact of the options on the Stage and Project Plans, Business Case and risks.	
Seek Project Board advice where necessary.	5.6 'Give Ad Hoc Direction'
Select the most appropriate option.	
Check that it will keep the plans within tolerances.	
Implement the corrective actions via a new or revised Work Package and update the Stage Plan, if the work is within tolerances.	
Have any necessary changes made to the affected Configuration Item Records, such as change in producer, cross-references.	A.5

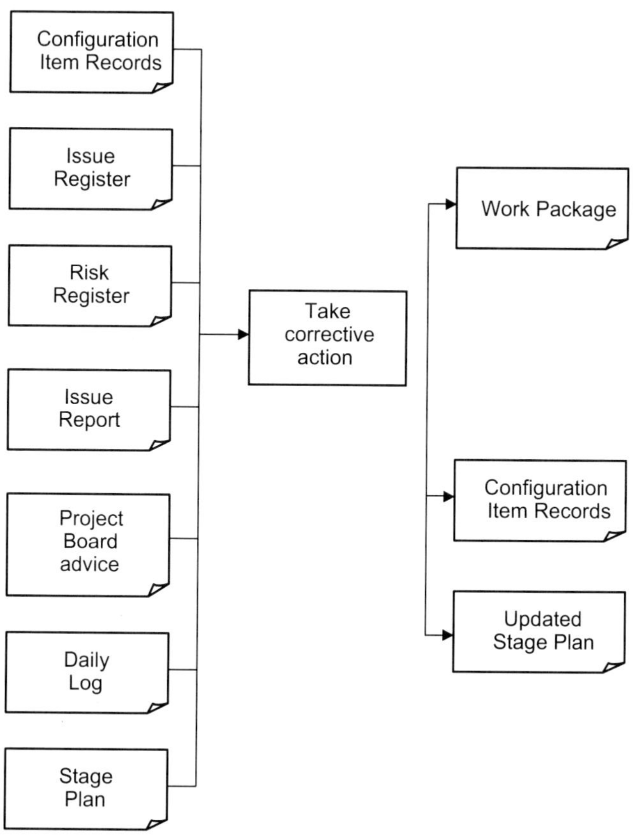

FIGURE 6.9 Take corrective action

Chapter 7

Managing Product Delivery (MP)

7.1 WHAT DOES THE PROCESS DO?

- Agrees work requirements with the Project Manager.
- Does the work.
- Keeps the Project Manager informed on progress, quality and any problems.
- Gets approval for the finished work.
- Notifies the Project Manager that the work is finished (Figure 7.1).

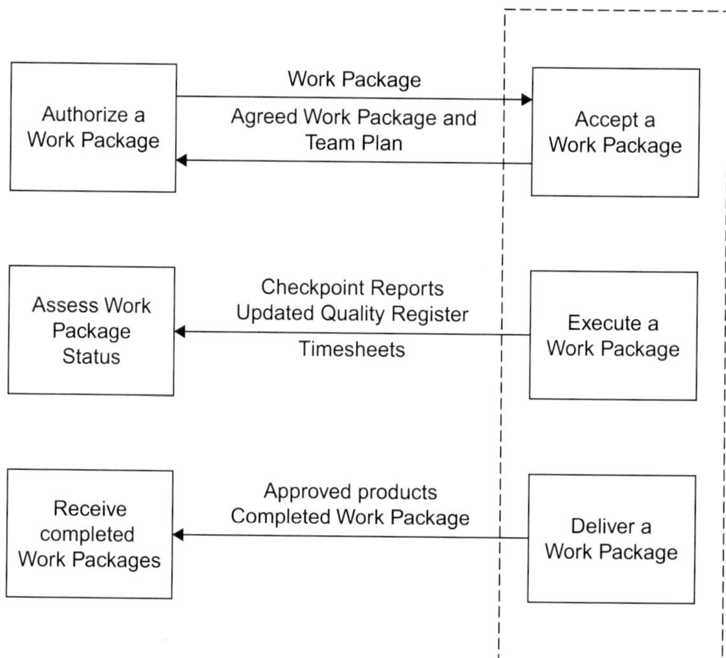

FIGURE 7.1 Managing Product Delivery

7.2 WHY?

Where work is delegated by the Project Manager, there must be appropriate steps by the team or person to whom the work is delegated to indicate understanding and acceptance of the work. While the work is being done, there may be a need to report progress and confirm quality checking. When the work is complete there should be an agreed way of confirming the satisfactory completion.

7.3 ACCEPT A WORK PACKAGE

7.3.1 What Does the Activity Do?

- Agrees the details of a Work Package with the Project Manager.
- Plans the work necessary to complete the Work Package.
- Performs the management of risk against the Work Package Plan.
- Negotiates the time resource requirements or the target date.
- Agrees the quality requirements of the product(s) in the Work Package, the reporting requirements and any tolerance margins or constraints.
- Confirms how approval and handover of the finished product(s) is to be done (Figure 7.2).

7.3.2 Why?

There must be an understanding and agreement between a Team Manager (or an individual) and the Project Manager on any delegated work, constraints, interfaces, reporting requirements and tolerances. The Team Manager has to be satisfied that the Work Package requirements are reasonable and achievable.

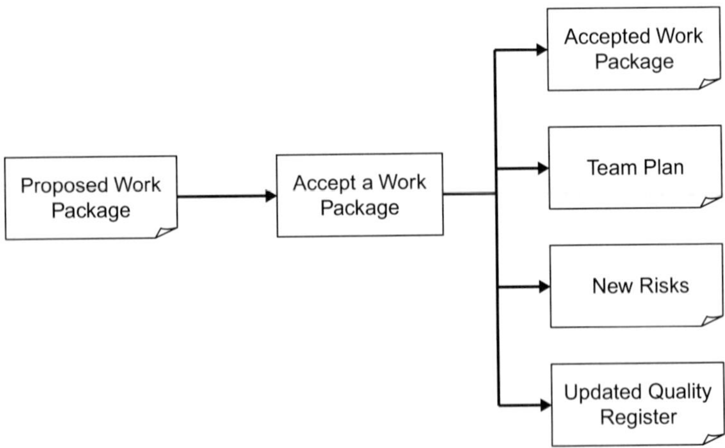

FIGURE 7.2 Accept a Work Package

7.3.3 Responsibility

Normally the responsibility will lie with a Team Manager to agree a Work Package with the Project Manager. If there are no Team Managers, the person who will do the work reports directly to the Project Manager, and this person would be responsible.

7.3.4 How?

This is achieved by taking the following actions:	Links to other parts of the book
Agree with the Project Manager on what is to be delivered.	
Obtain any referenced documents.	
Ensure that the quality requirements are clear.	
Identify in conjunction with Project Assurance any independent people who must be involved in quality checking.	
Identify any target dates and/or constraints for the work.	
Identify any reporting requirements.	
Understand how the products of the Work Package are to be handed over when complete.	A.30
Make a Team Plan to do the work (often this will be done as part of the activity *Plan a Stage,* within the process *Managing a Stage Boundary,* in order to have an accurate Stage Plan).	
Check the plan against the Work Package.	
Advise the Project Manager of any changed or new risks caused as a result of the Team Plan.	
Ensure that the Quality Register is updated with any additional participants identified and target dates from the Team Plan.	A.27
Adjust the plan or negotiate a change to the Work Package so that the Work Package is achievable.	
Agree suitable tolerance margins for the Work Package.	

7.4 EXECUTE A WORK PACKAGE

7.4.1 What Does the Activity Do?

- Manages the development/supply of the products/services defined in the Work Package.
- Obtains approval of the products developed/supplied.
- Hands over the products to whoever is responsible for Configuration Management (Figure 7.3).

7.4.2 Why?

Having agreed and committed to work in the activity *Accept a Work Package*, this activity covers the management of that work until its completion.

7.4.3 Responsibility

The process is the responsibility of the Team Manager.

7.4.4 How?

This is achieved by taking the following actions:	Links to other parts of the book
Allocate work to team members (if there is a Team Manager).	
Ensure that work is conducted according to the procedures and techniques defined in the Work Package.	
Capture and record the effort expended.	
Monitor progress against the tolerances agreed for the work.	
Monitor and control the risks, advising the Project Manager of any new risks.	Risk theme
Evaluate progress and the amount of effort still required to complete the product(s) of the Work Package.	
Feed progress reports back to the Project Manager at the frequency agreed in the Work Package.	Checkpoint Reports
Ensure that the required quality checks are carried out.	
Ensure that any personnel identified in the Work Package or Quality Register are involved in the quality checking.	A.30 and A.27
Ensure that the Quality Register is updated with results of all quality checks, following the procedure specified in the Work Package.	Quality theme
Obtain approval for the completed products according to the direction given in the Work Package.	
Transfer the products and control their release to the project's Configuration Librarian.	
Ensure that the relevant Configuration Item Records are kept up-to-date.	A.5
Update the Team Plan to reflect progress.	
Raise issues to advise the Project Manager of any problems.	

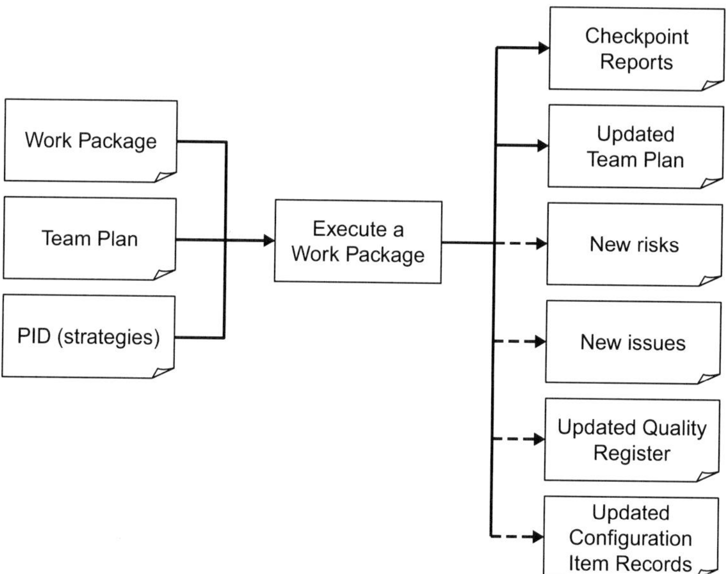

FIGURE 7.3 Execute a Work Package

7.5 DELIVER A WORK PACKAGE

7.5.1 What Does the Activity Do?

- Advises the Project Manager of the completion of the work (Figure 7.4).

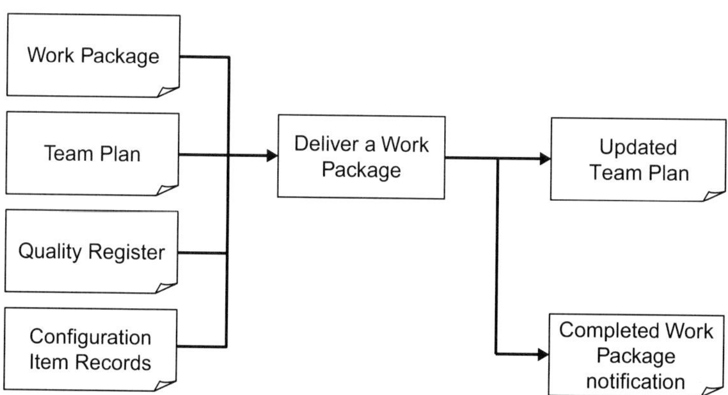

FIGURE 7.4 Deliver a Work Package

7.5.2 Why?

There has to be a process to deliver the requested product(s) and document the agreement that the work has been done satisfactorily.

7.5.3 Responsibility

Team Manager. If there is no Team Manager, then the responsibility lies with either an individual or the Project Manager, depending on to whom the Work Package was allocated.

7.5.4 How?

This is achieved by taking the following actions:	Links to other parts of the book
Confirm that the Quality Register has been updated with details of a successful check on the quality of the product(s).	A.27
Update the Team Plan to show completion of the Work Package.	
Follow the procedure in delivering completed products to the destination defined in the Work Package.	
Advise the Project Manager that the Work Package is complete.	

Chapter 8

Managing a Stage Boundary (SB)

8.1 WHAT DOES THE PROCESS DO?

- Confirms to the Project Board which products planned to be produced in the current Stage Plan have been delivered.
- Gives reasons for the non-delivery of any products which were planned (in the case of deviation forecasts).
- Verifies that any useful lessons learned during the current stage have been recorded in the Lessons Log.
- Provides information to the Project Board to allow it to assess the continued viability of the project.
- Obtains approval for the next Stage Plan or the Exception Plan.
- Ascertains the tolerance margins to be applied to the new plan (Figure 8.1).

8.2 WHY?

The ability to authorize a project to move forward a stage at a time is a major control for the Project Board. There is also a need for a process to create a plan to react to a forecast deviation beyond tolerances. This process aims to provide the information needed by the Project Board about the current status of the Project Plan, Business Case and risks to enable them to judge the continuing worth of the project and commitment to a new plan.

8.3 PLAN THE NEXT STAGE

8.3.1 What Does the Activity Do?

- Prepares a plan for the next stage (Figure 8.2).

8.3.2 Why?

In order to adequately control a stage the Project Manager needs a plan in which the detailed activities go down to the level of a handful of days.

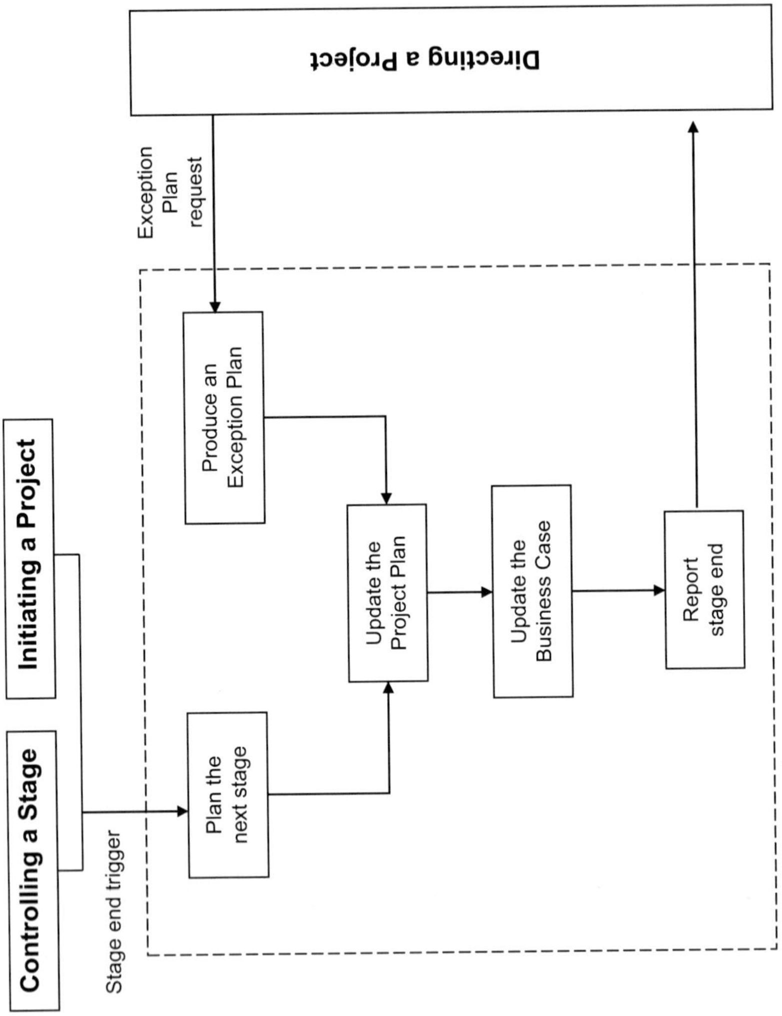

FIGURE 8.1 Managing a Stage Boundary

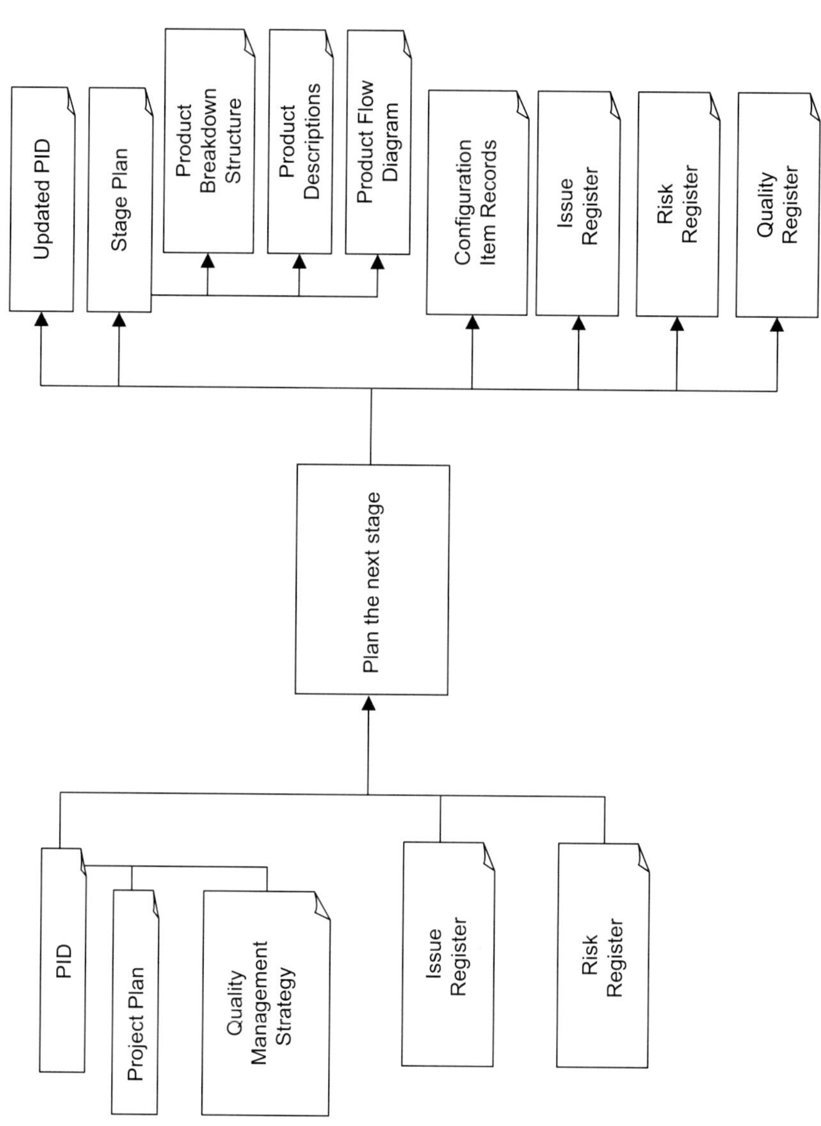

FIGURE 8.2 Plan the next stage

8.3.3 Responsibility

The Project Manager is responsible, but will need help from Project Support, the Project Board and Team Managers. Any Project Assurance functions should review the plan to ensure products have suitable and timely quality checks with appropriate resources assigned.

8.3.4 How?

This is achieved by taking the following actions:	Links to other parts of the book
Check for any changes to the customer's quality expectations and acceptance criteria.	14.3.1
Check the project approach for any guidance on how the products of the next stage are to be produced.	3.7
Check the Issue Register for any issues which will affect the next Stage Plan.	A.12
Review the Project Plan for the products to be produced in the next stage.	
Review the Risk and Issue Registers for entries that may affect the next stage.	A.29 and A.12
Use the Product-based Planning technique to create the draft Stage Plan.	Appendix C
Document any changes to the personnel of the project management team.	
Discuss the draft plan with those who have Project Assurance responsibilities for the Senior User and Senior Supplier in order to include quality-checking activities.	
Review the Quality Management Strategy for the quality standards and procedures to be used.	A.26
Add any formal quality reviews and any other quality checks required for Project Assurance purposes.	Appendix D
Identify (as a minimum) the chair of each formal quality review.	
Working with those with Project Assurance responsibility, identify the required reviewers for each formal quality review.	
Enter details of quality checks and involved personnel in the Quality Register.	A.27
Ensure that the plan includes all required management products.	
Create or update Configuration Item Records for the products of the next stage.	A.5
Check the plan for any new or changed risks and update the Risk Register.	A.29
Modify the plan, if necessary, in the light of the risk analysis.	

8.4 UPDATE THE PROJECT PLAN

8.4.1 What Does the Activity Do?

- Updates the Project Plan with the actual costs and schedule from the stage that has just finished, plus the estimated cost and schedule of the next Stage Plan (Figure 8.3).

8.4.2 Why?

As one stage is completed and the next one planned, the Project Plan must be updated. The Project Board needs to have the most up-to-date information on likely project costs and a schedule on which to partially base its decision on whether the project is still a viable business proposition.

8.4.3 Responsibility

The Project Manager is responsible, but may have help from Project Support.

8.4.4 How?

This is achieved by taking the following actions:	Links to other parts of the book
Ensure that the current Stage Plan has been updated with final costs and dates.	
Create a new version of the Project Plan ready to be updated.	A.16
Update the Project Plan with the actual costs and dates of the current stage.	
Update the Project Plan with the estimated costs, resource requirements and dates of the next stage or Exception Plan.	
Update any later stages of the Project Plan on the basis of any relevant information made available since the last update.	
Check to see if events mean that the project approach has to be modified.	
Check to see if events require any changes to the Quality Management Strategy.	A.26
Check the latest version of the Project Initiation Documentation for any change to strategies or the project management team that might affect the Project Plan.	A.23
Update the Risk and Issue Registers if new or changed issues or risks have been identified.	

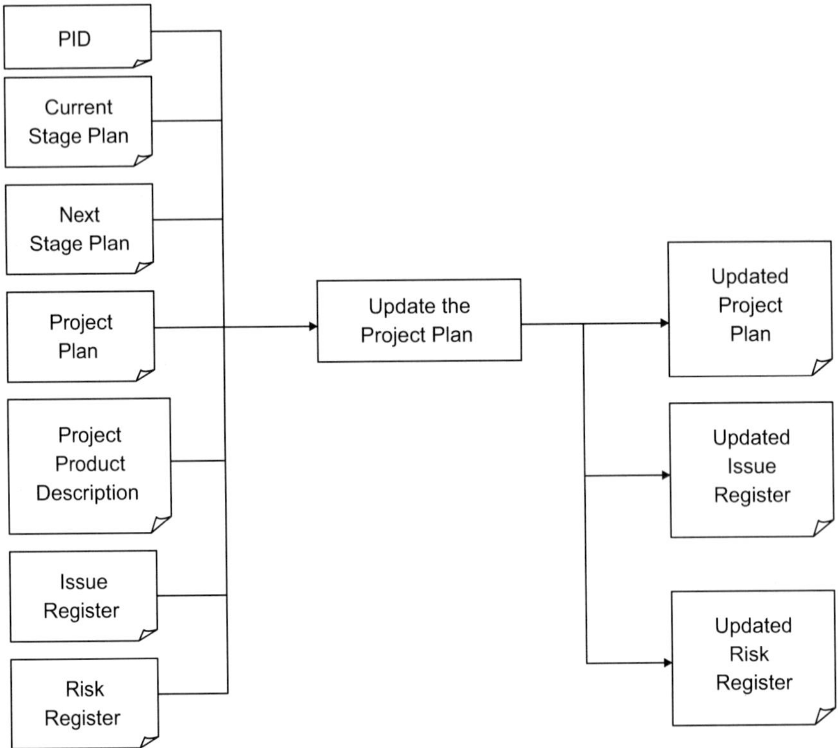

FIGURE 8.3 Update the Project Plan

8.5 UPDATE THE BUSINESS CASE

8.5.1 What Does the Activity Do?

- Modifies the Business Case, where appropriate, on the basis of information from the updated Project Plan.
- Checks the known risks to project success for any change to their circumstances and looks for any new risks.
- Updates the Benefits Review Plan with the results of any benefits reviews carried out in the stage (Figure 8.4).

8.5.2 Why?

The whole project should be business-driven, so the Project Board should review a revised Business Case as a major part of the check on the continued viability of the project.

Part of the assessment of the project's viability is an examination of the likelihood and impact of potential risks.

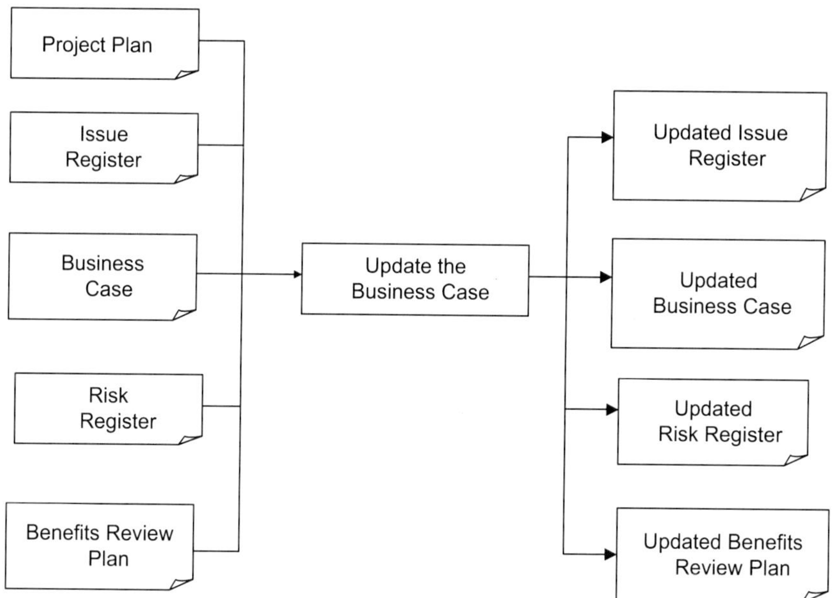

FIGURE 8.4 Update the Business Case

8.5.3 Responsibility

The Project Manager and whoever has responsibility for the Executive's Project Assurance for the project.

The Project Manager collates the information on risks, but each known risk should have been allocated to an 'owner', the person best placed to monitor that risk. (N.B. Not necessarily the person who will have to make a decision if the risk occurs, but the best placed to keep an eye on the risk.)

8.5.4 How?

This is achieved by taking the following actions:	Links to other parts of the book
Create a new version of the Business Case ready to be updated.	A.2
Review the impact of any approved changes on the expected benefits.	
Review the expected costs in the investment appraisal against the new forecast in the updated Project Plan.	

Continued

This is achieved by taking the following actions:	Links to other parts of the book
Review the financial benefits in the investment appraisal against any new forecasts.	
Review the reasons in the Business Case and check that there has been no change or that no new reasons have come to light.	
Modify the new version of the Business Case in the light of any changes to forecast benefits.	
Update the Benefits Review Plan with the results of any benefits reviews carried out in the current stage.	A.1
Check that the project's risk exposure remains within risk tolerances.	
Check if the project's risk appetite has changed.	
Ensure that the Risk Register is up-to-date with the latest information on the identified risks.	A.29
Ensure that any new risks identified in creating the next Stage Plan have been entered in the Risk Register.	
Assess all open risks to the project, as defined in the Risk Register.	
Decide if the next Stage Plan needs to be modified to avoid, reduce or monitor risks.	
Create contingency plans for any serious risks which cannot be avoided or reduced to manageable proportions.	
Update the Issue and Risk Registers if required.	

8.6 REPORT STAGE END

8.6.1 What Does the Activity Do?

- Reports on the results of the current stage.
- Forecasts the time and resource requirements of the next stage, if applicable.
- Gives a view on the continuing viability of the project to meet the Project Plan and Business Case.
- Assesses the overall risk situation.
- Looks for a Project Board decision on the future of the project (Figure 8.5).

8.6.2 Why?

Normally the Project Board manages by exception and therefore only needs to meet if things are forecast to deviate beyond tolerance levels. But as part of its control the Project Board only gives approval to the Project Manager to

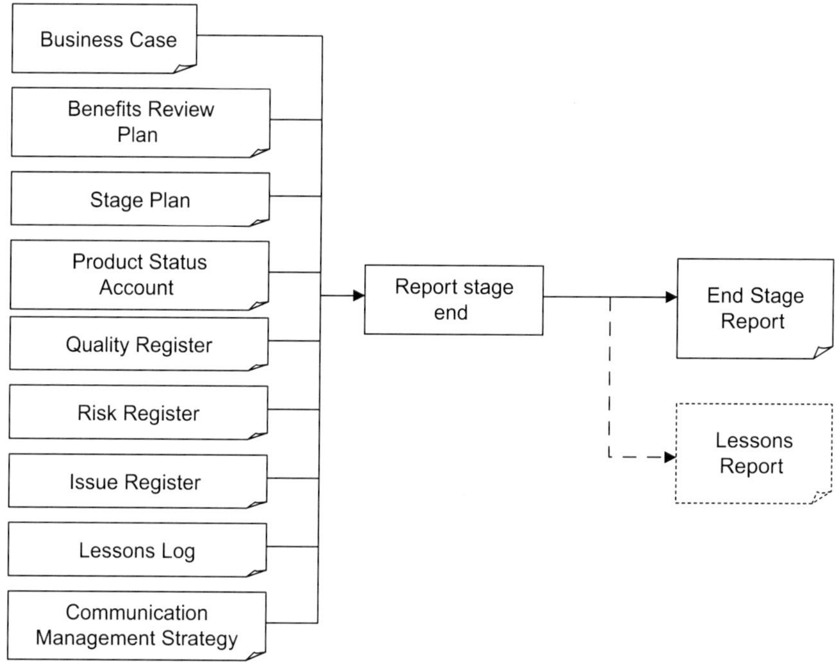

FIGURE 8.5 Report stage end

undertake one stage at a time, at the end of which it reviews the anticipated benefits, costs, timescale and risks and makes a decision whether to continue with the project or not.

8.6.3 Responsibility

The Project Manager is responsible.

8.6.4 How?

This is achieved by taking the following actions:	Links to other parts of the book
Report on the actual costs and time of the current stage and measure these against the plan which was approved by the Project Board.	
Report on the impact on the Project Plan of the current stage's costs and time taken.	

Continued

This is achieved by taking the following actions:	Links to other parts of the book
Report on any impact from the current stage's results on the Business Case.	A.2
Report on the status of the Issue Register.	A.12
Report on the extent and results of the quality work done in the current stage.	
Provide details of the next Stage Plan (if applicable).	
Identify any necessary revisions to the Project Plan caused by the next Stage Plan.	
Identify any changes to the Business Case caused by the next Stage Plan.	
Report on any benefits reviews carried out in the stage.	
Report on the risk situation.	
Recommend the next action (for example, approval of the next Stage Plan).	

8.7 PRODUCE AN EXCEPTION PLAN

8.7.1 What Does the Activity Do?

- Prepares a new plan at the request of the Project Board, to replace the remainder of the current plan in response to an Exception Report (Figure 8.6).

8.7.2 Why?

The Project Board approves a Stage Plan on the understanding that it stays within its defined tolerance margins. When an Exception Report indicates that the current tolerances are likely to be exceeded, it no longer has that approval. The Project Board may ask for a new plan to reflect the changed situation, which can be controlled within newly specified tolerance margins.

8.7.3 Responsibility

The Project Manager is responsible in consultation with the Project Assurance function.

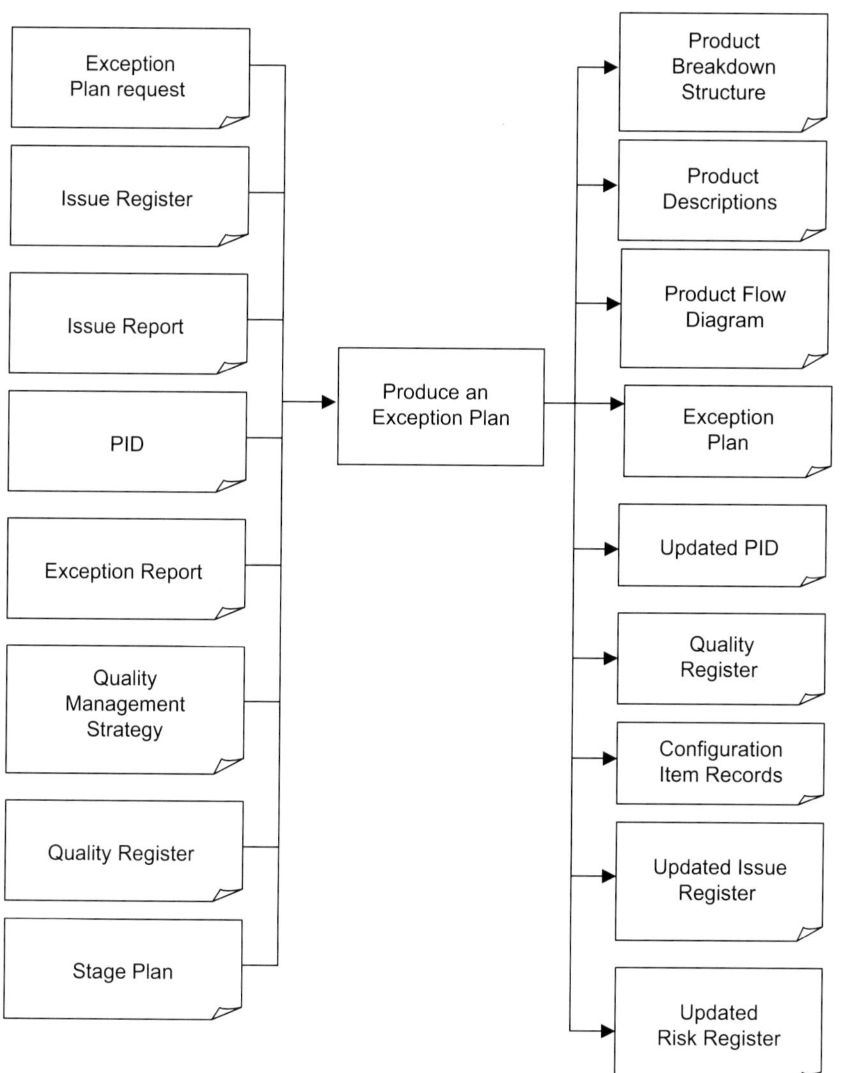

FIGURE 8.6 Produce an Exception Plan

8.7.4 How?

This is achieved by taking the following actions:	Links to other parts of the book
Record the Project Board request for an Exception Plan on the Issue Register and Issue Report.	A.12 and A.13
Consult with the Project Board on whether any changes are required to the Project Initiation Documentation, such as the: • customer's quality expectations; • project approach; • strategies; • project management team, such as suppliers or Project Assurance, or simply resource needs.	A.23
Extract from the current Stage Plan the incomplete products.	
Examine the Exception Report for any newly identified products or changes to existing ones.	A.10
Create a Product Breakdown Structure, any new or revised Product Descriptions and a Product Flow Diagram for the Exception Plan.	Appendix C
Review the Quality Management Strategy to understand the quality requirements, standards and activities that need to be added to the Exception Plan.	A.26
Complete the Exception Plan with activities, resources and scheduling.	Plans theme
Update the Quality Register with details of the planned checks and personnel.	A.27
Create any new Configuration Item Records and check existing ones that are included in the Exception Plan for any required updates.	A.5
Review the Exception Plan for new or changed risks or issues.	

Chapter 9

Closing a Project (CP)

9.1 WHAT DOES THE PROCESS DO?

- Checks that all required products have been delivered and accepted.
- Checks that support and maintenance teams are prepared to take over the running of the project outcome.
- Checks that all issues have been dealt with.
- Records any recommendations for subsequent work on the product.
- Passes on any useful lessons learned during the project.
- Reviews project performance against the Project Initiation Documentation.
- Recommends closure of the project to the Project Board.
- Confirms plans to measure the achievement of the project's Business Case (Figure 9.1).

9.2 WHY?

Every project should come to a controlled completion.

In order to have its success measured, a project must be brought to a close when the Project Manager believes that it has met the objectives set out in the Project Initiation Documentation.

There should be an agreed plan to judge achievement of the claimed benefits when it is appropriate to do so.

9.3 PREPARE PLANNED CLOSURE

9.3.1 What Does the Activity Do?

- Updates the Project Plan with the final costs and times from the final Stage Plan.
- Gets agreement from the customer that the acceptance criteria have been met.

- Confirms acceptance of the project's product from the customer and those who will support the product during its operational life.
- Checks that all issues are closed.
- Obtains agreement from the Project Board that project resources can be released (Figure 9.2).

9.3.2 Why?

The customer, Project Manager and supplier must agree that a project has met its objectives before it can close.

There must be a check that there are no outstanding problems or requests.

The project documentation, particularly agreements and approvals, should be preserved for any later audits.

9.3.3 Responsibility

The Project Manager and any Project Support staff assigned to the project.

9.3.4 How?

This is achieved by taking the following actions:	Links to other parts of the book
Update the Project Plan with actuals from the final stage.	
Obtain a Product Status Account and review the Project Product Description to: • ensure that all products have been completed and accepted by the customer; • get the customer's agreement that the acceptance criteria have been met.	A.21
Check that all issues have been closed and any incomplete ones transferred as follow-on action recommendations.	
Check that any open risks that might affect the products in their operational environment have been transferred as follow-on action recommendations.	
Ensure that, where applicable, those who will be responsible for maintenance and support of the products are ready to accept the product.	
Prepare a request to the Project Board to release project staff and set a date for receipt of final invoices from suppliers.	

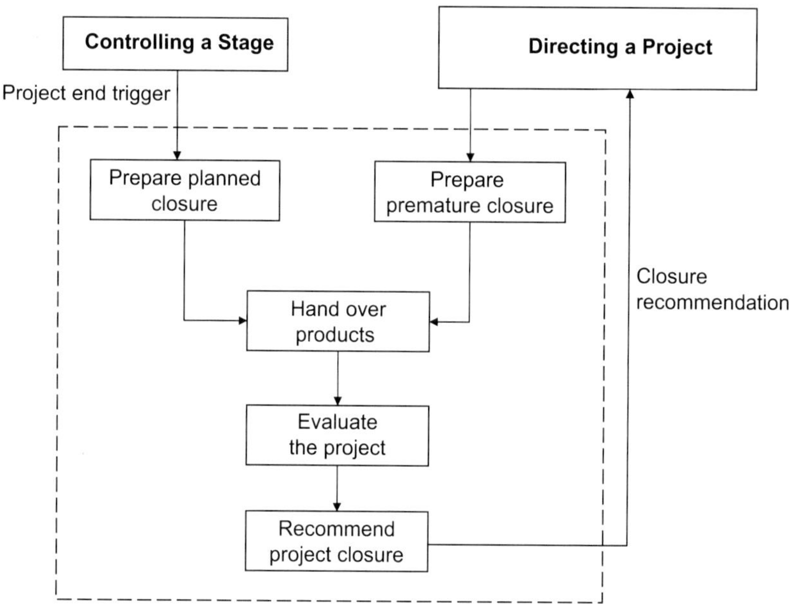

FIGURE 9.1 Closing a Project

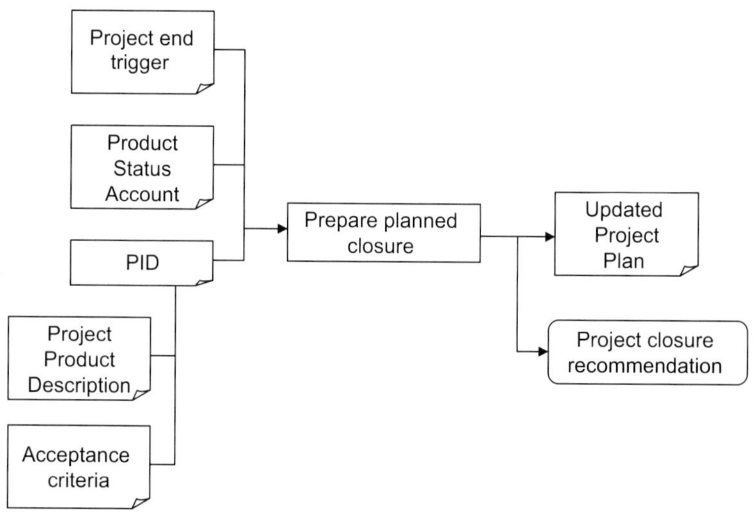

FIGURE 9.2 Prepare planned closure

9.4 PREPARE PREMATURE CLOSURE

9.4.1 What Does the Activity Do?

- Identifies any finished or unfinished products that can be used.
- Raises any problems caused by the premature termination of the project via the Project Board to corporate/programme management (Figure 9.3).

9.4.2 Why?

The project and its products should not simply be abandoned. Every effort should be made to salvage anything useful from the terminated project.

9.4.3 Responsibility

The Project Manager is responsible. Input should be sought from any Project Assurance roles used.

9.4.4 How?

This is achieved by taking the following actions:	Links to other parts of the book
Update the Exception Report (if there is one), the Issue Report and Issue Register to note the instruction to prematurely close the project.	A.10, A.13 and A.12
Update the Project Plan with final details of costs and times from the Stage Plan.	
Obtain a Product Status Account to identify which products: • have already been approved; • are under development, especially those that will still require work – for example, buildings to be made safe and secure; • may be useful to other projects.	A.21
Agree with the Project Board any work required from examination of the Product Status Account. This work may require an Exception Plan and approval from the Project Board.	
Check that all issues have been closed and any incomplete ones transferred as follow-on action recommendations.	
Check that any open risks that might affect the operational environment have been transferred as follow-on action recommendations.	
Ensure that, where applicable, those who will be responsible for maintenance and support of the products are ready to accept those products that were completed or are in a state where use can be made of them.	
Ensure that the reason for premature closure is recorded in the Lessons Log.	A.14
Prepare a request to the Project Board to release project staff and set a date for receipt of final invoices from suppliers.	

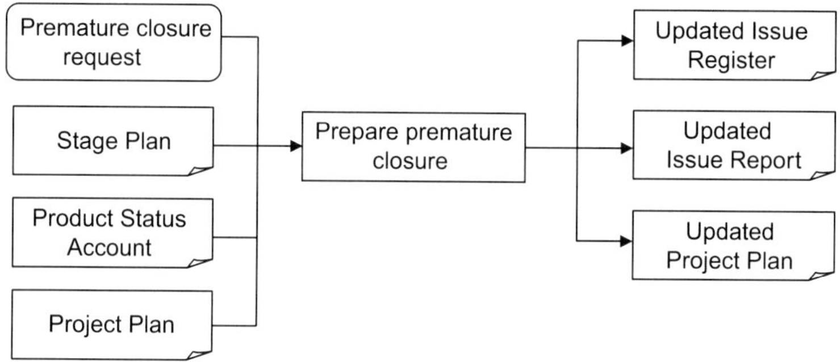

FIGURE 9.3 Prepare premature closure

9.5 HAND OVER PRODUCTS

9.5.1 What Does the Activity Do?

- Passes the project's products to the relevant operational and maintenance environment.
- Updates the Benefits Review Plan to show how and when those benefits that will only be achieved after an amount of operational use are to be calculated (Figure 9.4).

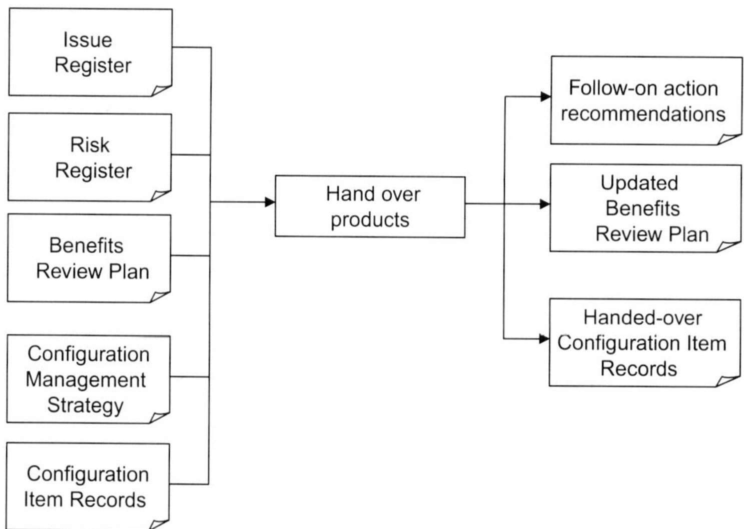

FIGURE 9.4 Hand over products

9.5.2 Why?

There must be a controlled handover of the project's products to those who will operate and maintain the finished product.

9.5.3 Responsibility

The Project Manager is responsible but must liaise with the customer and supplier to ensure a smooth and complete handover.

9.5.4 How?

This is achieved by taking the following actions:	Links to other parts of the book
Ensure there are follow-on action recommendations for any incomplete issues or risks that might affect operational use of the products.	
Check that the Benefits Review Plan contains measurements for all claimed benefits that cannot be checked until after a period of operational use of the products.	A.1
Check the Configuration Management Strategy to confirm how products are to be handed over to the customer.	A.6
Check that a suitable operational and maintenance environment is ready and prepared to accept the handover.	
Transfer the products to the customer.	
Update the Configuration Item Records.	A.5
Check if the configuration library is to be moved to a new site.	

9.6 EVALUATE THE PROJECT

9.6.1 What Does the Activity Do?

- Assesses the project's results against its objectives.
- Provides statistics on the performance of the project.
- Records useful lessons that were learned (Figure 9.5).

9.6.2 Why?

One way in which to improve the quality of project management is to learn from the lessons of past projects.

As part of closing the project, the Project Board needs to assess the performance of the project and the Project Manager. This may also form part of the customer's appraisal of a supplier, to see if the contract has been completed or to see if that supplier should be used again.

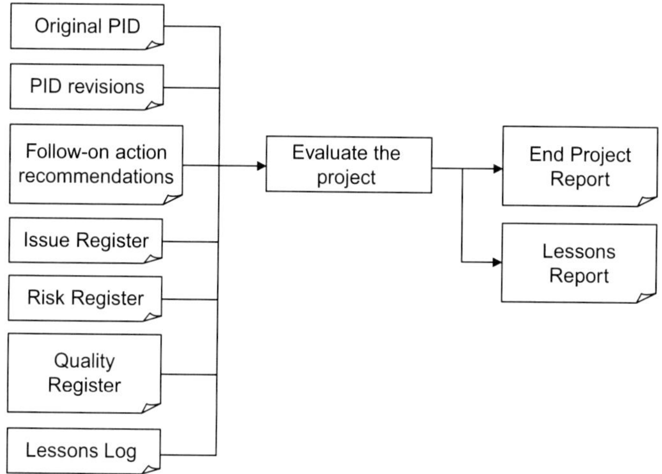

FIGURE 9.5 Evaluate the project

9.6.3 Responsibility

The Project Manager, Project Support and any quality assurance or centre of expertise personnel used.

9.6.4 How?

This is achieved by taking the following actions:	Links to other parts of the book
Review the original Project Initiation Documentation and the changes to it to understand what the project was supposed to achieve.	A.23
Write the End Project Report: • Evaluate the project performance against the expectations described in the Project Initiation Documentation, including the Project Plan and tolerances. • Evaluate the management, quality and technical methods, tools and processes used. • Examine the Risk Register and actions taken and record any useful comments. • Examine the Issue Register and actions taken and record any useful comments. • Examine the Quality Register and record any useful comments.	A.8
Assemble the items in the Lessons Log into the Lessons Report.	A.15

9.7 RECOMMEND PROJECT CLOSURE

9.7.1 What Does the Activity Do?

- Sends a recommendation for closure of the project to the Project Board.
- Closes all of the project's registers and logs.
- Archives all of the project's documentation (Figure 9.6).

9.7.2 Why?

Projects must come to a controlled finish with no loose ends.

9.7.3 Responsibility

The Project Manager, Project Support and any quality assurance or centre of expertise personnel used.

9.7.4 How?

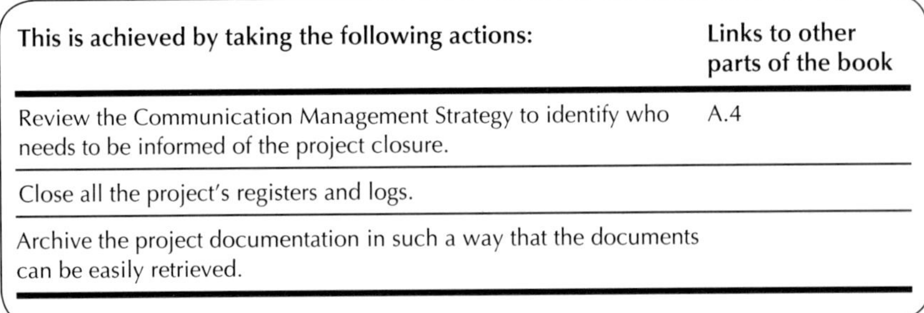

This is achieved by taking the following actions:	Links to other parts of the book
Review the Communication Management Strategy to identify who needs to be informed of the project closure.	A.4
Close all the project's registers and logs.	
Archive the project documentation in such a way that the documents can be easily retrieved.	

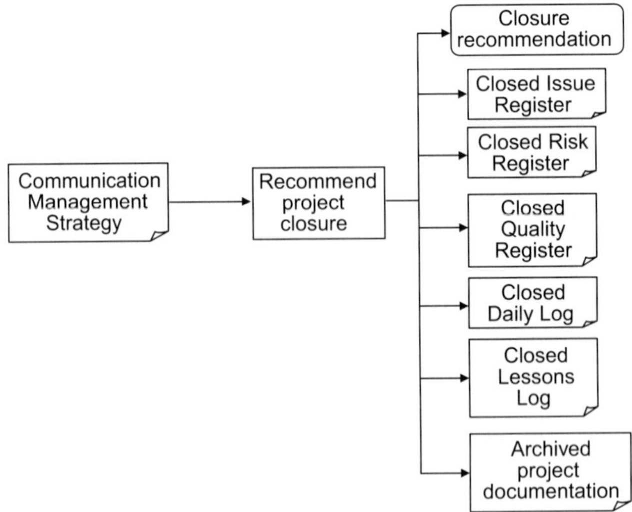

FIGURE 9.6 Recommend project closure

Chapter 10

Business Case

10.1 PHILOSOPHY

PRINCE2's philosophy is that the driving force of a project is its Business Case. No project should start without a valid Business Case; a project should be terminated if its Business Case becomes invalid.

A project's Business Case must include all the business changes, costs and impacts of the final product. Examples of this might include retraining members of staff, the provision of new premises and equipment and the costs of changeover to the new product.

The Executive is the owner of the Business Case. It is the Executive's responsibility to ensure that the Business Case remains aligned with the company's business strategy. Having said this, the Senior User is responsible for specifying the benefits, which is reasonable, because they will be responsible for realizing the benefits when the finished product is delivered. The Executive must check that the claimed benefits are realistic and represent good value for the project's investment.

10.2 BUSINESS CASE OVERVIEW

In an ideal world there would be a Business Case within the project mandate. Certainly the Project Brief must have at least the reasons why the project should be done as part of its outline Business Case. This would be checked by the Project Board as part of its decision on whether to enter the initiation stage.

During initiation the Business Case is expanded and completed. Costs are input to it from the Project Plan; a summary of risks is added, together with an overview of the options considered for meeting the business problem and reasons for the selection of the chosen option. An investment appraisal is created to show the benefits and savings that the new product is expected to achieve. (Appendix A contains a Business Case Product Description, showing the recommended contents of a Business Case.)

10.2.1 Business Case Options

The options mentioned here are not those considered when creating the project approach. The Business Case options are the different ways that were considered to solve the business problem. For example, if the business problem is that sales are dropping, options might be:

- Do nothing.
- A TV advertising campaign.
- Newspaper advertisements.
- Buying out a competitor.
- Lowering prices.
- Making a New Year calendar advertising the company's products.

If the last one is the chosen option, the project approach would look at how to provide the calendar.

'Do nothing' should always be the first business option. It provides a basis for quantifying the other options. What would happen to the business problem if nothing was done? What would be the potential losses? What are the costs of continuing as we are today? This can be compared against the costs and potential savings and benefits of each other option. After the 'Business Case' for each option has been considered, the recommended option should also be documented in the Business Case, together with the reasons for choosing it.

Wherever possible, benefits and savings should be defined in a measurable form. Careful measurements of the current situation should be taken in order to later discover whether use of the new product has achieved the benefits and savings.

The expected benefits will influence the products to be provided by the project. Mapping benefits to outcomes to required products helps decision-making in the planning and control of the project. No products should be there that do not directly or indirectly enable the expected benefits to be achieved.

10.2.2 Expected Dis-benefits

The PRINCE2 2009 manual uses this term in the Business Case to describe negative outcomes or consequences of the project. I prefer to use 'negative outcomes', 'negative effects' or even 'negative benefits'. Whichever phrase you use, it describes the bad results expected either during the project or when using the project outcome. For example, a project that turns a motorway into a toll road would have a negative outcome, because of the number of drivers leaving the motorway and driving through already-congested towns to avoid paying a toll.

CARTOON 10.1 Discounted Cash Flow

10.2.3 Benefits Tolerance

Stating benefits in measurable terms helps the setting of benefits tolerance – for example, a sales increase of 15–25%, or a reduction in road casualties by 5–10% for a project to provide a pedestrian crossing.

10.2.4 Investment Appraisal

This compares the development and operational costs against the expected savings and benefits. It normally evaluates these over a period of years or the life of the product. The customer will define the range to be used and may have accounting rules on how the investment appraisal is to be calculated.

10.2.5 Use of the Business Case

The Business Case forms part of the Project Initiation Documentation. The Project Board must be sure that the Business Case is valid before authorizing the project.

A review of the Business Case is part of every Project Board decision, such as at each end stage assessment, consideration of an Exception Report and confirmation of project closure. This means that the Business Case must be maintained throughout the project. For example, it is updated in the *Managing a Stage Boundary* process with the latest information from the revised Project Plan.

10.2.6 Benefits Review Plan

The Business Case feeds the claimed benefits into the Benefits Review Plan. This plan defines how, when and with what resources measurement of benefit achievement should be done. It may not be possible to realize most or all benefits until the products have been in operational use for some time, maybe months. This is one reason why benefits have to be stated in measurable terms and why measurements should be taken at the beginning of the project, so that progress in achieving them can be seen.

The Benefits Review Plan is created in the activity *Refine the Business Case* (part of the *Initiating a Project* process), and updated at the end of each stage in the activity *Update the Business Case* (part of the *Managing a Stage Boundary* process) and when closing the project (see the activity *Handing over Products* in the process *Closing a Project*).

If part of a programme, the Benefits Review Plan may be held and managed by the programme.

Some benefits may be achieved within the life of the project. In such cases, this is reported by the Project Manager in the End Stage Report (in the activity *Report Stage End*, part of the *Managing a Stage Boundary* process). The Executive is responsible for ensuring that any benefits reviews done within the project are planned and executed.

For post-project benefits reviews the responsibility passes from the Executive to corporate/programme management. This is because the project management team will have been disbanded and the benefits review will have to be funded and resourced. Corporate/programme management will expect those who were the Senior Users to provide evidence of benefit achievement.

Post-project reviews should also consider whether there are any side effects or bottlenecks caused by use of the end product and a review of user opinions of the outcome.

10.3 LINKS

A basic Business Case should appear in the project mandate or be developed as part of preparing the Project Brief.

There is a major link with the initiation stage, in which the Project Manager should finalize the Business Case before the Project Board decides whether the project should be undertaken.

The Business Case should be revised at the end of each stage as part of the *Managing a Stage Boundary* process (also in the event of raising an Exception Plan). This feeds into the end stage assessment, which is the review by the Project Board in the *Authorize a Stage or Exception Plan* activity as part of its decision on whether to continue with the project.

The impact on the Business Case is assessed for each major issue as part of the activity *Capture and Examine Issues and Risks*.

Achievement of the Business Case is finally judged when implementing the Benefits Review Plan after project closure.

The implications of risk management should be linked to the Business Case.

Chapter 11

Organization

11.1 PHILOSOPHY

A project needs a different organization structure from line management. It needs to be more flexible and is likely to require a broad base of skills for a comparatively short period of time. A project is often cross-functional and may need to combine people working full time on the project with others who have to divide their time between the project and other duties. The Project Manager may have direct management control over some of the project staff, but may also have to direct staff that report to another management structure (Cartoon 11.1).

The management structure of the customer will very often be different from that of the supplier. They will have different priorities, different interests to protect, but in some way they must be united in the common aims of the project.

The PRINCE2 organization for any project is based on a customer/supplier relationship. The customer is the person or group who wants the end product, specifies what it should be and, usually, pays for the development of that product. The supplier is whoever provides the resources to build or procure the

CARTOON 11.1 Responsibility

end product. This is true even if the customer and supplier work for the same company. If this is the case they may still, for example, report to different lines of management, have different budgets and therefore have a different view of the finances of the project. The customer will be asking, 'Will the end product save me money or bring in a profit?' The supplier will be asking if the provision of appropriate resources will earn a profit.

11.2 THE THREE PROJECT INTERESTS

The following are the decisions and commitments that a project needs to make:

- Budget and resource commitment.
- Specification of needs.
- Alignment with company strategies.

The project controllers must represent the three bodies that contribute to the project:

- Business (money, company strategy).
- User (what are the requirements?).
- Supplier (production of the specialist products) (Figure 11.1).

11.2.1 Business

The justification of any project depends upon it meeting a business need. The outcome of a project should match company strategy. A project should provide value for money. The business view should have a decision-making role in a project to ensure that these three prerequisites are present at the start of a project and are maintained throughout the project. The Executive looks after the business interests.

11.2.2 User

Users of the final products, on the other hand, are interested in getting as many of their requirements met as they can, which may clash at times with the need to get value for money. PRINCE2 therefore makes a distinction between the

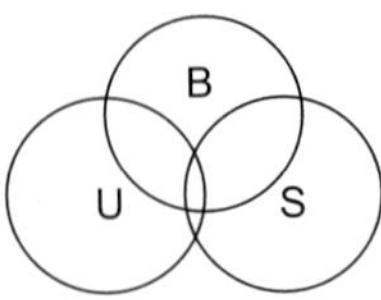

FIGURE 11.1 Business, user and supplier

business interests and those who will use the project's outputs. The user role on the Project Board represents those who will:

- specify the desired outputs;
- use the project outputs to realize the benefits;
- operate and maintain the project's outputs;
- be affected by the outputs.

These interests are part of the Senior User role on the Project Board. Remember that you may need more than one person to represent different groups of users. Alternatively, a small project may be able to combine this role with that of the Executive.

11.2.3 Supplier

The Senior Supplier role on the Project Board represents those who will provide the project's outputs. There may be more than one supplier. You must be careful to appoint managers who can commit the required resources. There may be in-house and external suppliers. There may be one major supplier and many smaller suppliers. You do not want too many to share the Senior Supplier role. Can one major supplier commit the resources of smaller suppliers by means of contracts with them? If there are several suppliers who will not agree to have another supplier make commitments on their behalf, is it better to have the customer's purchasing manager take the Senior Supplier role and control all the suppliers through contracts?

If the selection of a supplier is an early part of the project, here again the purchasing manager may take the Senior Supplier role until a supplier is chosen.

The customer/supplier philosophy works for most projects. If a company has decided to create a product for a given market, then the customer and user role is normally taken by the marketing function to represent the perceived end users of the product.

11.3 FOUR LAYERS OF MANAGEMENT

When designing what the project organization should be, the PRINCE2 philosophy is to consider the four layers of management. According to the size and importance of the project, you may not need all four to be represented, but that should be a decision you take when you understand the philosophy and can compare it to the needs of a specific project (Figure 11.2).

The project management team structure allows for the *possible* inclusion of the four layers of management.

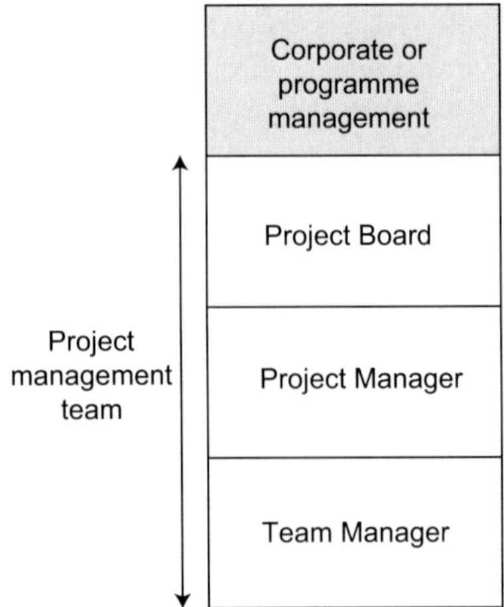

FIGURE 11.2 Four layers of management

11.3.1 Layer One

This layer is concerned with the business strategy. This layer provides a vision of what the company should look like and what it should be doing in the future. It has to coordinate all the projects going on to change the company to the vision that they have for it. For each project they appoint a Project Board to act on their behalf within certain constraints. I will address these constraints in the Progress theme.

11.3.2 Layer Two

This layer is called the Project Board. This consists of the roles that are needed to take those decisions that are too big for the Project Manager's authority level. Examples of such questions the Project Board would answer are:

- Is the proposed solution in line with company strategy?
- Is the project within tolerance of its planned timeframe and/or budget?
- Should they continue or close the project?
- Do they want to pay for this major change request?
- Does the product meet their requirements?

11.3.3 Layer Three

Layer three is the Project Manager role, the day-to-day planning, monitoring and control of the project.

11.3.4 Layer Four

If a project is large enough to need more than one team working on it, the teams form layer four. Geography may be a factor in deciding whether you need Team Managers. If the developers are in groups some distance away from each other, it is very difficult to manage them all personally. Skill set may be another reason for separate teams.

The other case is where the solution is to be provided by a third party. The external supplier will want to manage its own resources.

11.4 PROJECT MANAGEMENT TEAM STRUCTURE

To fulfil the philosophy described at the start of this chapter, PRINCE2 has a project management team structure.

Appendix B contains full role descriptions for each member of the project management team. A summary is given below, in Figure 11.3.

It would be good if we could create a generic project management structure that could be tailored to any project. Without knowing anything about a project's size or complexity we could understand the same organizational terms, and by fitting names to these understand quickly who does what. But if we were to have one structure for all sizes of project, it would be important that we made it flexible, a structure that would be adequate for large as well as small projects. The only way in which we can do this is to talk about *roles* that need to be filled, rather than jobs that need to be allocated on a one-to-one

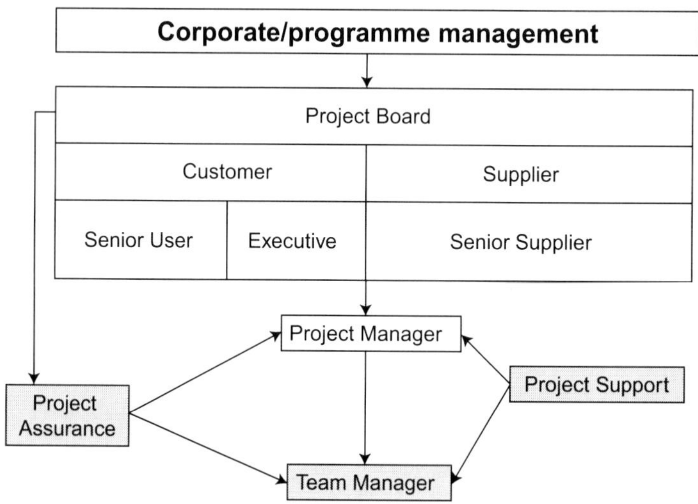

FIGURE 11.3 Project management team structure

basis to individuals. In order to be flexible and meet the needs of different environments and different project sizes, our structure will define roles that might be allocated to one person, shared with others or combined according to a project's needs. Examples are given later in the chapter.

The structure allows for the *possible* inclusion of the four layers of management (see 11.3). Whether they are all needed depends on the specific project.

Corporate/programme management hand the decision-making for a project to the Project Board. The Project Board members are busy with their own jobs and have not got the time to look after the project on a day-to-day basis. They delegate this to the Project Manager, reserving for themselves the key stop/go decisions. If they are too busy or do not have the current expertise, they can appoint someone to a Project Assurance role to monitor an aspect of the project on their behalf. A typical example here would be the participation of a company's quality assurance function on behalf of the Senior User or the Senior Supplier. Another example of the assurance role would be a role for internal audit.

Depending on the project environment or the Project Manager's expertise, he or she might need some support. This might be purely administrative tasks, such as filing or note taking, but it also includes specialist jobs, such as configuration management or expertise in the planning and control software tool that is to be used on the project.

The following sections describe each role in the project management structure. These can be used as the basis for discussion of an individual's job and tailored to suit the project's circumstances. The tailored role description becomes that person's job description for the project. Two copies of an agreed job description should be signed by the individual, one for retention by the individual, the other to be filed in the project file.

11.4.1 Project Board

11.4.1.1 General

The Project Board is appointed by corporate/programme management to provide overall direction and management of the project. The Project Board is accountable for the success of the project, and has responsibility and authority for the project within the limits set by corporate/programme management. The Project Board is the project's 'voice' to the outside world and is responsible for any publicity or other dissemination of information about the project.

11.4.1.2 Specific Responsibilities

The Project Board approves all major plans and authorizes any major deviation from agreed Stage Plans. It is the authority that signs off the completion of each stage as well as authorizes the start of the next stage. It ensures that required resources are committed, arbitrates on any conflicts within the project or negotiates a solution to any problems between the project and external bodies. In addition, it approves the appointment and responsibilities of the Project Manager and any delegation of its assurance responsibilities.

According to the size, complexity and risk of the project, the Project Board may decide to delegate some of their responsibilities to one or more separate Project Assurance roles. (Project Assurance is defined in more detail later in this chapter.)

11.4.2 Executive

The Executive is ultimately responsible for the project, supported by the Senior User and Senior Supplier. The Executive has to ensure that the project is consistent with company strategy and value for money, ensuring a cost-conscious approach to the project, balancing the demands of business, user and supplier. Throughout the project the Executive 'owns' the Business Case (Cartoon 11.2). The Executive is responsible for overall business assurance of the project, i.e. that it remains on target to deliver products that will achieve the expected business benefits, and the project will complete within its agreed tolerances for budget and schedule.

11.4.3 Senior User

The Senior User is responsible for the specification of the needs of all those who will use the final product of the project, user liaison with the project team and for monitoring that the solution will meet those needs within the constraints of the Business Case.

CARTOON 11.2 Executive

The role represents the interests of all those who will use the final product of the project, those for whom the product will achieve an objective or those who will use the product to deliver benefits. The Senior User role commits user resources and monitors products against requirements. This role may require more than one person to cover all the user interests. For the sake of effectiveness, the role should not be split between too many people.

Where the project's size, complexity or importance warrants it, the Senior User may delegate the responsibility and authority for some of the assurance responsibilities to one or more Project Assurance roles.

11.4.4 Senior Supplier

The Senior Supplier represents the interests of those designing, developing, facilitating, procuring, implementing, operating and maintaining the project products. The Senior Supplier role must have the authority to commit or acquire any supplier resources required.

If necessary, more than one person may be required to represent the suppliers.

The Senior Supplier is responsible for the specialist assurance of the project. The specialist assurance role responsibilities are to:

- advise on the selection of technical strategy, design and methods;
- ensure that any specialist and operating standards defined for the project are met and used to good effect;
- monitor potential changes and their impact on the correctness, completeness and assurance of products against their product description from a technical perspective;

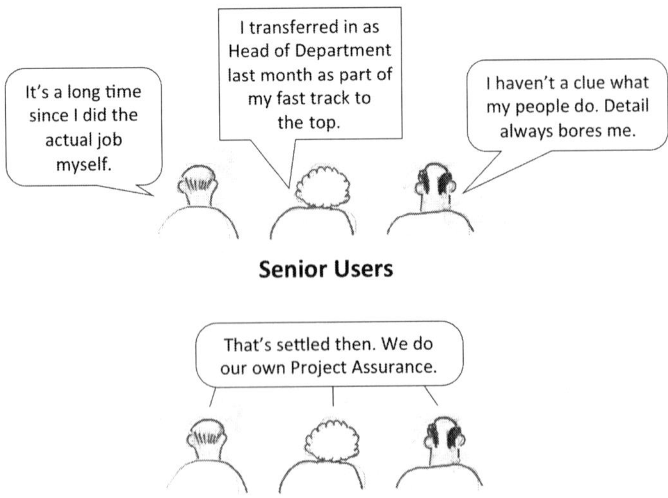

CARTOON 11.3 Senior Users

- monitor any risks in the specialist and production aspects of the project;
- ensure quality control procedures are used correctly so that products adhere to technical requirements.

If warranted, some of this assurance responsibility may be delegated. Depending on the particular customer/supplier environment of a project, the customer may also wish to appoint people to Project Assurance roles to monitor supplier activities.

11.4.5 Project Manager

The Project Manager has the authority to run the project on a day-to-day basis on behalf of the Project Board within the constraints laid down by the Board. In a customer/supplier environment the Project Manager will normally come from the customer organization.

The Project Manager's prime responsibility is to ensure that the project produces the required products, to the required standard of quality and within the specified constraints of time and cost. The Project Manager is also responsible for the project producing a result that is capable of achieving the benefits defined in the Business Case.

11.4.6 Team Manager

The allocation of this role to one or more people is optional. Where the project does not warrant the use of a Team Manager, the Project Manager takes the role.

The Project Manager may find that it is beneficial to delegate the authority and responsibility for planning the creation of certain products and managing a team of technicians to produce those products. There are many reasons why it may be decided to employ this role. Some of these are the size of the project, the particular specialist skills or knowledge needed for certain products, geographical location of some team members and the preferences of the Project Board.

The Team Manager's prime responsibility is to ensure production of those products defined by the Project Manager to an appropriate quality, in a timescale and at a cost acceptable to the Project Board. The Team Manager reports to and takes direction from the Project Manager.

The use of this role should be discussed by the Project Manager with the Project Board and, if the role is required, planned at the outset of the project. This is discussed later in the pre-project preparation and kick-off processes.

11.4.7 Project Assurance

The Project Board members do not work full-time on the project; therefore, they place a great deal of reliance on the Project Manager. Although they receive regular reports from the Project Manager, they may want a more independent view of progress. For example, the supplier may have a quality assurance function charged with the responsibility to check that all projects are adhering to their quality system.

All of these points mean that there is a need in the project organization for a monitoring of all aspects of the project's performance and products independent from the Project Manager. This is the Project Assurance function.

To cater for a small project, we start by identifying these Project Assurance functions as part of the role of each Project Board member. According to the needs and desires of the Project Board, any of these assurance responsibilities can be delegated, as long as the recipients are independent of the Project Manager and the rest of the project management team. Any appointed assurance jobs assure the project on behalf of one or more members of the Project Board.

It is not mandatory that all Project Assurance roles be delegated. Each role which is delegated may be assigned to one individual or shared. The Project Board decides when a role needs to be delegated. It may be for the entire project or only part of it. The person or persons filling a role may be changed during the project at the request of the Project Board. Any use of these roles needs to be planned at initiation stage, otherwise resource usage and costs for the roles could easily get out of control.

There is no stipulation on how many Project Assurance roles there are. Each Project Board role has Project Assurance responsibilities. Again, each project should determine what support, if any, each Project Board role needs to achieve this assurance.

CARTOON 11.4 Project Assurance

For example, an international standards group, such as the International Organization for Standardization (IOS), may certificate the supplier's work standards. A requirement of the certification is that there will be some form of quality assurance function that is required to monitor the supplier's work. Some of the Senior Supplier's assurance responsibilities may be delegated to this function. Note that they would only be delegated. The Project Board member retains accountability. Any delegation should be documented. Project Assurance covers all interests of a project, including business, user and supplier. It has to be independent of the Project Manager; therefore, the Project Board cannot delegate any of its Project Assurance responsibilities to the Project Manager.

11.4.8 Project Support

The provision of any Project Support on a formal basis is optional. It is driven by the needs of the individual project and Project Manager. Project Support could be in the form of advice on project management tools and administrative services, such as filing or the collection of actual data. Where set up as an official body, Project Support can act as a repository for lessons, and a central source of expertise in specialist support tools.

One support function that must be considered is that of configuration management. Depending on the project size and environment, there may be a need to formalize this, and it quickly becomes a task with which the Project Manager cannot cope without support. See the Change theme for details of the work.

CARTOON 11.5 Project Support

Chapter 12

Plans

It is commonly accepted that one of the most common causes of projects failing to deliver benefit is a neglect of the planning process.

12.1 PHILOSOPHY

A plan is the backbone of every project and is essential for a successful outcome. Good plans cover all aspects of the project, giving everyone involved a common understanding of the work ahead. My friends at Duhig Berry used the following picture to provide a formal definition of a plan (Cartoon 12.1).

CARTOON 12.1 Definition of a plan

A plan defines:

- the products to be developed or obtained in order to achieve a specified target;
- the steps required in order to produce those products;
- the sequence of those steps;
- any interdependencies between the products or steps;
- how long each step is estimated to take;
- when the steps take place;
- who will carry out the steps;
- where controls are to be applied.

A plan:

- shows in advance whether the target is likely to be achievable;
- shows what resources are needed to accomplish the work;
- shows how long the work will take;
- shows who is to do what and when;
- provides a basis for assessing the risks involved in the work;
- provides the base against which progress can be measured;
- provides the information on the Project Manager's intentions to be communicated to those concerned;
- can be used to gain the consent and commitment of those who have to contribute in some way.

There are many reasons put forward for this, one of the most common being that there is 'no time to plan'. What is really being said here is that there is a strong desire to start the 'real' work, especially if there is a deadline to be met. The other side of this is where senior management does not recognize the importance of planning, and will not make the necessary time available.

The next excuse given for failure to plan is that there is 'no need'. This is perhaps where:

- the job has been done before;
- the project is expected to take only a short time;
- the Project Manager prefers to keep all the details 'in their head'.

There are, of course, dangers in these 'reasons' for not planning. Projects are always different, with different people, size, complexity and environments. Short projects can become very long when you realize that you have forgotten something vital. The human brain can retain only a very small number of linked events over a period of several days. When you start adding the details of what is actually happening to what you had planned, it doesn't take long for a required event to get lost somewhere in the brain cells. Project Managers who say that they keep all the details in their head are simply 'fire-fighters'. They lurch from one crisis to the next, always having to put fires out. Sometimes they are hailed as whiz kids because they solve (or waste everybody's time working around) a problem. Most of the problems that they go around solving would not have been there if they had planned properly in the first place! Undertaking a project without planning is just leaving things to chance.

Often people are expected to plan a project with no knowledge of how to go about it. Sadly it is often the case that people are promoted into project management (hence planning) positions without being given the necessary education and training to allow them to do the job effectively. Planning is something that needs to be learned. It is not an inherent skill with which people are born. There are specific techniques (critical path analysis, resource levelling, use of a planning tool, etc.) that need to be learned. Without expertise in these areas, planners are unlikely to do a good job.

The last excuse is that planning is *no fun*! What this means is that planning is hard work. There is a great desire to 'get going' with the stimulating business of the technical challenge.

12.2 HIERARCHY OF PLANS

Figure 12.1 introduces the PRINCE2 hierarchy of plans.

At the outset of a project, it is always difficult to plan in detail the activities and resource requirements for the production of all the products required. How accurately can you plan your own activities that you will be doing six months from now? Three months from now? Why should we think it would be an easy task to plan the work for one or more teams of people for the next year (or however long the project may take)? It is nevertheless necessary to provide overall estimates for the project in terms of duration and cost so that approval to proceed can be gained.

These will now be examined in more detail.

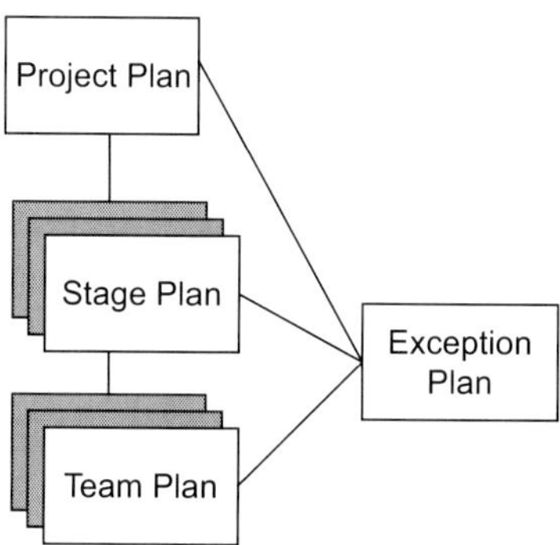

FIGURE 12.1 Plan hierarchy

12.2.1 Project Plan

The highest level is the Project Plan, which is created at the start of the project and updated at the end of each stage. The initial Project Plan is a part of the Project Initiation Documentation. The Project Plan is a mandatory plan in a PRINCE2 project.

The Project Board does not want to know about every detailed activity in the project. It requires a high-level view. This allows the Project Board to know:

- how long the project will take;
- what the major deliverables or products will be;
- roughly when these will be delivered;
- which people and other resources will have to be committed in order to meet the plan;
- how control will be exerted;
- how quality will be maintained;
- what risks there are in the approach taken.

The Project Board will control the project using the Project Plan as a yardstick of progress (Cartoon 12.2).

CARTOON 12.2 Authorize the project

12.2.2 Stage Plan

Having specified the stages and major products in the Project Plan, each stage is then planned in a greater level of detail. Each Stage Plan is prepared, as previously mentioned, just before the end of the previous stage.

Stage Plans are mandatory, and unless a project is very small it will be easier to plan in detail one stage at a time. Another part of the philosophy that makes stage planning easier is that a stage is planned shortly before it is due to start, so you have the latest information available on actual progress to date.

When planning a stage the major products in the Project Plan that are to be created during that stage are taken and broken down (typically) into a further two or three levels of detail.

Stage Plans have the same format as the Project Plan.

The Project Manager uses the Stage Plans to track progress on a daily basis through regular progress monitoring.

12.2.3 Team Plan

Team Plans are optional. Their use or otherwise is dictated by the size, complexity and risks associated with the project.

Team Plans are the lowest level of detail and specify activities down to the level of a handful of days, say ten at most. Team Plans may or may not contain the narrative sections associated with the higher levels.

Team Plans will be needed when internal or external teams are to do portions of the work. Part of the Project Manager's job is to cross-relate these plans to the Project and Stage Plans.

12.2.4 Exception Plan

Finally, there is the Exception Plan. This is produced when a plan is predicted to exceed the time and/or cost tolerances agreed between the planner and the next higher level of authority. If a Team Plan is forecast to deviate beyond tolerances, the Team Manager may need to produce the Exception Plan and get approval for its introduction from the Project Manager. If a Stage Plan is forecast to deviate, the Project Manager will produce an Exception Report and the Project Board may require an Exception Plan to replace the current Stage Plan. If the Project Plan threatens to go beyond its tolerances, the Project Board must take the Exception Report to higher management, who might ask for a new Project Plan.

The Exception Plan takes over from the plan it is replacing and has the same format.

12.3 THE PRINCE2 APPROACH TO PLANNING

PRINCE2 offers a standard way in which to produce any level of plan (Figure 12.2). This means that all plans will have the same format and method of development. The process is based around the PRINCE2 technique of Product-based Planning (see Appendix C).

12.3.1 Designing a Plan

This process is carried out only once per project, at the start. It defines the standards to be used in all future plans. The result should be a consistent set of plans. The activities in designing a plan are the following:

- Decide on what levels of plan are needed for the project, i.e. Project Plan, Stage Plans, Team Plans.
- Ascertain if the organization or programme uses a particular planning tool as standard.
- Identify the planning tool to be used in the initial Project Plan, part of the Project Initiation Documentation.
- Identify what estimating method(s) are available and suitable for the project.
- Ensure that the estimating method(s) chosen contain allowances for issue and risk analysis, telephone calls, ad hoc meetings, learning curves, experience, etc.
- Discuss with the Project Board whether there should be a change budget set aside.

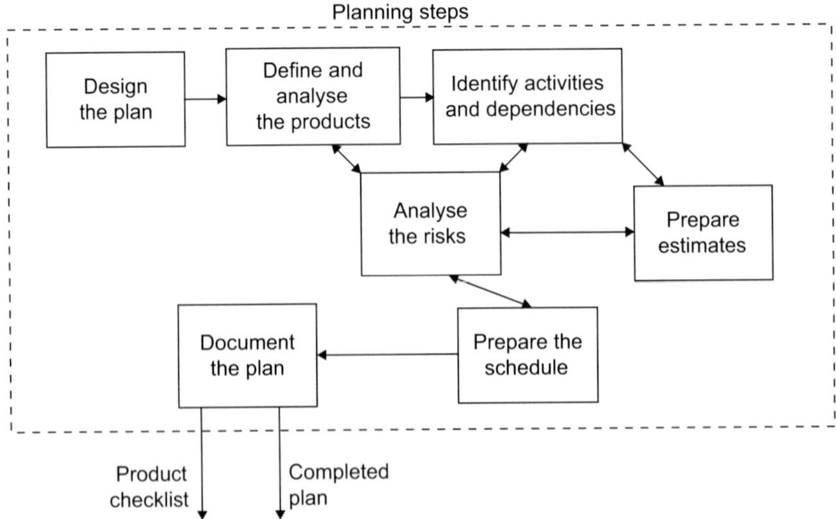

FIGURE 12.2 The PRINCE2 planning steps

- Discuss with the Project Board whether there should be a separate allowance for any anticipated contingency plans.

12.3.2 Defining and Analysing Products

The PRINCE2 approach to planning is product based. By defining the products and their quality requirements everyone can see and understand the required plan result. It means that whoever has to deliver a product knows in advance what its purpose is, to what quality it has to be built and what interfaces there are with other products.

The steps are the following:

- Identify the products required, using a Product Breakdown Structure.
- Write Product Descriptions for them.
- Draw a Product Flow Diagram showing the sequence of delivery and dependencies between the products.
- Optionally produce a Product Checklist.

The first three of these form the PRINCE2 Product-based Planning technique (see Appendix C).

The planner is responsible for identifying the products. This will be either the Project Manager or a Team Manager, depending on the type of plan being produced. The users of any of the products to be delivered within the plan should be involved in writing the Product Descriptions, particularly in defining the quality criteria.

12.3.3 Identifying Activities and Dependencies

For Stage and Team Plans the Product Flow Diagram may still be at too high a level for the purposes of estimation and control. This optional process allows a further breakdown into the activities to produce each product, based on the Product Flow Diagram, until each activity will last only a handful of days.

The planner is responsible, and this will be either the Project Manager or a Team Manager. Depending on the type of plan being produced the planner should do the following:

- Consider if a product in the Product Flow Diagram is too big to estimate or would need such a large amount of effort that it would be difficult to control against that estimate.
- Where a product is too big, break it down into the activities needed to produce it. This should continue down to the level where an activity is less than ten days' effort, ideally no more than five days'.
- Where a product has been broken down into several activities, put the activities into their correct sequence.
- Review the dependencies between products and refine them to give dependencies between the new activities. For example, where Product Flow Diagram

dependencies went from the end of one product to the start of the next, is there now an opportunity to overlap or start some activities on a product before all the activities on its preceding product have been done?

12.3.4 Estimating

The objective is to identify the resources and effort required to complete each activity or product.

This is the responsibility of the Project Manager, but there may possibly be expert help available from Project Support.

- Examine each activity/product and identify what type of resources it requires. Apart from human resources there may be other resources needed, such as equipment. With human resources, consider and document what level of skill you are basing the estimate on.
- Judge what level of efficiency you will base your estimates on, what allowance for non-project time you will need to use.
- Estimate the effort needed for each activity/product.
- Understand whether this is an estimate of uninterrupted work, to which allowances must be added, or whether it already includes this.
- Document any assumptions you have made – for example, the use of specific named resources, levels of skill and experience, the availability of user

CARTOON 12.3 Estimating

resources when you need them. Check the assumptions with those who have such knowledge, such as the Senior Supplier and Senior User.

12.3.5 Scheduling

A plan can only show whether it can meet its targets when the activities are put together in a schedule against a timeframe, showing when activities will be done and by what resources. Therefore, the following activities should be undertaken:

- Draw a planning network.
- Assess resource availability. This should include dates of availability as well as what the scale of that availability is. Any known information on holidays and training courses, etc., should be gathered.
- Allocate activities to resources and produce a draft schedule.
- Revise the draft to remove as many peaks and troughs in resource usage as possible.
- Negotiate a solution with the Project Board for problems, such as too few or too many resources, or the inability to meet fixed target dates.
- Add in management and quality activities or products (Stage and Team Plans only).
- Calculate resource utilization and costs.

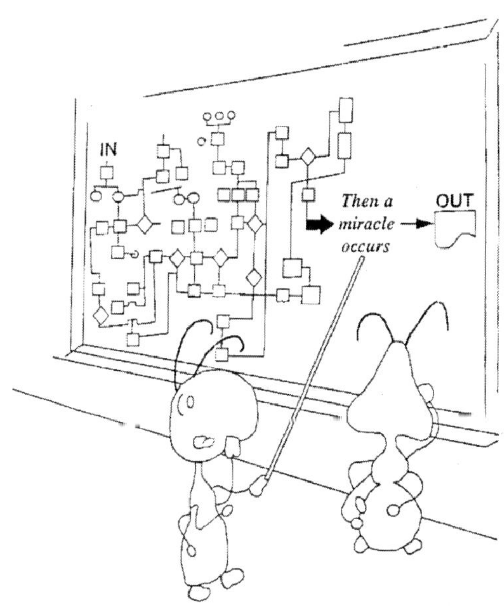

'Good work .... but I think we need just a little more detail right here'

CARTOON 12.4 Scheduling

12.3.6 Analysing Risks

You should not commit to a plan without considering what risks are involved in it, and what impact the plan might have on risks already known.

- Look for any external dependencies. These always represent one or more risks – for example, they may not arrive on time, they may be of poor quality, or be wrong in some other way.
- Look for any assumptions you have made in the plan – for example, the resources available to you. Each assumption is a risk.
- Look at each resource in the plan. Is there a risk involved? For example, that a new resource doesn't perform at the expected level, or that a resource's availability is not achieved.
- Are the tools or technology unproven?
- Take the appropriate risk actions. Where appropriate, revise the plan. Make sure that any new or modified risks are shown in the Risk Register.

12.3.7 Completing a Plan

A plan in diagrammatic form is not self-explanatory. It needs text.

- Agree tolerance levels for the plan.
- Document what the plan covers, the approach to the work and the checking of its quality.
- Document any assumptions you have made.
- Add the planning dates to the Product Checklist (if used).
- Publish the plan.

Chapter 13

Progress

13.1 INTRODUCTION

The purpose of the Progress theme is to describe the mechanisms that will monitor a project, compare actual progress against what was planned, forecast future events and control any deviations from the plan.

The Progress theme supports the PRINCE2 principles of managing by stages, managing by exception and continued business justification.

Project control involves measuring actual progress against the planned targets. This covers the six tolerance areas of time, cost, scope, quality, benefits and risk.

There are two diagrammatic ways of looking at controls. A project needs a controlled start, controlled progress and a controlled finish. This is represented in Figure 13.1.

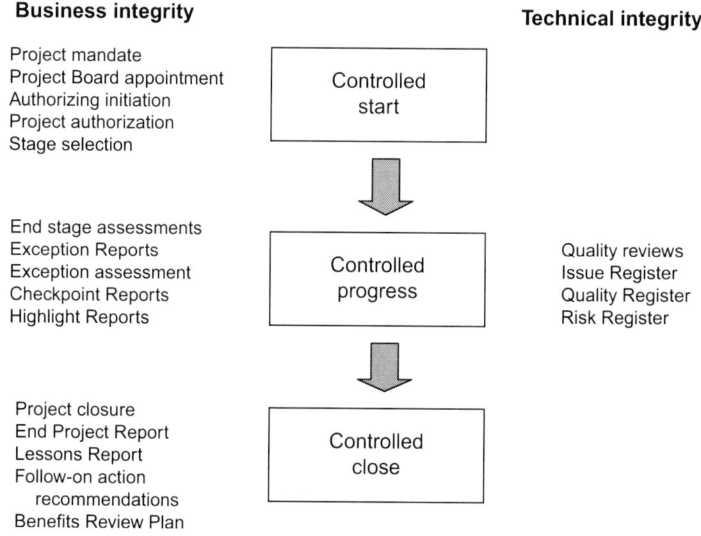

FIGURE 13.1 Controlled start, progress and finish

13.1.1 Progress Philosophy

Good control doesn't happen by accident – The control needs of a project need to be assessed and appropriate mechanisms put in place.

Control needs planning – You can't tell whether you are behind or ahead of schedule, or above or below budget, unless you have a plan against which you can compare. Setting up project controls is part of the planning process. Failure to plan monitoring and control activities means that they probably won't get done.

Effective monitoring techniques support good control decisions – Without accurate, timely information, project management is blundering about in the dark and constantly reacting to problems rather than preventing or reducing them in advance.

Control needs to be appropriate to the project – As with all other aspects of project management, the level and formality of control should be appropriate for the project.

In setting up any practically based project control system we will need to put something in place that can, as the project is progressing, answer several fundamental questions.

What was expected to happen?	This is where plans are vital. Without them it is not possible to begin!
What *has* happened?	Accurate and timely status information is required if this question is to be answered.
What is the difference?	Comparison of plans against actuals gives us this.
How serious is it?	Without some benchmark which defines 'serious', this cannot be decided. Tolerance is the key here. (See the later explanation.)
What can be done about it?	Having got reliable information about all the preceding questions, sensible decisions at the proper level of authority can now be made.

Figure 13.2 looks at controls from the view of the management levels.

I shall take each one in turn and discuss it under the same headings used for other project management themes.

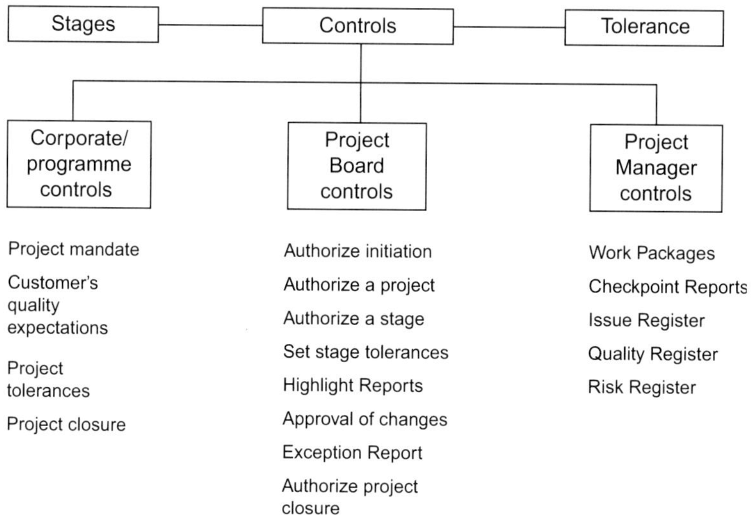

FIGURE 13.2 Controls

13.2 STAGES

13.2.1 Stages Philosophy

The Project Board only gives approval to the Project Manager to proceed with one stage at a time. At the end of each stage, before it approves a detailed plan to produce the products of the next stage, the Project Board verifies that the project's continuation can still be justified by examining the status of:

- The Business Case.
- Risks.
- The Project Plan.

A PRINCE2 project must have at least two stages: initiation and the specialist work of the project. According to size and risk, the second stage may be broken down into more stages (Figure 13.3).

13.2.2 Project Board Reasons for Stages

The Project Board wants to be in control without spending all its time on the project. It needs to feel it is making the big decisions, guaranteeing that it will be warned of any major problems in advance, and doesn't want to feel that it has 'a tiger by the tail', in that once started, the project cannot be stopped if it turns sour.

With risky projects there is the need to pause and make sure that the risks are still controllable, so risky projects are likely to have more, smaller stages.

Why plan in stages?

How can we make sure we stay in control?
How can we limit the risks?
How can we stop it if it goes wrong?
Where are the key decision points?
Alignment within a programme

Too much time planning
How far ahead is it sensible to plan?
Too many unknowns
Too much guesswork

Project
Manager

FIGURE 13.3 Why plan in stages?

The key criterion for decision-making in business terms is the viability of the Business Case. Is the justification for what we are doing still valid? If it is not valid, the project may be in jeopardy. If it is valid, then it should go forward. These decisions are made in the light of the strategic or programme objectives.

Stages give the Project Board opportunities at formal moments in the project to decide whether the project is no longer viable, and if not close it down.

Stage-limited commitment: At the end of each stage the Project Board only approves a detailed plan to produce the products of the next stage. The Project Plan is updated, but this is mainly for the guidance of the Project Board and will become more accurate as more stages are completed.

The stage-limited commitment, which is sometimes referred to as a 'creeping commitment', is especially important for large projects with a rapidly changing environment that makes it almost impossible to develop an accurate plan for the total project at the outset. However, this type of commitment requires that the provider of the funds for the project must accept that the estimate for the completion of the system will inevitably change with time.

Sign-off of interim end-products: At the end of each stage, the interim end-products are reviewed by all affected organizational functions, particularly those that will use the end-products in order to develop the products of the next stage.

In theory, at the end of each stage, the Project Board can call for cancellation of the project because of the existence of one or more possibly critical situations. For example, the organization's business needs may have changed to the point at which the project is no longer cost effective. A project may also be cancelled if the estimated cost to complete the project exceeds the available funds. In practice, however, cancellation of a project becomes progressively more difficult to justify as increasing amounts of resources are invested.

13.2.3 Project Manager Reasons for Stages

The Project Manager does not want to spend huge amounts of time at the outset trying to plan a long project in sufficient detail for day-to-day control. Trying to look ahead – say, nine months – and plan in detail what will happen and who will do what is almost certain to be wrong. It is much easier to plan just the next few weeks in detail and have only a high-level plan of the whole project.

Stage ends are needed to obtain from the Project Board the required commitment of resources, money and equipment to move into the next stage.

13.2.4 Initiation Stage

However large or small the project, it is sensible to begin a project with an initiation stage. This is where the Project Board and Project Manager decide if there is agreement on:

- what the project is to achieve;
- why it is being undertaken;
- who is to be involved and in what role;
- how and when the required products will be delivered.

This information is documented in the Project Initiation Documentation. This version is then 'frozen', and used by the Project Board as a benchmark throughout the project and at the end to check the progress and deliveries of the project.

13.3 TOLERANCE

13.3.1 Tolerance Philosophy

- Tolerances are the permissible deviation from a plan without having to refer the matter to the next higher level of authority.

No project has ever gone 100% to plan. There will be good days and bad days, good weeks and bad weeks. If the Project Board is going to 'manage by exception' it doesn't want the Project Manager running to it, saying 'I've spent a pound more than I should today' or 'I've fallen half a day behind schedule this week'. But equally the Project Board doesn't want the project to overspend by a million Euros or slip two months behind schedule without being warned. So where is the dividing line? What size of deviation from the plan is acceptable without having to go back to the Board for a decision? These deviations are the tolerances.

The second philosophical point about tolerances is that we do not wait for tolerances to be exceeded; we forecast this, so that the next higher level of authority has time to react and possibly prevent or reduce the deviation (Cartoon 13.1(A) and (B)).

CARTOON 13.1 (A) and (B) Tolerances

13.3.2 Tolerance Overview

The elements of tolerance are time, cost, scope, risk, benefits and quality.

Within the four levels of project management, the following takes place:

- Corporate/programme management set the project tolerances within which the Project Board has to remain.
- The Project Board agrees stage tolerances with the Project Manager.
- The Project Manager agrees tolerances for a Work Package with a Team Manager.

Figure 13.4 helps explain the concept.

As long as the plan's actual progress is within the tolerance margins, all is well. As soon as it can be *forecast* that progress will deviate outside the tolerance margins, the next higher level of authority needs to be advised.

13.3.3 Tolerance Detail

Project tolerances should be part of the project mandate handed down by corporate/programme management. If they are not there, it is the Executive's job during initiation to find out from corporate/programme management what they are.

The Project Board sets stage tolerances for the Project Manager within the overall project tolerances that they have received. The portion allocated to a stage should depend on the risk content of the work and the extent of the unknowns (such as technologies never used before, resources of unknown ability or tasks never attempted before).

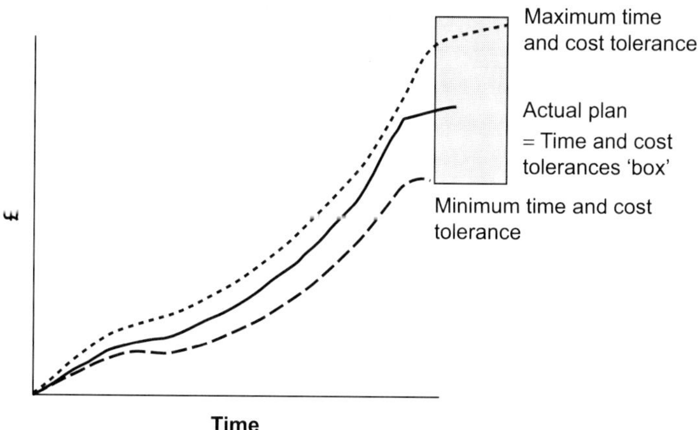

FIGURE 13.4 Example of time and cost tolerances

CARTOON 13.2 Cost tolerances

The Project Manager negotiates appropriate tolerances for each Work Package with the Team Manager. Again these tolerances will be within the stage tolerances set for the Project Manager.

13.4 MANAGEMENT CONTROLS

Management controls work around the three areas of getting a project off to a controlled start, controlling progress and bringing the project to a controlled close. Let's take a look at the necessary management controls following our concept of up to four levels of management: corporate/programme management, Project Board, Project Manager and Team Manager.

13.4.1 Corporate/Programme Management Controls

13.4.1.1 Philosophy

Corporate/programme management will have many things on their mind and will want to spend the minimum of time on any one project while still retaining control. This is the start of 'management by exception'. They agree the overall project objectives and time and cost objectives with the Executive of the Project Board and say, 'Get on with it. As long as you are on course, just send us progress information, but come back to us if you forecast that you are moving outside the limits we have agreed with you.'

13.4.1.2 Executive Appointment

For the maximum amount of confidence in their Project Board, corporate/programme management should normally appoint one of their members to be the Executive. They can appoint people to other Project Board roles or leave the selection to the Executive.

13.4.1.3 Project Mandate

Corporate/programme management is responsible for the creation of the project mandate, which they will pass to the Executive of the Project Board. This gives them control over the project's objectives, scope and constraints.

13.4.1.4 Customer's Quality Expectations

As part of the project mandate corporate/programme management should specify their quality expectations of the final product. This should cover such things as packaging or presentation, performance, reliability and maintainability.

13.4.1.5 Project Tolerances

Corporate/programme management set the project tolerances. This allows them to define the circumstances under which the Project Board must refer problems to them for a go/no go decision, rather than make the decision itself. It is the Executive's job to ensure this information is made available at the outset of a project as part of the project mandate or creation of the Project Brief.

13.4.1.6 Project Closure

The Executive must gain confirmation from corporate/programme management that the project mandate has been satisfied.

13.4.2 Project Board Controls

13.4.2.1 Philosophy

The Project Board wants to 'manage by exception', i.e. agree a Stage Plan with the Project Manager and then let him/her get on with it without any interference or extra effort – unless the plan goes wrong.

13.4.2.2 Overview of Project Board Controls

The Project Board 'owns' the project, and its members – not the Project Manager – are ultimately accountable for the success of the project. This is why the Project Board members must have the requisite authority to commit resources and make decisions.

Project Board members will be busy with their other jobs, and therefore will want to spend the minimum amount of time controlling the project commensurate with making sure that the project meets its objectives within the defined constraints.

13.4.2.3 Controlled Start

Authorize Initiation

The Project Board examines the initiation Stage Plan to see if it reflects the work needed to initiate the project. This will be affected by any previous work done if the project is part of an overall programme.

The project mandate should contain the project objectives, customer quality expectations and project approach, among other things. One of the first tasks in PRINCE2 is to add any missing information, then turn the project mandate into the Project Brief. It is therefore very important for the Project Board to examine this document and be satisfied with its contents before agreeing to initiate the project.

Authorize the Project

The Project Initiation Documentation is the internal 'contract' for the project, documenting what the project is to do, why it should be done (the Business Case) and who is responsible for what, when and how products are to be delivered. There has to be agreement by customer and supplier on its contents before commitment to the project by the Project Board. If a viable Business Case does not exist, the Project Board should not proceed with the project.

13.4.2.4 Controlled Progress

Authorize a Stage

An end stage assessment happens (surprise, surprise!) at the end of each management stage, where the Project Board assesses the continued viability of the project and, if satisfied, gives the Project Manager approval to proceed with the next stage.

The Project Board defines the maximum deviations allowed from the Stage Plan without the Project Manager having to return to the Board for a decision on action to be taken. This is the key element of 'management by exception'.

The Project Board must be aware of the need to avoid technical or irrelevant discussions and to focus on the management aspects which, when taken as a whole, inform its decision on whether to proceed or not. As a rule of thumb, an end stage assessment should not last more than two hours. A sensible Project Manager will have been in touch with the Project Board, either verbally or through Highlight Reports, making sure that the members know what is coming and finding out what they think about the future of the project. 'No surprises' is the best way to ensure short end stage assessments.

The detail of the next Stage Plan may often cause modification of the Project Plan. The Project Board checks the figures against both the previous version of the Project Plan and the revised version to see what changes have been made. Any changes should be justified (for example, against approved requests for change) before approval of the Stage Plan.

The 'bottom line' is whether the project is still predicted to deliver sufficient benefits to justify the investment, i.e. is the Business Case still sound?

The other aspects of the end stage assessment are:

- Current progress checked against the Project Plan.
- Current stage completed successfully (all products delivered and accepted).
- Confirmation that all delivered stage products have passed their pre-defined quality checks.
- Next Stage Plan examined against the Project Plan and authorized.
- 'Approval to proceed' form signed by all Project Board members.

The Project Board must sign the 'Approval to proceed' form so that the project cannot drift without approval into the next stage.

Highlight Reports

The best way of characterizing 'management by exception' is the expression 'no news is good news'. At a frequency defined by the Project Board in the Project Initiation Documentation, the Project Manager has to send a Highlight Report to the Project Board to confirm achievements towards meeting the Stage Plan.

The frequency of Highlight Reports is determined by the Project Board during initiation, and should relate to the commitment and level of risk in the stage.

The Project Manager prepares Highlight Reports, using progress information provided by the team members and analysed at the checkpoints.

The principal focus of the Highlight Report is to identify:

- products completed during the current reporting period;
- products to be completed in the next period;
- any real or potential problems.

CARTOON 13.3 Highlight Report

Other limited narrative information, such as the budget and risk status, can be added – up to a total of one page of paper.

Change Request Approval

Having approved the objectives and products required in the Project Initiation Documentation, it is only right that the Project Board should have to approve any changes to them. Once requested changes have been estimated for the effort and cost of doing them, the customer has to decide on their priority, whether they should be done and whether the money to do them can be found. As for all the other decisions, it needs an assessment of the impact on the Project Plan, the Business Case and the risk situation.

Exception Report Review

If the Project Manager can forecast that the plan will end outside its tolerance margins, an Exception Report must be sent immediately to the Project Board, detailing the problem, options and a recommendation.

It should be stressed that if the project is not collecting reliable progress information, it will be difficult to know when that point has been reached.

Authorize an Exception Plan

If the Project Board, on reading the Exception Report, decides to accept a recommendation to proceed on the basis of a modified plan, it will ask the Project Manager to produce an Exception Plan, which replaces the remainder of the plan.

The Project Manager should prepare an Exception Plan and present it to the Project Board for approval at an exception assessment, identical to an end stage assessment. The less formal approach says that there may not be a need for a meeting, but the Project Manager still needs to get his/her plan of remedial action approved by the Project Board.

13.4.2.5 Controlled Close

Authorize Project Closure

As part of its decision on whether to close the project, the Project Board receives an End Project Report from the Project Manager, summing up the project's performance in meeting the requirements of the Project Initiation Documentation plus any approved changes.

The Project Board uses the original Project Initiation Documentation to confirm that the project has achieved its original objectives, including the required quality. Any requests for change that were made after the Project Initiation Documentation was 'frozen' when the project was authorized are included, and their impact on the Project Plan, Business Case and risks is assessed.

The End Project Report provides statistics on Issue Reports and their impact on the project, plus statistics on the quality of work carried out. It is created by the Project Manager and submitted to the Project Board.

Follow-on Action Recommendations

Follow-on action recommendations form part of the End Project Report. They describe any unfinished business at the end of the project.

For example, there may have been a number of requests for change that the Project Board decided not to implement during the project, but which were not rejected. Not all expected products may have been handed over, or there may be some known problems with what has been delivered. Risks in the use of the final product may have been identified during the project.

The follow-on action recommendations allow the Project Board to direct any unfinished business to the person or group whose job it will be to have the recommendations considered for action after the current project has ended.

The Project Board is presented with a list of all outstanding actions that are to be handed to the group that will support the product in its operational life.

These may be requests for change that the Project Board decided not to implement during the life of the current project or risks identified during the project that may affect the product in use. The Project Board has to confirm that all outstanding issues have been captured, and satisfy itself that nothing on the list should have been completed by the project.

Lessons Report

As another part of the End Project Report the Project Manager has to present a report on what project management (and possibly technical) aspects of the project went well, and what went badly. The Project Board has the job of ensuring that this is passed to an appropriate body that will disseminate the report to other projects and possibly modify the relevant standards. It is important that an appropriate group is identified. There may be a project management support group or a quality assurance group.

(If any lessons are found earlier in the project, the Project Manager may decide to add a Lessons Report to the End Stage Report if this will benefit other projects earlier than waiting until the end of the project.)

Benefits Review Plan

Usually, many products need time in use before the achievement of their expected benefits can be measured. Corporate/programme management will be responsible for ensuring that these measurements take place. The Project Manager has to provide a plan for how, when and by whom these measurements are to be done.

Benefits reviews occur outside the project and, as such, are not part of the project.

Any corrective work identified by a benefits review would be done during product use and maintenance. Any problems may not be with the product itself, but organizational ones, needing such solutions as retraining.

The benefits reviews can occur perhaps six, twelve or eighteen months after the project has finished, depending on the nature of the product.

Customer Acceptance

The Project Manager should provide confirmation of customer acceptance of the end product(s) before asking the Project Board to allow the project to close.

Operational and Maintenance Acceptance

The Project Manager must present evidence to the Project Board of the willingness of those who will operate and maintain the product in its operational life to accept the final product. This includes documentation and training.

13.5 PROJECT MANAGER CONTROLS

13.5.1 Philosophy

A project is broken down into stages. The Project Manager is in day-to-day control of a stage, and carries on with a stage until its end without needing further approval from the Project Board unless:

- there is a forecast of an exception beyond tolerance limits;
- changes have been requested for which extra resources are needed.

13.5.2 Overview of Project Manager Controls

The basic idea is to:

- agree with the Project Board what is to be done and the constraints within which the job has to be done;
- get approval from the Project Board for a plan to do the work;
- direct teams or individuals to do the necessary work;
- confirm with the customer that the products meet requirements;
- report back that the work has been done.

Breaking a project into stages, using tolerance levels and agreeing the need for any Highlight Reports with the Project Board complements this basic concept.

13.5.3 Controlled Progress

13.5.3.1 Quality Register

Details of all planned quality work are entered in the Quality Register, and updated with actual results of the quality work. The Project Manager monitors the register on a regular basis.

13.5.3.2 Work Packages

A Work Package is an agreement between the Project Manager and either an individual or a Team Manager to undertake a piece of work. It describes the work, agreed dates, standards to be used, quality and reporting requirements. No work can start without the Project Manager's approval via a Work Package, so it is a powerful schedule, cost and quality control for the Project Manager.

13.5.3.3 Team Plans

Where the Project Manager is dealing with several teams, as part of agreement on a Work Package, the Project Manager has to agree the Team Plan to produce the products involved. This is then reflected in the Stage Plan.

The Project Manager can use this to confirm that the plan is reasonable, will fit within the stage tolerances given by the Project Board, and that it contains adequate quality work.

13.5.3.4 Checkpoint Reports

This is a report from a team to the Project Manager. It is sent at a frequency agreed in the Work Package.

A specific aim of a Checkpoint Report is to check all aspects of the Work Package against the Team and Stage Plans to ensure that there are no nasty surprises hiding. Useful questions to answer are: 'What is not going to plan?' and 'What is likely not to go to plan?' The crucial question that underlies the objective of the meeting is: 'Are we still likely to complete the stage within the tolerances laid down by the Project Manager?'

Checkpoints should be taken as frequently as the Project Manager requires. They may coincide with the Project Manager's need to consider re-planning. The checkpoint frequency is determined in the Work Package.

The information gathered at a checkpoint is used by the Project Manager to form the basis of the next Highlight Report.

13.5.3.5 Issue Register

The Issue Register is a key control document for the Project Manager, keeping track of all problems and change requests. It usually contains the answer to Project Board questions such as: 'Why is the project going to cost more/take longer than you said in the Project Initiation Documentation?'

13.5.3.6 Risk Register

The status of risks should be monitored regularly. Risks are formally reviewed at each stage end, but should also be checked as part of the impact analysis of major requests for change.

13.5.3.7 Stage Plan

The Stage Plan is the document against which the Project Manager is controlling a stage.

13.5.3.8 Configuration Management

Configuration management is the identification of the products to be created/used by the project and their tracking and control. This provides the Project Manager with the status of products.

13.5.3.9 Daily Log

Apart from the Stage Plan a Project Manager needs a diary to record significant events, or remind him or herself of informal issues or other tasks to deal with in the coming week.

The Project Manager keeps a Daily Log in which to record important events, decisions, happenings or statements. This is partly a defence mechanism in case some time later the other person forgets that they said something, but also to become part of the Project Manager's monitoring that an action promised actually happens.

It is also useful for the Project Manager to set up a number of monitoring activities for the coming week.

Before the start of each week the Project Manager should take a look at the Stage Plan, the Risk Register, the Issue Register and the Quality Register. This should provide a number of monitoring points for action during the week, such as:

- What is on the critical path of my plan that is supposed to finish during the week? Is it going to finish on time? (Or else when?) Did it finish on time?
- Should the status of any risks be checked this week? Is it time to give a risk owner a nudge to follow up on the risk's status?
- Are there any outstanding issues that I should be chasing which are out for impact analysis or for consideration by the customer?

13.5.4 Controlled Close

13.5.4.1 Acceptance Criteria

If all customer acceptance criteria can be ticked, this puts the Project Manager in a strong position to say that the project has achieved its objectives and can close.

CARTOON 13.4 Daily Log

13.5.4.2 Configuration Item Records

The Configuration Librarian does a check on all products produced and their status. This confirms that all products have been approved, a necessary check before work to close the project can begin.

13.5.4.3 Issue Register

All issues should have either been dealt with or have Project Board agreement to being held over and passed to the operational support group. The Project Manager must check the status of all issues as part of closing the project.

The Issue Register is used together with the Project Initiation Documentation to check how the original objectives of the project were modified. It is also used to match against the follow-on action recommendations to ensure that there are no loose ends.

13.5.4.4 Quality Register

The Quality Register gives an assessment of whether the appropriate quality work was put into the project's products and whether there is an audit trail available.

13.6 EVENT-DRIVEN AND TIME-DRIVEN CONTROLS

Some of the PRINCE2 controls described in this chapter are event-driven; others are time-driven. Below is a table, showing which controls are time-driven and which event-driven.

	Event-driven	Time-driven
Project initiation	✓	
Stages	✓	
Management by exception	✓	
End stage assessment	✓	
Highlight Report		✓
Exception Report	✓	
Work Package	✓	
Checkpoint Report		✓
Risk Register	✓	
Quality Register	✓	
Issue Register	✓	

Chapter 14

Quality

14.1 PHILOSOPHY

The Quality theme supports the 'product focus' principle and addresses the quality methods and responsibilities not only for the technical products, but also for the management of the project. Only after establishing product quality criteria and quality control activities and resourcing can the full costs and timescales be estimated for the Project, Stage and Team Plans.

The ISO9000 definition of quality is:

> The totality of features and inherent or assigned characteristics of a product, person, process, service or system that bear on its ability to show that it meets expectations or satisfies stated needs, requirements or specification.

Many people get worried by some of the words in this definition, such as the word 'inherent'. What is hidden there? Basically, it means inbuilt or natural. An example might be a definition of the requirement for a lawn. The requirement would not have to say that the lawn should be green, because that is 'inherent'. The specification for a wheel might not need to specify that it should be round, because this is 'inherent' in a wheel.

14.2 QUALITY OVERVIEW

It is likely that both the supplier and the customer will have quality standards already in place – a Quality Management System (QMS). Both may also have staff responsible for ensuring that these standards are used (quality assurance). Depending on the environment into which the final product will be delivered, there may be other legal or environmental standards to be reached. An example here would be a car's emission levels if we were building a new car. All of these need to be matched against the customer's quality expectations, the anticipated project timeframe, the cost and the solution method. Out of this comparison we should get a list of the development standards, the testing methods and the tools to be used.

These quality requirements need to be related to the various products that the project will create or use. We then need to get down to putting into our detailed plans the work necessary to ensure that quality is built in and tested, who will do this and when.

After this we need to consider an audit trail of our quality work. How do we prove to the customer that the necessary quality work has been done?

14.3 THE QUALITY AUDIT TRAIL

Step	Product	Process/ technique/theme
Ascertain the customer's quality expectations	Project mandate or Project Brief	Starting up a Project
Define the project's acceptance criteria	Project Product Description	Starting up a Project
Write a Quality Management Strategy	Project Initiation Documentation	Initiating a Project
Add quality work and resources to a Stage Plan	Stage Plan	Managing a Stage Boundary
Identify planned quality check dates	Quality Register	Managing a Stage Boundary
Define a product's quality criteria	Product Descriptions	Product-based Planning
Explain the quality requirements for each piece of work	Work Package	Controlling a Stage
Report back on the quality work performed	Quality Register	Managing Product Delivery
Check that quality work is being done correctly	Quality Register	Controlling a Stage
Control changes	Issue	Change Control
Keep track of changes to products	Configuration records	Configuration Management

14.3.1 Customer's Quality Expectations

This is a definition in measurable terms of what must be done for the final product to be acceptable to the customer and members of staff who will be affected.

The customer's quality expectations should be made clear in the project mandate at the very outset of the project. If it is not sufficiently clear, the Project Manager should clarify the expectations when preparing the Project

Brief (during *Starting up a Project*). The expectations should be measurable. 'Of good quality' may sound fine, but how can it be measured? Expectations of performance, reliability, flexibility, maintainability and capability can all be expressed in measurable terms.

Quality is one corner of a triangle, as shown in Figure 14.1. The customer has to decide where, within the triangle, the project's main focus is to be. Does it incline more towards the cost, the time or the quality? This simple exercise shows that the three items are interlinked. If you want the product to be cheap, that may have an adverse effect on the quality, and so on.

14.3.2 Acceptance Criteria

A definition in measurable terms of those aspects of the final product which it must demonstrate for the product to be acceptable to the customer and staff who will be affected by the product.

Expectations of performance, reliability, flexibility, maintainability and capability can all be expressed in measurable terms.

Acceptance criteria measurements defined when starting up the project may need refining. This can happen during initiation and at the end of each stage.

14.3.3 The Quality Management Strategy

The next step is to decide how the project is going to meet the customer's quality expectations for the product. The Quality Management Strategy is created during initiation. Other inputs to this should be the standards to be used to guide the development of the product and test its ability to meet the quality expectations. The supplier should have standards, but the customer may also have standards that it insists on being used. Such standards have to be compared against the quality expectations to see which are to be used. There may be gaps where extra standards have to be obtained or created. The customer has the last say in what standards will be used to check the products. There may also be regulatory standards to be met.

The Quality Management Strategy identifies the standards to be used and the main quality responsibilities. The latter may be a reference to a quality assurance function (belonging to the customer, supplier or both). The Quality Management Strategy refers to the establishment of the Quality Register and its purpose.

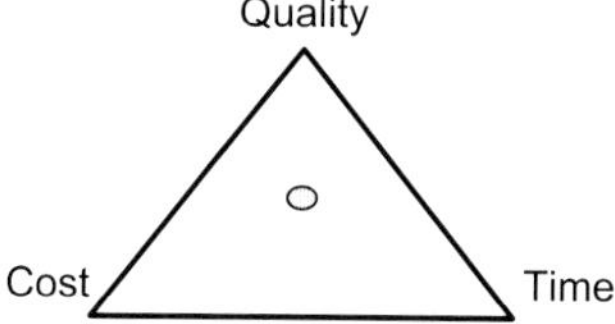

FIGURE 14.1 The quality, cost and time triangle

Product Descriptions are written for the key products shown in the Project Plan. These include specific quality criteria against which the products will be measured.

14.3.4 The Project Product Description

This is created in the *Starting up a Project* process as part of the Project Brief and is a prerequisite to selecting the project approach. (Will the approach provide all the products at the required quality and meet the acceptance criteria?) It is reviewed during initiation and at each stage boundary. It is a summary of the project's final product. It defines what the project must deliver in order to be accepted by the customer, including:

- Purpose of the final product.
- Its set of products.
- The customer's quality expectations.
- Acceptance criteria.
- Project quality tolerances.

It is officially the responsibility of the Senior User, but usually the Project Manager writes it in consultation with the Senior User and Executive. A full description of its contents can be found in Appendix A.

14.3.5 Adding Quality to Each Stage Plan

Each stage needs its own quality plan containing lower-level detail than the Quality Management Strategy. This identifies the method of quality checking to be used for each product of the stage. The plan also identifies responsibility for each individual quality check. For example, for each quality review the chair and reviewers are identified. This gives an opportunity for those with Project Assurance roles to see each draft Stage Plan and input its needs for checking and the staff who should represent it at each check.

If they were not done as part of the Quality Management Strategy, any major products developed in the stage have Product Descriptions written for them.

14.3.6 Product Descriptions

A Product Description should be written for each major product to be produced by the project. Among other information the description should contain:

- Title.
- Purpose.
- Composition (what are the themes of the product?).
- Derivation (what is the source of the themes?).
- Format (what does the product have to look like?).
- Quality criteria (what quality does the product have to display?).
- Quality tolerance.

- Quality method (how will the product be tested that it meets the quality criteria?).
- The skills or resources required to check the quality.

The Product Description is the first place where we start thinking about the quality of the product, how we will test the presence of its quality and who we might need in order to test that quality.

The Product Description is an important part of the information handed to a Team Manager or individual as part of a Work Package.

Any time that a product that has been approved by the Project Board has to be changed, the Product Description should also be checked to see if it needs an update.

14.3.7 Quality Tolerance

The quality tolerance of a product is defined as a range of values within which the quality criteria can vary and still be acceptable. For example, 'the white wine must be stored at 6°C, with a tolerance of 5°C–7°C', or 'time taken to process the order must be no more than 30 seconds, with a tolerance margin of −10 seconds to +0 seconds'.

14.3.8 Quality Register

The Quality Register is a summary of planned tests, tests carried out, personnel involved in carrying out the tests and the results of the tests. The initial entry is by the Project Manager when a Stage Plan is created. The Team Manager may wish to add the names of extra reviewers and the actual results as the quality checking is done. This information is normally passed to Project Support to make the actual updates to the register, but this is defined in the Configuration Management Strategy.

14.3.9 Quality File

There should be one quality file for each project. The Project Manager is responsible for setting up the Quality Register and quality file and checking that either Team Managers or individuals are feeding information into the file. If Project Support has been appointed to the project, it is important that the duties with regard to the quality file are clearly defined between this role and the Project Manager. Normally Project Support will be allocated the duties of logging and filing all the documents.

The quality file should contain the Quality Register, the master copy of the Product Descriptions and the forms that are produced as part of the quality controls applied during the life of the project. It is an important part of the audit trail that can be followed by the user or an independent quality assurance body to assess what quality checking has been carried out and how effective it has been. As such, it is a deliverable product.

CARTOON 14.1 Quality Register

Wherever possible, the originals of documents should be filed in the quality file. A copy can be filed if the original has to be circulated for signature or comments, but on its return the original should be replaced in the quality file.

The quality file should have sections for:

- Quality Register.
- Quality review invitations.
- Quality review results.

Each quality check should have a unique number to provide the basis for statistics on how many quality checks have been carried out.

On filing the section on quality review invitations there should be a check that there is no change to the planned review date. If there is, the Project Manager should be notified.

When all corrective actions on the action list have been taken and the list signed off by the chair of the review, it is filed in the quality file. If the review was terminated prematurely, the review documents such as follow-on action list, annotated product copies and question lists should all be filed in the quality file.

14.4 QUALITY REVIEW

A quality review is a peer review of the quality of a product against its Product Description, including its quality criteria. It deserves a full description, so rather than making this a long chapter I have put it in Appendix D.

Chapter 15

Risk

15.1 PHILOSOPHY

A project brings about change, and change brings risks. Risks are inevitable in every project. Risk can be formally defined as 'the chance of exposure to the consequences of future events'.

It is not uncommon to hear people say, 'This is a high-risk project.' This statement by itself is of limited interest or value. We need far more detail. What are the actual risks? What are their causes? What is the probability of the risk occurring? How serious would the impact of that occurrence be? What can be done about it?

15.2 RISK OVERVIEW

The management of risk is one of the most important ongoing parts of the Project Board's and Project Manager's jobs. We should remember that *occasionally* there may be the risk of something beneficial happening to a project. We need to be prepared to take advantage of such risks occurring. However, most risks to be considered are those that might bring bad news, and it is on these risks that we shall concentrate in this chapter.

So the focus of our risk attention is on the likelihood of something happening that we would wish to avoid. In a project, risk is anything that causes the project to end in such a way that it does not fully meet its identified targets and objectives.

Risks need to be:

- Identified.
- Assessed.
- Controlled.

The effect of failure to deliver a project on time and to an acceptable cost and level of quality can be disastrous. Although the cost of managing risk may appear significant, the cost of *not* managing risk effectively can be many times greater.

Only by fully recognizing and understanding the risks that exist can potential problems and opportunities be understood and addressed. Both the likelihood of things happening and the consequences if they do occur must be understood by the project management team in order to have this true appreciation of the risk situation. The Project Board then needs to choose a course of action that can be taken to improve the situation.

It should be recognized that it may be desirable to accept some risks in order to obtain additional benefits to the project. *Note:* the option to take no action may sometimes be appropriate. This means that a decision is made that the perceived level of risk is acceptable.

How effectively a risk can be managed depends on the identification of its underlying causes and the amount of control that the project management team can exert over those causes. It is more effective to reduce the potential cause of a risk than to wait for that risk to materialize and then address its impact.

The impact of a risk that materializes should not be mistaken for the underlying cause of the risk. For example, *cost escalation* on a project is an ever-present risk impact. Expenditure should be monitored to determine the underlying causes of *why* costs are escalating.

It is important that the management of risk is considered as a continuous process throughout the life of a project. Once potential risks have been identified they need to be monitored until such time as either they cease to be material, or their effect has been reduced or mitigated as a result of management intervention. The potential for new risks being introduced with time, or in consequence of actions taken, also needs to be considered throughout the project life cycle. The obvious – and what should be considered the minimum – number of times for risk assessment and management are:

- Project initiation.
- End stage assessment.

Depending on the project's criticality and size, risks should be examined regularly – for example, each month.

In broad terms, the Project Manager is responsible for seeing that risk analysis is done, and the Project Board is responsible for the management of risk (the decisions on courses of action to take). In practice the Project Manager may take decisions on certain risks where the consequences are within the tolerance margins, but even then it would be wise to advise the Project Board in the Highlight Report of any such decisions.

It is good practice to appoint one individual as responsible for monitoring each identified risk, the person best placed to observe the factors that affect that risk. According to the risk, this may be a member of the Project Board, someone with Project Assurance duties, the Project Manager, the Team Manager or a team member.

There are many methods of risk management on the market and quite a few software packages that will help you with a standard set of questions and 'forms' to come to a view of the risk situation of your project. To my mind, far more important than which method you choose is *when* you should carry out assessment of risk. Too many projects look at the risk situation at the beginning of a project, then forget about it for the rest of the project (or until a risk comes up and smacks them in the face!).

I suggest that you do the following:

- Carry out risk assessment at the start of a project. Make proposals on what should be done about the risks. Get agreement on whether to start the project or not.
- Review the risks at the end of every stage. This includes existing risks that might have changed and new risks caused by the next Stage Plan. Get agreement on whether to continue into the next stage.
- Appoint an owner for every risk. Build into the Stage Plan the moments when the owners should be monitoring the risks. Check on the owners to see that they are doing the job and keeping the risk status up-to-date.
- Review every request for change for its impact on existing risks or the creation of a new risk. Build the time and cost of any risk avoidance or reduction, for example, into your recommendation on the action to be taken.
- Inspect the risks at the end of the project for any that might affect the product in its operational life. If there are any, make sure that you notify those charged with looking after the product. (Use the follow-on action recommendations for this.)

These points should be enough for you to keep control of the risk situation. If you have very long stages (which I do not recommend) and very few requests for change, you may decide to review risks on a monthly basis.

There is one other point of philosophy about risk. When considering actions, you have to consider the cost of taking action against the cost of not taking action.

15.3 RISK MANAGEMENT STRATEGY

During initiation a Risk Management Strategy should be developed, describing how risk management is to be embedded in the various project management activities. The contents of the strategy are identified in Appendix A, but it is worth a few extra words about some of its contents.

15.3.1 Risk Tolerance

Before deciding what to do about risks, the Project Board must consider the amount of risk it can tolerate. Another name for risk tolerance is 'risk appetite'. The view of how much the project is prepared to put at risk will depend on a number of variables. A project may be prepared to take comparatively large risks in some areas and none at all in others, such as risks to company survival, exceeding budgets or target date and fulfilling health and safety regulations.

Risk tolerance can be related to the five other tolerance parameters: risk to completion within *timescale* and/or *cost*, and to achieving product *quality*, project *scope* and the *benefits* within the boundaries of the Business Case.

Risk tolerances have to be considered carefully to obtain the optimum balance of the cost of a risk occurring against the cost of limiting or preventing that risk. The organization's overall risk tolerance must also be considered as well as that of the project.

15.3.2 Risk Responsibilities

The Project Board has two responsibilities:

- To notify the Project Manager of any external risk exposure to the project.
- To make decisions on the Project Manager's recommended reactions to risk.

The Project Board makes the key decisions on risk management. Remember, the Project Board represents all the parties: the customer, the user and the supplier.

The Project Manager has the responsibility to ensure that risks are identified, recorded and regularly reviewed. The Project Manager is responsible for ensuring that the appropriate level of information is gathered from all sources to enable a true assessment of a risk to be made. The customer and supplier may each have a different set of risks to which they feel exposed, or will have a different view of a risk and the alternative actions. The customer will try to protect the achievement of its Business Case and get the supplier to take the risks (or bear the cost of any preventive or avoiding action). The supplier will try to protect the expected profit margin and therefore take the opposite view.

15.4 RISK REGISTER

PRINCE2 uses a Risk Register to record and keep track of each identified risk. A Product Description of a Risk Register is provided in Appendix A. The Risk Register is created during project initiation. If any risks are identified in the process *Starting up a Project*, these are recorded in the Project Manager's Daily Log and transferred to the Risk Register when the latter is created.

Although the Risk Register is the Project Manager's responsibility, its maintenance will usually be delegated to Project Support. The procedures for registering risks and maintaining the Risk Register are defined in the Risk Management Strategy.

15.5 RISK MANAGEMENT PROCEDURE

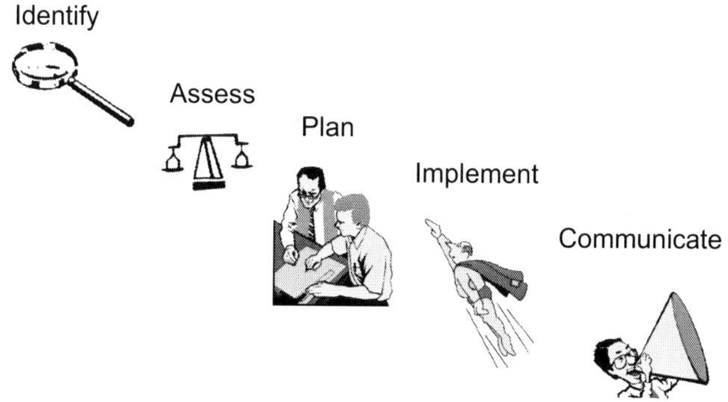

FIGURE 15.1 The five risk management steps

15.5.1 Risk Identification

This should be a straightforward statement of the risk. PRINCE2 suggests these activities in risk identification (Figure 15.1):

- Record identified threats and opportunities in the Risk Register.
- Prepare early-warning indicators to allow monitoring of these potential risks.
- Get stakeholder views on the identified risks.

People can sometimes get confused and identify the impact of a risk as the risk or as extra risks. For example, there may be a risk that bad weather will delay the date for completion of an extra factory. Failure to meet the demands for products would be an impact of that risk, not the actual risk or an extra risk. In order to have a clear and unambiguous risk statement, consider the following risk aspects:

- Cause.
- Event.
- Effect.

15.5.1.1 Risk Cause

What is the source of the risk? What is the trigger or situation that would cause the risk?

15.5.1.2 Risk Event

What might happen as a result of the cause?

15.5.1.3 *Risk Effect*

What would be the impact of the event?

15.5.1.4 *Example of Threat Identification*

If we get heavy and prolonged rain (risk cause), the river might burst its banks (risk event), flooding the housing estate we are building (risk effect).

15.5.1.5 *Example of Opportunity Identification*

The forecast series of channel port blockades by French fishermen (risk cause) would cause cancellation of many car ferry crossings (risk event), increasing the attractiveness of the channel tunnel (risk effect).

15.5.2 Risk Assessment

Risk assessment breaks down into two steps: estimation and evaluation.

15.5.2.1 *Risk Estimation*

Risk estimation judges a risk by:

- Probability.
- Impact.
- Proximity.

Probability

- How likely is the threat or opportunity to occur?

Impact

It is not enough to simply say, 'The impact will be high.' Impact should be judged under the headings of:

- Time.
- Cost.
- Quality.
- Benefits.
- People/resources.

Many people also confuse the impact of the risk with the impact of risk responses. For example, situations such as 'bad weather causing a delay to factory completion will cost money for overtime to make up the lost time or payment to outsource production until the factory is completed' are not impacts of the risk. They are part of the assessment of responses to the risk.

Proximity

- How soon might the risk or opportunity occur? Something that might happen next week might get priority over a more important risk that might happen in three months' time. The impact of a risk might vary according to when it is likely to happen.

15.5.2.2 Risk Evaluation

The aim here is to collate all the risks and assess the net effect of all identified risks and opportunities. This will allow comparison with the project risk tolerance set by the Project Board and may affect the continued business justification.

15.5.3 Plan

This step identifies and evaluates a range of responses to the threats and opportunities.

The identification of suitable responses covers:

- Assessing the acceptable level of each risk.
- Generating alternative paths of action for risks which do not meet acceptability criteria.
- Assessing the reality of the countermeasures in the light of the project and company environment.

The subsections below give a standard list of the types of alternative responses to risk in order of preference

15.5.3.1 Threats

Response	Definition	Example
Avoid	Change something in the project so that either the threat can no longer occur or will have no impact if it does	Certain chemicals, if mixed, cause a fire, so store them in separate buildings
Reduce	Take action ahead of a risk occurring to reduce its probability	Operators may make errors because they have not read the instruction manual before using the product, so we will insist that they pass a test before being certificated to use the product
	Take action ahead of a risk occurring to reduce its impact	There is a threat of a rail strike, so arrange to travel by taxi

Continued

Response	Definition	Example
Fallback	Create a fallback plan for what action to take to reduce the impact if the risk occurs	If the new style of exam is not ready on time, we will continue using the old style
Transfer	Responsibility for some or all of the financial impact of a risk is accepted by a third party	The Rembrandt picture is insured for £3 million Put liquidated damage clauses in the supplier contract for any product failure
Accept	A conscious decision not to take action on a risk because the risk is so unlikely to occur or the cost of its occurring is so small or the cost of reduction actions is so great that it is not worth taking the preventative or reduction action	We accept the risk that unseasonal storms might wash out the national golf open championship in early summer

15.5.3.2 Opportunities

Response	Definition	Example
Share	The customer and supplier agree to share the profits or losses of a joint venture, possibly within defined limits	You write a book for me and we agree to share the profits when they rise above the production costs
Exploit	Ensuring that an opportunity does occur and that the impact (benefits) will be realized	A large company has just had a major project failure. Create a marketing campaign to persuade it to take on your project management method
Enhance	This can be either enhancing the probability of an opportunity occurring or enhancing the impact if an opportunity should occur	We could offer a price reduction to swap old for new when the new model becomes available If our major competitor does stop offering its Dover–Calais service, we could increase the price of our service by 10%
Reject	A deliberate decision not to take an identified opportunity, perhaps because of the risk of diverting essential resources or insufficient financial incentive	We might increase early sales by beating a competitor to the launch of a product, but the shortening of timescales to do so would put our quality in jeopardy

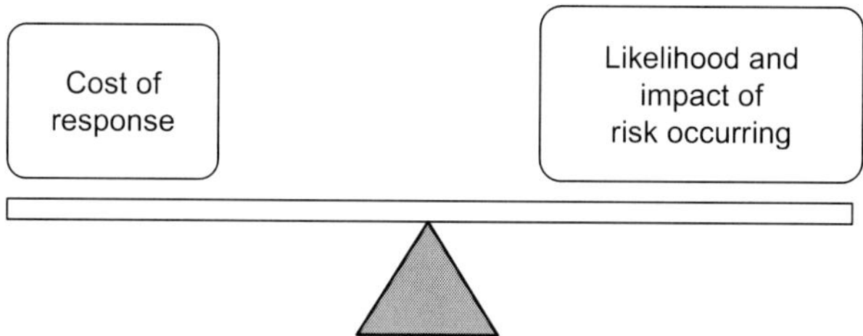

FIGURE 15.2 Risk balance

Sometimes more than one risk response is required in order to completely respond to a risk. Sometimes the response to one risk can cause knock-on effects to other risks or create new ones.

15.5.4 Implement

This step ensures that the planned actions are taken, their effectiveness monitored and, where necessary, any corrective action is taken.

In the implementation step of risk management the revised version of the PRINCE2 manual uses two role names: 'risk owner' and 'risk actionee' (a name that I must admit to disliking).

15.5.4.1 Risk Owner

This is a named individual who is made responsible for the monitoring and control of an assigned risk, including the implementation of the agreed response actions.

15.5.4.2 Risk Actionee

The person assigned to carry out a risk response action is called a 'risk actionee', supporting and taking direction from the risk owner.

In many cases both roles may be given to the same person. The risk owner should be the person most capable of managing the risk. I worry that this can be confused with the Project Manager's management tasks, and prefer the old definition of a risk owner as the person best suited to keep an eye on the risk.

15.5.5 Communicate

This is a continuous process. It ensures that all relevant members of the project and stakeholders are kept aware of the situation of the risk. It is not normally necessary to create reports that are in addition to the regular PRINCE2 reports. Risk status should be conveyed in:

- Checkpoint Reports.
- Highlight Reports.
- End Stage Reports.
- End Project Reports.
- Lessons Reports.

The Communication Management Strategy will define the most appropriate method of communicating with stakeholders.

15.6 RISK PROFILE

A graphic way of viewing risks is in a summary risk profile. An example is shown in Figure 15.3. This puts risks, using their unique identifiers, in a table of low-to-high probability and impact. In the example, the top right-hand corner contains risks with a high probability and high impact. The thick black line shows the risk tolerance level, so any risks to the right of that are beyond the risk tolerance levels. Such a table is a snapshot of known risks at a certain time and would need to be updated regularly. Updating it may show trends in known risks.

15.7 LINKS

There are many links to the PRINCE2 processes:

- Planning the Next Stage (*Managing a Stage Boundary* process)
  When a draft plan has been produced, it should be examined for risks before being published.
- Capture and Examine Issues and Risks (*Controlling a Stage* process)
  One aspect of examining new Issue Reports is to see if they cause new risks or modify existing risks.

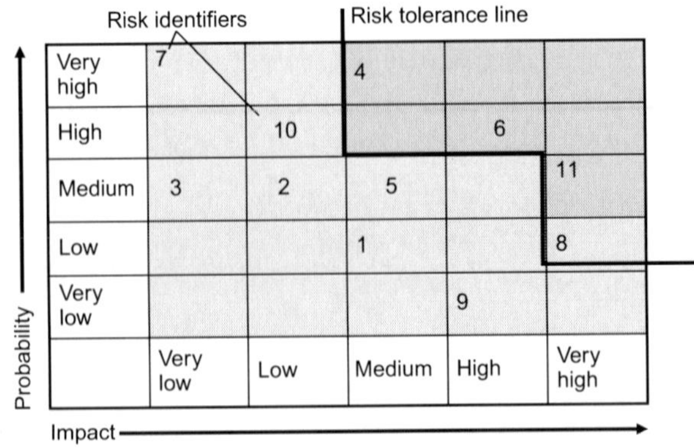

FIGURE 15.3 Risk profile

- Review the Stage Status (*Controlling a Stage* process)
  Part of this process is to check if the status of any risks has changed since the last review.
- Report Highlights (*Controlling a Stage* process)
  If *Controlling a Stage* detects a change in the risk situation, the Project Manager should advise the Project Board of the change in the next Highlight Report.
- Take Corrective Action (*Controlling a Stage* process)
  If a risk status becomes worse, the Project Manager may be able to take corrective action within the tolerance limits.
- Escalate Issues and Risks (*Controlling a Stage* process)
  Where the event described in a risk either has happened or is about to happen, the Project Manager may forecast that the results will cause the stage to deviate beyond its tolerances. This would be escalated to the Project Board in an Exception Report.
- *Directing a Project* process.
  The Project Board should consider the risk situation before making all its decisions.

Chapter 16

Change

16.1 PHILOSOPHY

Change consists of two closely linked activities: change control and configuration management. Neither can function effectively without the other. Change directly supports the principles of 'focus on products' and 'manage by exception' and indirectly the 'continued business justification' principle.

16.1.1 Change Control

No matter how well a project has been planned, if there is no control over changes, this will destroy any chance of bringing the project in on schedule and to budget. In any project there will be changes for many reasons – for example:

- Government legislation has changed, and this must be reflected in the product specification.
- The users change their mind on what is wanted.
- Because the development cycle is making the user think more and more about the product, extra features suggest themselves for inclusion.
- There is a merge of departments, change of responsibility and company merger or takeover which radically alters the project definition.
- The supplier finds that it will be impossible to deliver everything within the agreed time or cost.
- The supplier cannot meet an acceptance criterion, such as performance.
- A product delivered by an outside contractor or another project fails to meet its specification.

All of the above examples need a procedure to control them and their effect on the project. This procedure must make sure they are not ignored, but that no changes are implemented which have not been approved by the appropriate level of management or Change Authority. This includes the Project Board.

16.1.2 Configuration Management

No organization can be fully efficient or effective unless it manages its assets, particularly if the assets are vital to the running of the organization's business. A project's assets have to be managed likewise. The assets of the project are the products that it develops. The name for the combined set of these assets is a configuration. The configuration of the final deliverable of a project is the sum total of its products.

In the foreword to its Product Configuration Management System (PCMS), SQL Software wrote: 'If the product you develop has more than one version, more than a few components or more than one person working on it, you are doing configuration management. The only question is how well you are doing it.'

Configuration management is needed to manage the creation, safekeeping and controlled change to the project's products.

In PRINCE2 the procedures to control change and configuration are contained in the Configuration Management Strategy.

CARTOON 16.1 Configuration Librarian

16.2 CONFIGURATION MANAGEMENT STRATEGY

The Configuration Management Strategy is created during the initiation of a project. There is a Product Description of its composition in Appendix A. The strategy defines:

- the configuration management procedure;
- the issue and change control procedure;
- roles and responsibilities for the two activities;
- any tools and techniques to be used;
- a scale for prioritizing issues;
- a scale for rating the severity of issues, linking this to the management level required to handle each level;
- use and membership of a Change Authority and its change budget.

The severity rating of issues raises the question of whether to use a Change Authority. The use of a severity rating is to allow decisions to be made on what level of management should make a decision on an issue.

16.2.1 Change Authority

It is part of the Project Board's responsibility to review and approve requests for change and off-specifications. If many of these are expected, the Project Board may decide to delegate the task, within limits, to a Change Authority. This can be an individual or a group. Examples would be those given Project Assurance roles, a group of users or the Project Manager.

16.2.2 Change Budget

There is no point in having a Change Authority if it has no money with which to pay for any approved work. Therefore, the change budget is a sum of money to pay for the analysis of requests for changes or off-specifications. The Executive might have had to negotiate this with corporate or programme management during initiation. It is given to the Change Authority by the Project Board, which normally puts two limits on its use: the amount that can be spent on a single change, and the amount of the budget that can be spent in one stage. Anything outside these limits has to be referred to the Project Board.

The use of a Change Authority with its budget can greatly reduce the number of calls on it for decisions. The use of a Change Authority and the budget it is to be allocated are documented as part of the Configuration Management Strategy.

16.3 OVERVIEW OF ISSUE AND CHANGE CONTROL

An Issue Report is the formal way into a project of any inquiry, complaint or request (outside the scope of a quality review question list). It can be raised by anyone associated with the project. Issues fall into three groups:

1. A desired new or changed function.
2. A failure of a product in meeting some aspect of the user requirements. In such cases the report should be accompanied by evidence of the failure and, where appropriate, sufficient material to allow someone to re-create the failure for assessment purposes.
3. A problem or concern.

In other words, there is no limit to the content of an issue beyond the fact that it should be about the project (Cartoon 16.2).

Any error found during a quality review normally goes on a follow-on action list. There are two exceptions to this:

1. Where an error is found during quality review which belongs to a different product from the one under review.
2. Where work to correct an error found during quality review cannot be done during the agreed follow-on action period.

Such errors are recorded as issues as the way of getting them into the change control procedures.

When considering the procedures for handling issues, there is the possibility that the subject will be outside the scope of the project. An example might be a fault in a component that is used in many products across the department. Although it is being used in the project, it clearly has a wider implication. There should be a procedure to close the issue as far as the project is concerned and transfer it to a departmental level. The same approach applies if the project

CARTOON 16.2 Project issue

is part of a programme and an error is found in a quality review that affects other projects in the programme.

All possible changes should be handled by the same issue and change control procedure. Apart from controlling possible changes, this procedure should provide a formal entry point through which questions or suggestions can also be raised and answered.

It is particularly important that the librarian identifies any *baselined* configuration items that will need to change. This is because the Project Board has already been told of the completion of those items. The Project Board must therefore approve any change to such items.

16.4 ISSUE AND CHANGE CONTROL PROCEDURE

The procedure has five steps:

1. Capture.
2. Examine.
3. Propose.
4. Decide.
5. Implement.

16.4.1 Capture

The first step is to carry out a brief analysis, just enough to decide what type of issue it is, and whether it can be managed formally or informally. The outcome is usually one of the following:

- The issue is proposing a change to a baselined configuration item. The issue is a request for change, and the decision can only be made by the Project Board (or Change Authority if one has been appointed).
- The issue requests a change to the agreed user specification, acceptance criteria or a Product Description. The issue is a request for change, and the decision can only be made by the Project Board (or Change Authority if one has been appointed).
- A product does not meet its specification. The issue is an off-specification.
- The issue asks a question or voices a concern, but will not lead to a product change.

16.4.1.1 Informal

The latter type of issue can be immediately resolved and doesn't require further analysis, or decision from the Project Board/Change Authority. These issues can be logged by the Project Manager in the Daily Log and dealt with informally.

16.4.1.2 Formal

Issues needing more analysis and/or are considered more serious should be handled formally. An Issue Report should be raised, preferably by the originator, and this should be entered on the Issue Register by the Configuration Librarian, who will allocate a unique identifier to the issue and pass a copy back to the originator and another to the Project Manager. The issue is now classed as 'Open'.

16.4.2 Examine

The Project Manager allocates the issue to the person or team best suited to perform a full impact analysis on it. The issues are evaluated in terms of their impact on:

- Time.
- Cost.
- Quality.
- Scope.
- Benefits.
- Risks.

The impact analysis of an issue should cover all aspects – business, user and supplier – with the aim of making recommendations to the Project Manager on their resolution.

The Project Manager should review all open issues. He or she may do this alone, with a senior technical member of the team and/or with those carrying integrity responsibilities. The frequency of such meetings will depend on the volume of issues being received, but meetings should be held regularly and with sufficient frequency to ensure that no inordinate delay occurs in taking action.

All Issue Reports have to be closed by the end of the project or transferred to follow-on action recommendations, part of the End Project Report. The transfer of an issue to these recommendations can only be done with the approval of the Project Board.

16.4.2.1 Request for Change

A request for change records a proposed modification to the user requirements. The request for change requires an impact analysis to see how much work is involved. Senior team members with the appropriate skills and experience normally do this. The configuration library holds information that will help to identify what other products or configuration items will be affected.

16.4.2.2 *Off-specification*

An off-specification is used to document any situation where the product is failing to meet its specification in some respect.

The Configuration Librarian allocates the next unique issue identifier from the register and sends a copy of the issue to its author. Senior team members carry out an impact analysis with the help of the Configuration Librarian to discover which products are affected by the off-specification.

16.4.3 Propose

With the results of the impact analysis available, the next step is to look at alternative actions and propose the best response.

The alternatives are costed and the impact on the Stage Plan's budget and schedule assessed. Before a decision can be made the Project Manager will want to know the answer to two questions:

1. Can the work be done within the tolerance levels of the current plan? For this reason it is best that a batch of requests is studied, to give a wider view of the effect on the plans.
2. Does the advantage of taking action outweigh the costs of doing so?

In preparation for the decision, the off-specifications or requests for change should be awarded a priority rating. This can be one of four:

- High.
- Medium.
- Low.
- Cosmetic.

16.4.4 Decide

16.4.4.1 *Request for Change*

In order for the request for change to be implemented, it must be approved by either the Project Manager or the Project Board. Whose decision it is will be documented in the Configuration Management Strategy, and depends on the following:

- If it is not a change to a configuration item that has already been *baselined* and the work can be done within the current plan's *tolerances*, the Project Manager *can* make the decision to implement it. Alternatively, it can be passed to the Project Board (or Change Authority if one has been appointed) for its decision. Since experience shows that there will be a lot of changes during the project, it is a good idea to make the Project Board decide on any changes other than trivialities. This keeps the Board aware of how many changes are being requested and their cumulative impact on the

schedule and cost. If the Stage Plan runs into trouble later, it is usually too late for the Project Manager to get any sympathy about a claim that lots of requests for change have been implemented without asking for more time or money. The answer will usually be: 'Why didn't you ask us? We could have cancelled or delayed some of them.' *It is important to note here that tolerances are not there to pay for small requests for change.* The Project Manager should only implement a small change without asking for extra time and money if work on the relevant product has not yet started and inclusion of the requested change will not cost extra.
- The decision must be made by the Project Board or Change Authority if the change is to one or more configuration items that the Project Board has already been told are complete (to any baseline, not necessarily the final one). More than anything, this is to retain the confidence level of the Board. If it has been told that something is finished and later finds out that it has been changed without consultation, its sense of being in control evaporates.
- If the work to do the request for change cannot be done within the tolerance levels of the current Stage Plan, the decision on action *must* come from the Project Board. The Project Manager must submit an Exception Report with the request for change. This may lead to a request for an Exception Plan showing the new schedule and cost for the rest of the stage.

If the Project Board retains the authority to approve changes, then the Senior User is the key role in any request to implement the changes. All those requests for change that have not been decided by the Project Manager are passed to the Senior User. It should be the Senior User's job to put them in order of priority for consideration by the Board.

The Project Board's decision may be to:

- approve implementation of the request for change. If the change required an Exception Plan, then this means approving the Exception Plan;
- delay the request for change to an enhancement project after the current one is finished;
- defer a decision until a later meeting;
- ask for more information;
- cancel the request for change.

If the Project Board has delegated the responsibility for decision on Issue Reports to a Change Authority, then the Change Authority will make the decisions described above. The decision should be documented on the Issue Report and in the Issue Register.

Whenever the status of an issue changes, for example from 'open' to 'closed', a copy of the Issue Report should be sent to the originator.

16.4.4.2 Off-specification

As with requests for change, the decision on what action is to be taken is made by either the Project Manager or Project Board or Change Authority. If the off-specification is because of a failure within the Project Manager's responsibility, the onus is on the Project Manager to correct the problem within tolerances. Similarly, if the error is because of a Team Manager's failure to fulfil an agreed Work Package, the onus is on the Team Manager (or the supplier if the team is from an external company) to correct the error without asking the Project Manager for more time or money. Other situations can be dealt with as follows:

- If the off-specification does not involve a change to a configuration item that has already been baselined and the work can be done within the current plan's tolerances, the Project Manager should make the decision to implement it.
- If the off-specification requires changes to one or more configuration items which the Project Board have already been told are complete (to any baseline, not necessarily the final one), the Project Board or Change Authority must make the decision.
- If the work to do the off-specification cannot be done within the tolerance levels of the current Stage Plan, the decision on action must come from the Project Board. The Project Manager must submit an Exception Report with the off-specification. If the Project Board accepts the need for the extra work, it will request an Exception Plan showing the new schedule and cost for the rest of the stage.

The Project Board's decision may be to:

- correct the fault. If the work required an Exception Plan, then this means approving the Exception Plan;
- delay correction of the fault to an enhancement project after the current one is finished;
- defer a decision until a later meeting;
- ask for more information.

The decision should be documented on the off-specification and Issue Register, and an updated copy filed. Whenever its status changes, a copy should be sent to the originator.

16.4.5 Implement

The Project Manager is responsible for scheduling any approved changes. This work will possibly involve the issue of a new version of one or more products by Project Support.

On receipt of a completed request for change or off-specification, Project Support should ensure that any amended products have been re-submitted to the configuration library. The finalized request should be stored in the quality file, and the originator advised. The Issue Register should be updated with the final details and the originator advised.

16.5 CONFIGURATION MANAGEMENT

16.5.1 Philosophy

Configuration management is regarded as a boring subject, but it affects the quality of the project work and, if it is done badly, it can kill any hopes that you had of a successful project.

16.5.2 Purpose

The purpose of configuration management is to identify, track and protect the project's products as they are developed.

16.5.3 Configuration Management Strategy

During initiation a Configuration Management Strategy should be written. This covers both configuration management and change control.

The first step in this is to check if there are corporate/programme policies and procedures that cover this area.

The contents of a Configuration Management Strategy are:

- Procedures covering the identification of products, where master copies are to be kept and how they are to be controlled, and details of status accounting and configuration auditing.
- The issue and change control procedures.
- Configuration management and change control responsibilities.
- Record retention.
- Any tools, software or techniques to be used.

Configuration management is closely linked to the management of changes to the project's products. It must be possible to retrieve at any time any version of a product and any revision of the components that make up that product. Configuration management must ensure that the resulting product will always be built in an identical manner. Product enhancements and special variants create the need to control multiple versions and releases of the product. All these have to be handled by configuration management.

As an example of this, consider the car that you drive. It will have a unique number. The manufacturer will make many minor modifications to the assembly of that car over the years without changing the name of the model. Let's imagine that you have a Ford Mondeo. If you at some time need a replacement facia panel, the unique number will allow the storeroom to identify which model of facia was used in the assembly of your car.

16.5.4 Baselines

Baselines are moments in a product's development when it and all its components have reached an acceptable state, such that they can be 'frozen' and used as a base for the next step. The next step may be to release the product to the customer, or it may be that you have 'frozen' a design and will now construct the products from that design.

Products constantly evolve and are subject to change as a project moves through its life cycle and, later on, in the operational life of the product. A Project Manager will need to know the answer to many questions, such as:

- What is the latest agreed level of specification to which we are working?
- What exact design are we implementing?
- What did we release to site X last January?

In other words, a baseline is a frozen picture of what products and what versions of them constituted a certain situation. A baseline may be defined as a set of known and agreed configuration items under change control from which further progress can be charted. This description indicates that you will baseline only products that represent either the entire product or at least a significant product.

A baseline is created for one of a number of reasons:

- To provide a sound base for future work.
- As a point to which you can retreat if development goes wrong.
- To represent a standard configuration against which supplies can be obtained (for example, purchase of identical personal computers for a group).

The baseline record itself should be a product, so that it can be controlled in the same way as other products. It is a baseline identifier, date, reason and list of all the products and their version numbers that comprise that baseline. Because of its different format it is often held in a separate file.

16.5.5 Product Status Account

Product status accounting provides a complete statement of the current status and history of the products generated within the project or within a stage. The purpose of this is to provide a report on:

- the status of one or all configuration items;
- all the events which have impacted those products.

This allows comparison with the plans and provides tracking of changes to products.

For the purpose of status accounting, the configuration management method should be able to produce reports on such things as:

- the history of development of a particular item;
- the number of requests for change which were approved during a specific period of time;

- the person who is responsible for an item;
- items in the design baseline that have been changed since it was approved;
- items that have had changes approved but not yet implemented.

16.5.6 Configuration Item Record

The Composition section of the Product Description in Appendix A.5 gives a list of potential information about a product that should be considered against the needs of the project. You need to consider each project's size, importance and the company standards in deciding the set of information that is needed. The first three fields are essential.

Project identifier	A unique identifier allocated by either the configuration management software or the Configuration Librarian to identify all products of the project
Item identifier	Unique identifier for a single product
Current version number	The number of this particular version of the product. This is usually linked to a baseline. You may wish to divide this into version and sub-version number – for example, '3.1'

Chapter 17

Tailoring PRINCE2 to the Project Environment

As stated in the Introduction, PRINCE2 can be applied to any kind or size of project, i.e. the basic philosophy is always the same. The method should be tailored to suit the size, importance and environment of the project. PRINCE2's common sense philosophy says, 'Do not use a sledgehammer to crack a walnut', but equally do not agree important things informally where there is any chance of a disagreement later over what was agreed.

A company may be reading about the PRINCE2 method and saying to itself, 'But we only have short, simple projects. How can we justify using everything in this method?' The answer is to tailor the method.

The 2009 manual uses two terms, embedding and tailoring, that we should understand and then move on. 'Embedding' refers to the adoption of PRINCE2 across an organization. A company may already have in place an effective change control mechanism, tools and procedures and therefore may wish to use these instead of the change control part of PRINCE2. It may have its own configuration management tools and department. It may have a specific way of creating a Business Case. PRINCE2 should be modified to use these documents and procedures as part of this embedding. I have written several 'project management handbooks' for organizations, where they have modified terminology, combined processes and inserted their own documents, etc. Every project in the organization then used this embedded variation of PRINCE2.

Tailoring is done by a project management team to adapt the method to the context of a specific project.

17.1 GENERAL APPROACH TO TAILORING

Tailoring does not consist of dropping parts of the method. PRINCE2 is a series of interlinked themes, roles and processes. Simply dropping bits will leave gaps and create flaws. So what we want is a scaled version of the method that suits the needs of a project, not over-bureaucratic but offering the required level of control.

17.1.1 Tailoring Principles

The PRINCE2 principles should always be applied.

17.1.2 Adapting the Themes

This is in line with 'embedding'. It incorporates any useful or mandatory terminology, standards, documents or procedures from the company or – in the case where you are a supplier – that the customer asks you to use. You may not have a local document, but senior management do require one or more specific points of information that are not in the PRINCE2 Product Descriptions. You can simply add these to form your version of a document. For example, your version of a Work Package may require additional information, such as contract number and terms and conditions.

If the project is part of a programme, the project may be required to use the programme's strategies, standards and procedures. This would affect:

- Quality.
- Plans.
- Risk.
- Change.
- Progress.

17.1.3 Adapting the Roles

PRINCE2 expects you to adapt the standard role descriptions to the needs of each specific project. In any given company, this may entail moving responsibilities from one role and adding them to another. That brings up a good rule to follow. Responsibilities can be moved, but they shouldn't be dropped. Someone has to take each responsibility. In the spirit of PRINCE2, this doesn't mean moving all the Project Board's responsibilities to the Project Manager!

In small projects, it may be sensible to combine some of the roles, such as Executive and Senior User. The Project Manager may carry out the Project Support and Configuration Librarian roles or get a team member to do them. There may be no need for Team Managers in many small projects.

In a programme environment, the programme board may choose to appoint one of its members as Executive for all or some of the projects in the programme. Possible candidates are the programme manager and business change managers. The programme's design authority may fulfil the role of Change Authority to ensure that changes are viewed for their impact across the programme. If you need more information on programme organization, the APMG bookshop has the MSP manual (*Managing Successful Programmes*) with full details.

17.1.4 Adapting the Processes

All the processes should be used to some extent. In a programme environment, where a lot of start-up information is provided to the project, it may be acceptable to combine the *Starting up a Project* and *Initiating a Project* processes. In a small project it may be possible to combine the processes of *Controlling a Stage* and *Managing Product Delivery*.

Appendix A

Product Descriptions

This appendix contains suggested Product Description outlines for the PRINCE2 management products. Care should be taken to scrutinize them and tune them to any site or project's specific needs. Some headings have been omitted because they will be specific to the individual project, such as Identifier, Allocated To, Quality Check Skills and People Required. These should be added for 'real' Product Descriptions.

A.1 BENEFITS REVIEW PLAN

Purpose

The purpose of the benefits review is to find out:

- whether the expected benefits of the product have been realized;
- whether the product has caused any problems in use;
- the enhancement opportunities that have been revealed by use of the product.

Each expected benefit is assessed for:

- the level of its achievement so far;
- any additional time needed for the benefit to materialize;
- unexpected side effects, beneficial or adverse, which use of the product may have brought; these are documented, with explanations of why these were not foreseen.

Recommendations are made to realize or improve benefits, or counter problems.

Composition

- The benefits that are to be measured.
- Who is accountable for the expected benefits?
- How and when each benefit is to be measured.

- Required resources.
- The baseline measurements of each benefit taken at the start of the project against which the expected improvement is to be gauged.
- Questionnaire to judge the perception of the users.

General comments should be obtained about how the users feel about the product. The type of observation will depend on the type of product produced by the project, but examples might be its ease of use, performance, reliability, contribution it makes to their work and suitability for the work environment.

Form(at)

Site reporting standards.

Derivation

- Business Case.
- Project Product Description.

Quality Criteria

- Covers all benefits mentioned in the Project Brief and Business Case.
- Covers all changes approved during the project life cycle.
- Includes discussions with representatives of all those affected by the end product.
- Describes each benefit in a tangible, measurable form.

Quality Method

Formal quality review against the Project Brief, Business Case and Issue Register.

A.2 BUSINESS CASE

Purpose

To document the reasons and justification for undertaking a project, based on the estimated cost of development and the anticipated business benefits to be gained. The Project Board will monitor the ongoing viability of the project against the Business Case.

The Business Case may include legal or legislative reasons why the project is needed.

Composition

- Business reasons for undertaking the project.
- Options considered.

- Reasons for choosing the selected option.
- Business benefits expected to be gained from development of the product.
- Negative consequences of the project.
- Benefits tolerance.
- Summary of the main risks.
- Development cost and timescale.
- Investment Appraisal.

(These may refer to the programme Business Case if it is part of a programme.)

Form(at)

The Business Case forms part of the Project Initiation Documentation.

Derivation

Information for the Business Case is derived from:

- Project mandate/Project Brief (reasons).
- Project Plan (costs and timescale).
- The customer.

Quality Criteria

- Can the benefits be justified?
- Do the cost and timescale match those in the Project Plan?
- Are the reasons for the project consistent with corporate or programme strategy?

Quality Method

Quality review with the Executive and anyone appointed to the Executive's Project Assurance role.

A.3 CHECKPOINT REPORT

Purpose

To report at a frequency defined in the Work Package the progress and status of work for a team.

Composition

- Date of the checkpoint.
- Period covered by the report.
- Report on any follow-up action from previous reports.
- Products completed during the period.
- Quality work carried out during the period.

- Tolerance status.
- Products to be completed during the next period.
- Risk assessment.
- Other actual or potential problems or deviations from the plan.

Form(at)

According to the agreement between the Project Manager and Team Manager, the report may be verbal or written. It should contain the information given above, plus any extra data requested by the Project Manager.

Derivation

- Team Plan actuals and forecasts.
- Risk Register.
- Team member reports.

Quality Criteria

- Every team member's work covered.
- Includes an update on any unresolved problems from the previous report.
- Does it reflect the Team Plan situation?
- Does it reflect any significant change to the Risk Register?
- Does it reflect any change in a team member's work which has an impact on others?

Quality Method

Informal check by the Team Manager and those with Project Assurance responsibility.

A.4 COMMUNICATION MANAGEMENT STRATEGY

Purpose

The Communication Management Strategy identifies all parties who require information from the project and those from whom the Project requires information. The plan defines what information is needed and when it should be supplied.

Composition

- Interested parties (such as user groups, suppliers, stakeholders, Quality Assurance, Internal Audit).
- Information required by each identified party.
- Identity of the information provider.

- Frequency of communication.
- Method of communication.
- Format.

Form(at)

To the defined site standard for reports with the above content.

Derivation

- The Project Board.
- The Project Brief.
- The Project Initiation Documentation.
- The Quality Management Strategy.
- The project approach.

Quality Criteria

- Have all the listed derivation sources been checked?
- Has the timing, content and method been agreed?
- Has a common standard been agreed?
- Has time been allowed for communications in the Stage Plans?

Quality Method

Informal quality review between the Project Manager and those identified in the Communication Management Strategy.

A.5 CONFIGURATION ITEM RECORD

Purpose

A record of the information required about a product's status.

Composition

Not all information defined here may be needed for every project, but the list should be carefully studied to assess the benefit such information would have on the project, during the product's creation and in its operational life.

- The project identifier.
- Item (product) identifier.
- Latest version number.
- Item title and description.
- Type of product.
- Status.
- Stage when created.

- 'Owner' of the product.
- Person working on the product.
- Date allocated.
- Library or location where the product is kept.
- Source – for example, in-house, or purchased from a third-party company.
- Links to related products.
- Copyholders and potential users.
- Cross-reference to the Issue Report(s) that caused the change to this product.
- Cross-references to relevant correspondence.

Form(at)

Probably electronic, a database record.

Derivation

- Configuration Management Strategy.
- Product Breakdown Structure.
- Stage and Team Plans.
- Work Package.
- Quality Register.
- Issue Register.

Quality Criteria

- Does it accurately reflect the status of the product?
- Are all Configuration Item Records kept together in a secure location?
- Does the version number in the record match that of the actual product?
- Is the copyholder information correct?
- Do the copyholders have the latest version?

Quality Method

Audit by those with Project Assurance responsibility.

A.6 CONFIGURATION MANAGEMENT STRATEGY

Purpose

To identify how and by whom the project's products will be stored, controlled and protected.

Composition

- An explanation of the purpose of configuration management.

- A description of (or reference to) the configuration management method to be used. Any variance from corporate or programme standards should be highlighted together with a justification for the variance.
- Reference to any configuration management systems, tools to be used or with which links will be necessary.
- How and where the products will be stored (for example, project filing structure).
- What filing and retrieval security there will be.
- How the products and the various versions of these will be identified.
- Where responsibility for configuration management lies.

Form(at)

A word processor document containing headings as shown in the Composition section of this Product Description.

Derivation

Details of the plan might come from:

- the customer's quality management system (QMS);
- the supplier's QMS;
- specific needs of the project's products and environment;
- the project organization structure;
- any configuration management software in use or mandated by the customer.

Quality Criteria

- Responsibilities are clear and understood by both customer and supplier.
- The key identifier for project products is defined.
- The method and circumstances of version control are clear.
- The plan provides the Project Manager with all the product information required.

Quality Method

Formal quality review between the Project Manager, configuration management specialists and those with Project Assurance responsibility.

A.7 DAILY LOG

Purpose

To record required actions or significant events not caught by other PRINCE2 documents. It acts as the Project Manager's or a Team Manager's diary. Before creation of the Risk and Issue Registers, it is used to record any early risks or issues.

Composition

(The following are only suggestions.)

- Date of entry.
- Action or comment.
- Person responsible.
- Target date.
- Result.

Form(at)

This may be any form of notebook or electronic diary that is convenient for its user.

Derivation

- Risk Register.
- Stage Plan.
- Checkpoint Reports.
- Quality Register.
- Conversations and observations.

Quality Criteria

- Entries are understandable at a later date.
- Anything of a permanent nature is transferred to the appropriate record – for example, Issue Report.
- Date, person responsible and target date are always filled in.

Quality Method

Informal check by the owner as the log is referenced, plus a more formal inspection against the quality criteria at each stage end.

A.8 END PROJECT REPORT

Purpose

The report is the Project Manager's report to the Project Board (which may pass it on to corporate or programme management) on how the project has performed against the objectives stated in the Project Initiation Documentation and revised during the project. It should cover comparisons with the original targets, planned cost, schedule and tolerances, the revised Business Case and final version of the Project Plan.

The End Project Report also includes any follow-on action recommendations and the final Lessons Report.

Composition

- Assessment of the achievement of the project's objectives.
- Performance against the planned (and revised) target times and costs.
- The effect on the original Project Plan and Business Case of any changes which were approved.
- Any benefits achieved within the project life cycle.
- Final statistics on change issues received during the project and the total impact (time, money and benefits, for example) of any approved changes.
- Statistics for all quality work carried out.
- Follow-on action recommendations (changes proposed but not carried out and risks that might affect the operational product).
- Lessons Report (see its own Product Description).

Form(at)

To the defined site standard for reports with the above content plus any extra information requested by the Project Board.

Derivation

- The final Project Plan with actuals.
- The Project Initiation Documentation.
- Issue Register.

Quality Criteria

- Does the report describe the impact of any approved changes on the original intentions stated in the Project Initiation Documentation?
- Does the report cover all the benefits which can be assessed at this time?
- Does the quality work done during the project meet the customer's quality expectations?

Quality Method

Formal quality review between the Project Manager and those with Project Assurance responsibility.

A.9 END STAGE REPORT

Purpose

The purpose of the End Stage Report is to report on a stage that has just been completed, the overall project situation and sufficient information to ask for a Project Board decision on the next step to take with the project.

The Project Board uses the information provided in the End Stage Report to approve the next Stage Plan, amend the project scope, ask for a revised next Stage Plan, or stop the project.

Normally the End Stage Report for the last stage of a project is combined with the End Project Report.

Composition

- Current Stage Plan with all the actuals.
- Project Plan outlook.
- Business Case review.
- Risk review.
- Issue Report situation.
- Quality checking statistics.
- Report on any internal or external events which have affected stage performance.

Form(at)

Site report standards covering the information described above plus any extra data requested by the Project Board.

Derivation

Information for the report is obtained from:

- Stage Plan and actuals.
- Next Stage Plan (if appropriate).
- Updated Project Plan.
- Lessons Log.
- Quality Register.
- Completed Work Packages.

Quality Criteria

- Does the report clearly describe stage performance against the plan?
- Were any approved changes described, together with their impact?
- Does the report give an accurate picture of the quality testing work done in the stage?
- Does the report give an accurate review of the revised risk situation?
- Does the report give an accurate assessment of the ability of the project to meet its Business Case?

Quality Method

Informal quality review between the Project Manager and those with Project Assurance responsibility.

A.10 EXCEPTION REPORT

Purpose

An Exception Report is produced when costs and/or timescales for an approved Stage Plan are forecast to exceed the tolerance levels set. It is sent by the Project Manager in order to warn the Project Board of the adverse situation.

An Exception Report may result in the Project Board asking the Project Manager to produce an Exception Plan.

Composition

- A description of the cause of the deviation from the Stage Plan.
- The consequences of the deviation.
- The available options.
- The effect of each option on the Business Case, risks and project and stage tolerances.
- The Project Manager's recommendations.

Form(at)

Site report standard containing the information shown above.

Derivation

The information for an Exception Report is drawn from:

- Current Stage Plan and actuals.
- Project Plan and actuals.
- Deviation forecast.
- Issue Register.
- Risk Register.
- Quality Register.
- Checkpoint Reports.
- Project Board advice of an external event which affects the project.

Quality Criteria

- The Exception Report must accurately show the current status of stage and project budget and schedule, plus the forecast impact on both of the deviation.
- The reason(s) for the deviation must be stated.
- Options, including 'do nothing', must be put forward, together with their impact on objectives, plans, Business Case and risks.
- A recommendation must be made.

Quality Method

Informal review between the Project Manager, any Team Managers and those with Project Assurance responsibility.

A.11 HIGHLIGHT REPORT

Purpose

The Project Manager has to provide the Project Board with a summary of the stage status at intervals defined by them in the Project Initiation Documentation. A Highlight Report normally summarizes a series of Checkpoint Reports. The Project Board uses the report to monitor stage and project progress. The Project Manager also uses it to advise the Project Board of any potential problems or areas where the Project Board could help.

Composition

- Date.
- Project.
- Stage.
- Period covered.
- Budget status.
- Schedule status.
- Products completed during the period.
- Actual or potential problems.
- Products to be completed during the next period.
- Issue Report status.
- Budget and schedule impact of any changes approved so far in the stage.

Form(at)

Site reporting standards containing the above information plus any extra data requested by the Project Board.

Derivation

Information for the Highlight Reports is derived from:

- Checkpoint Reports.
- Stage Plan.
- Issue Register.
- Risk Register.

Quality Criteria

- Accurate reflection of Checkpoint Reports.
- Accurate summary of the Issue Register status.
- Accurate summary of the Stage Plan status.
- Highlights any potential problem areas.

Quality Method

Informal review between the Project Manager and those with Project Assurance responsibility.

A.12 ISSUE REGISTER

Purpose

The purpose of the Issue Register is to:

- allocate a unique number to each Issue Report;
- record the type of Issue Report;
- summarize the Issue Reports, their analysis and status.

Composition

- Issue Report number.
- Issue Report type (Issue, Request for Change, Off-specification).
- Author.
- Date created.
- Date of last update.
- Status.

Form(at)

Standard department form with the headings shown under 'Composition'.

Derivation

Issue Reports may be raised by anyone associated with the project at any time.

Quality Criteria

- Does the status indicate whether action has been taken?
- Are the Issue Reports uniquely identified, including to which product they refer?
- Is access to the Issue Register controlled?
- Is the Issue Register kept in a safe place?

Quality Method

Regular inspection.

A.13 ISSUE REPORT

Purpose

To record any matter that has to be brought to the attention of the project, and that requires an action. An Issue Report may be:

- Request for Change.
- Off-specification.
- Question.
- Statement of concern.

Composition

- Author.
- Date.
- Issue number.
- Type (Request for Change, Off-specification or Question).
- Description of the issue.
- Priority.
- Impact analysis.
- Decision.
- Signature of decision-maker(s).
- Date of decision.

Form(at)

Department style of form with the headings shown under 'Composition'.

Derivation

Anyone may submit an issue. Typical sources are users and specialists working on the project, the Project Manager and those with Project Assurance responsibility.

Quality Criteria

- Is the statement of the problem/requirement clear?
- Has all necessary information been made available?
- Have all the implications been considered?
- Has the Issue Report been correctly logged?

Quality Method

Check by the person responsible for the Issue Register.

A.14 LESSONS LOG

Purpose

The purpose of the Lessons Log is to be a repository of any lessons learned during the project that can be usefully applied to other projects. At the close of the project it is written up formally in the Lessons Report. Minimally, it should be updated at the end of a stage, but sensibly a note should be made in it of any good or bad point that arises in the use of the management and specialist products and tools at the time of the experience.

Composition

- What management and quality processes:
  - went well;
  - went badly;
  - were lacking.
- A description of any abnormal events causing deviations.
- Notes on the performance of specialist methods and tools used.
- Recommendations for future enhancement or modification of the project management method.
- Useful measurements on how much effort was required to create the various products.
- Notes on effective and ineffective quality reviews and other tests, including the reasons for them working well or badly.

Form(at)

Freeform, electronic or handwritten; the main concern is that the information can be recovered for use in the next End Stage Report and the Lessons Report at the end of the project.

Derivation

Information for the records in the Lessons Log is derived from:

- Observation and experience of the processes.
- Quality Register.
- Completed Work Packages.
- Risk Register.
- Highlight Report(s).
- Checkpoint Reports.
- Stage Plans with actuals.

Quality Criteria

- Each management control has been considered.
- The reasons for all tolerance deviations and corrective actions have been recorded.
- Input to the log is being done, minimally, at the end of each stage.
- Project Assurance and Project Support have been asked for their input.
- Statistics of the success of quality reviews and other types of test used are included.

Quality Method

Informal review on a regular basis and at each stage end by the Project Manager and those with Project Assurance responsibilities.

A.15 LESSONS REPORT

Purpose

The purpose of the Lessons Report is to pass on to other projects any useful lessons that can be learned from this project.

The data in the report should be used by an independent group, such as quality assurance, who are responsible for the site Quality Management System, to refine, change and improve project management and technical standards. Statistics on how much effort was needed for products can help improve future estimating.

Composition

- What management and quality processes:
  - went well;
  - went badly;
  - were lacking.
- An assessment of the efficacy of technical methods and tools used.
- Recommendations for future enhancement or modification of the project management method, including the reasons.
- Measurements on how much effort was required to create the various products.
- A description of any abnormal events causing deviations to targets or plans.
- An analysis of Issue Reports raised, their causes and results.
- Statistics on how effective quality reviews and other tests were in error trapping (for example, how many errors were found after products had passed a quality review or test).

Form(at)

Site reporting standards containing at least the above information.

Derivation

Information for the report is derived from:

- Observation and experience of the processes and techniques used.
- Checkpoint Reports.
- Observations of quality checks.
- Performance against plans.
- End Stage Reports.
- Any exception situations.

Quality Criteria

- Input to the report is being done, minimally, at the end of each stage.
- Every management control has been examined.
- A review of every specialist technique is included.
- Statistics of the success of quality reviews and other types of quality check used are included.
- The accuracy of all estimates and plans is included.
- Details of the effort taken for each product are given.
- The success of change control is reviewed.

Quality Method

Informal review at each stage end by the Project Manager and those with Project Assurance responsibilities; formal quality review by this group before presentation.

A.16 PLAN

Purpose

A mandatory plan which shows at a high level how and when a project's objectives are to be achieved. It contains the major products of the project and the activities and resources required.

It provides the Business Case with planned project costs, and identifies the management stages and other major control points.

The Project Board uses it as a baseline against which to monitor project progress and cost stage by stage.

It forms part of the Project Initiation Documentation.

Composition

- Plan description, giving a brief description of what the plan covers.
- Project prerequisites, containing any fundamental aspects which must be in place at the start of the project, and which must remain in place for the project to succeed.

- External dependencies.
- Planning assumptions.
- Project Plan, covering:
  - project-level Gantt or bar chart with identified management stages;
  - project-level Product Breakdown Structure;
  - project-level Product Flow Diagrams;
  - project-level Product Descriptions;
  - project-level activity network;
  - project financial budget;
  - project-level table of resource requirements;
  - requested/assigned specific resources.

Form(at)

Gantt or bar chart plus text.

Derivation

Project Brief.

Quality Criteria

- Is the plan achievable?
- Does it support the rest of the Project Initiation Documentation?

Quality Method

Formal quality review with the Project Manager and those with Project Assurance responsibility.

A.17 PRODUCT BREAKDOWN STRUCTURE

Purpose

- Identify all products to be developed and quality controlled.
- Provide a statement of how and when objectives are to be achieved by showing the products, activities and resources required for the scope of the plan. In PRINCE2 there are three levels of plan: project, stage and team. Team Plans are optional and may not follow the composition of this Product Description.
- Identify the project management activities required to control and report on the plan's work.

Composition

Top-to-bottom diagram showing a breakdown of all products to be developed during the life of the plan. External products must be included, clearly distinguished from those to be developed.

Form(at)

- Display from a planning and control tool.
- Spreadsheet, diagrams, mindmap or table.

Derivation

- Higher-level plan (if there is one).
- Product Descriptions.
- A statement of the final product(s) whose creation or procurement is to be planned.

Quality Criteria

- Are all external products and project products included?
- Is any product defined as external really the source of the product rather than the product (an error)?
- Is a product defined as external when, in fact, it is a project product provided by an external team (an error)?
- Is the Product Breakdown Structure consistent with the Product Checklist?
- Are management and specialist products identified and distinguished?
- Can Product Descriptions for the bottom-level products be written without further decomposition?
- Have enough bottom-level products been identified to meet management planning and control requirements?
- Will the combination of all the products identified fulfil the business need?
- Have all quality products been identified that meet the needs of the customer, audit and Project Assurance as described in the Quality Management Strategy?

Quality Method

Formal quality review against known required end-product(s).

A.18 PRODUCT CHECKLIST

Purpose

Lists the products to be produced within a plan, together with key status dates. Updated at agreed reporting intervals by the Project Manager and used by the Project Board to monitor progress.

Composition

- Plan identification.
- Product names (and identifiers where appropriate).
- Planned and actual dates for:
  - draft product ready;
  - quality check;
  - approval.

Form(at)

Standard department form with the headings defined under 'Composition'.

Derivation

Extracted from the Stage Plan.

Quality Criteria

Do the details and dates match those in the Stage Plan?

Quality Method

Informal review against the Stage Plan.

A.19 PRODUCT DESCRIPTION

Purpose

To define the information needed to describe each product to be created by the project.

Composition

- Title.
- Purpose:
  - An explanation of the purpose of the product.
- Composition:
  - A list of the various parts of the product – for example, chapters of the document.
- Form or format:
  - What the product should look like. If it is a document, the name of the template to be used.
- Derivation:
  - The sources of information for the product.
- Quality Criteria:
  - What quality measurements the product must meet.

- Quality Method:
  - What method of checking the product's quality is to be used, and what type of skill is required.

Form(at)

Standard department form with the headings defined under 'Composition'.

Derivation

- Project Brief.
- Project Initiation Documentation.
- Quality Management Strategy.
- Ultimate recipient of the product.

Quality Criteria

- Does it contain information under all the headings?
- Is there more than one purpose?
- Has the end user been involved in its writing?

Quality Method

Formal quality review.

A.20 PRODUCT FLOW DIAGRAM

Purpose

To show the required sequence of delivery of a plan's products and identify dependencies between those products, including any external products.

Composition

A diagram showing the product delivery sequence from top to bottom (or left to right) of the products that form the final product, plus the dependencies between those products. Arrows indicate dependencies between products. External products must be clearly distinguished from the products developed by the plan. The PRINCE2 convention is for project products to be shown as rectangles and external products as ellipses.

Form(at)

A chart normally flowing from top to bottom (or left to right depending on the shape of the visual medium used) with arrows connecting the various products to show the sequence of delivery and any inter-product dependencies.

Derivation

- Product Descriptions (derivation field).
- Product Breakdown Structure (external products).

Quality Criteria

- Is the final product from the Product Breakdown Structure (Product Breakdown Structure) shown as the end of the Product Flow Diagram?
- Are all external products identified and the dependencies understood?
- Are all bottom-level products on the Product Breakdown Structure identified on the diagram?
- Are all 'real' products identified on the Product Breakdown Structure shown on the Product Flow Diagram?
- Are all products identified in the Product Flow Diagram identified as products on the Product Breakdown Structure?
- Are the product names the same in both diagrams?
- Are there any products without dependencies?
- Have dependencies been identified at a level suitable to that of the plan of which the Product Flow Diagram is a part?
- Are the dependencies consistent with the derivation fields (from Product Description) of all the products?

Quality Method

Quality review.

A.21 PRODUCT STATUS ACCOUNT

Purpose

The Product Status Account provides information about the state of products. For example, the report could cover the entire project, a particular stage or a particular area of the project. It is particularly useful if the Project Manager wishes to confirm the version number of products or confirm that all products within a specific plan have reached a certain status, such as draft, tested or approved.

Composition

The composition will vary but will normally consist of the following information:

- Project Name.
- Product Type.
- Product Identifier.
- Version Number.

For each product identified the following additional information may be provided:

- Date Product Description baselined.
- Date product baselined.
- List of related products.
- Date on which a copy of the product was issued for change.
- Planned date for next baseline.
- Planned date of next release.
- Any relevant notes – for example, change pending, under review.

Form(at)

Normally a table with columns for product, status and date of last status change. The Project Manager may vary this and ask for any information held in the Configuration Item Record.

Derivation

Configuration Item Records.

Quality Criteria

- Covers all items requested.
- Accurate.

Quality Method

Verification against sample Configuration Item Records and actual products.

A.22 PROJECT BRIEF

Purpose

To briefly explain the reasons for the project, the customer's expectations and any limitations that apply.

Composition

The following is a suggested list of contents, which should be tailored to the requirements and environment of each project.

- Project Definition, explaining what the project needs to achieve:
  - Background.
  - Project objectives.
  - Project scope.
  - Outline project deliverables and/or desired outcomes.

  - Any exclusions.
  - Constraints.
  - Assumptions.
  - Project tolerances.
  - Users and stakeholders.
  - Interfaces.

- Outline Business Case:
  - Reason for the project.
  - Description of how this project supports business strategy, plans or programmes.

- Project Product Description.
- Project approach:
  - Defines the type of solution to be developed or procured by the project. It should also identify the environment into which the product must be delivered.
  - Type of solution – for example:
    - Off-the-shelf.
    - Built from scratch.
    - Modifying an existing product.
    - Built by one or more external suppliers.
    - Adding to/modifying a product developed by another project.
    - Built by company staff.
    - Built by contract staff under the supervision of the Project Manager.
  - Reason for the selection of approach – for example, part of a programme.
  - Implications on the project.

- Project management team structure.
- Role descriptions.
- References to associated documents or products.

If earlier work has been done, the Project Brief may refer to document(s), such as the outline Project Plan.

Form(at)

Site project request standards containing at least the information shown above.

Derivation

- Project mandate.
- If the project is part of a programme, the programme should provide the Project Brief.
- If no project mandate is provided, the Project Manager has to generate the Project Brief in discussions with the customer and users.

- Any significant change to the material contained in the Project Brief will thus need to be referred to corporate or programme management.

Quality Criteria

- Does it accurately reflect the project mandate?
- Does it form a firm basis on which to initiate a project (*Initiating a Project*)?
- Does it indicate how the customer will assess the acceptability of the finished product(s)?

Quality Method

Informal quality review between the Project Manager and Project Board during the process *Starting up a Project.*

A.23 PROJECT INITIATION DOCUMENTATION

Purpose

- Define the project.
- Form the basis for the ultimate assessment of the project's success and the project's management.

There are two primary uses of the document:

- Ensure that the project has a sound basis before asking the Project Board to make any major commitment to the project.
- Act as a base document against which the Project Board and Project Manager can assess progress, evaluate change issues and answer questions of the project's continuing viability.

Composition

The Project Initiation Documentation must answer the following fundamental questions:

- **What** is the project aiming to achieve?
- **Why** is it important to achieve it?
- **Who** is going to be involved in managing the project and what are their responsibilities?
- **How** and **when** is it all going to happen?

The following list should be seen as the information needed in order to make the initiation decisions.

- *Background*, explaining the context of the project, and steps taken to arrive at the current position of requiring a project.

- *Project Definition*, explaining what the project needs to achieve. Under this heading may be:
    - Project objectives.
    - Project deliverables and/or desired outcomes.
    - Project scope.
    - Constraints.
    - Exclusions.
    - Interfaces.
    - Assumptions.
- *Project Approach.*
- *Initial Business Case*, explaining why the project is being undertaken.
- *Project Organization Structure*, defining the project management team.
- *Quality Management Strategy*. (See the separate Quality Management Strategy Product Description.)
- *Initial Project Plan*, explaining how and when the activities of the project will occur. (For details of the Project Plan content see the separate Product Description.)
- *Project Tolerances*, showing tolerance levels for time, cost, quality, benefit, risk and resources. Tolerances for quality should already be in the Quality Management Strategy, and benefit tolerances in the Business Case, so a choice can be made to simply point to their presence in those documents rather than repeat them.
- *Project Controls*, stating how control is to be exercised within the project, and the reporting and monitoring mechanisms which will support this.
- *Communication Management Plan*. (See separate Product Description.)
- *Initial Risk Register*, summarizing at least all major risks and their current statuses.

Form(at)

Site report standards.

Derivation

- Customer's or supplier's project management standards.
- Customer's specified control requirements.

(Much of the information should come from the project mandate, enhanced in the Project Brief.)

Quality Criteria

- Does the document correctly represent the project?
- Does it show a viable, achievable project which is in line with corporate strategy, or overall programme needs?

- Is the project organization structure complete, with names and titles?
- Does it clearly show a control, reporting and direction regime that can be implemented and is appropriate to the scale, business risk and importance of the project?
- Has everyone named in the organization structure received and accepted their job description?
- Does the project organization structure need to say to whom the Project Board reports?
- Are the internal and external relationships and lines of authority clear?
- Do the controls cover the needs of the Project Board, Project Manager and any Team Managers?
- Do the controls satisfy any delegated Project Assurance requirements?
- Is it clear who will administer each control?

Quality Method

Formal quality review between the Project Manager and those with Project Assurance responsibility.

A.24 PROJECT MANDATE

The 2009 version of the PRINCE2 manual does not recognize the project mandate as a PRINCE2 product, since it has no control over its creation. However, I believe that it is useful to be able to show anyone about to create a project mandate what information, in an ideal world, should be in it.

Purpose

Project mandate is a term to describe an initial request for a project, which may require further work to turn it into a Project Brief.

Composition

The actual composition of a project mandate will vary according to the type and size of project and also the environment in which the mandate is generated. The following is a list of contents which would make up an 'ideal' mandate, and should be tailored to suit the specific project. An actual mandate may have much less information.

- Authority responsible.
- The customer(s), user(s) and any other known interested parties.
- Background.
- Outline Business Case (reasons).
- Project objectives.
- Scope.

- Constraints.
- Interfaces.
- Quality expectations.
- An estimate of the project size and duration (if known).
- A view of the risks faced by the project.
- An indication of who should be the project's Executive and Project Manager.
- Reference to any associated projects or products.

Form(at)

May be in any format.

Derivation

A project mandate may come from anywhere, but it should come from a level of management that can authorize the cost and resource usage.

Quality Criteria

- Does the mandate describe what is required?
- Is the level of authority commensurate with the anticipated size, risk and cost of the project?
- Is there sufficient detail to allow the appointment of an appropriate Executive and Project Manager?
- Are all the known interested parties identified?

Quality Method

Informal review between the Executive, Project Manager and the mandate author.

A.25 PROJECT PRODUCT DESCRIPTION

Purpose

The Project Product Description is a special form of Product Description that defines what the project must deliver in order to gain acceptance. It is used to:

- gain agreement from the user on the project's scope and requirements;
- define the customer's quality expectations;
- define the acceptance criteria, method and responsibilities for the project.

The Product Description for the project product is created in the *Starting up a Project* process as part of the initial scoping activity, and is refined during the *Initiating a Project* process when creating the Project Plan. It is used by the *Closing a Project* process as part of the verification that the project has delivered what was expected of it, and that the acceptance criteria have been met.

Composition

- *Title*: Name by which the project is known.
- *Purpose*: This defines the purpose that the project product will fulfil and who will use it. It is helpful in understanding the product's functions, size, quality, complexity, robustness, etc.
- *Composition*: A description of the major products to be delivered by the project.
- *Derivation*: What are the source products from which this product is derived? Examples are:
    - Existing products to be modified.
    - Design specifications.
    - A feasibility report.
    - Project mandate.
- *Development skills required*: An indication of the skills required to develop the product, or a pointer to which area(s) should supply the development resources.
- *Customer's quality expectations*: A description of the quality expected of the project product and the standards and processes that will need to be applied to achieve that quality. They will impact on every part of the product development, thus implying time and cost. The quality expectations are captured in discussions with the customer (business and user stakeholders). Where possible, expectations should be prioritized.
- *Acceptance criteria*: A prioritized list of criteria that the project product must meet before the customer will accept it – i.e. measurable definitions of the attributes that must apply to the set of products to be acceptable to key stakeholders (and, in particular, the users and the operational and maintenance organizations). Examples are: ease of use, ease of support, ease of maintenance, appearance, major functions, development costs, running costs, capacity, availability, reliability, security and accuracy or performance.
- *Project-level quality tolerances*: Specifying any tolerances that may apply for the acceptance criteria.
- *Acceptance method*: Stating the means by which acceptance will be confirmed. This may simply be a case of confirming that all the project's products have been approved or may involve describing complex handover arrangements for the project product, including any phased handover of the project's products.
- *Acceptance responsibilities*: Defining who will be responsible for confirming acceptance.

Derivation

- Project mandate.
- Discussions with the Senior User and Executive – possibly via scoping workshops.
- Request for proposal (if in a commercial customer/supplier environment).

Form(at)

A Product Description for the project product can take a number of formats, including:

- Document, presentation slides or mindmap.
- Entry in a project management tool.

Quality Criteria

- The purpose is clear.
- The composition defines the complete scope of the project.
- The acceptance criteria form the complete list against which the project will be assessed.
- The acceptance criteria address the requirements of all the key stakeholders (for example, operations and maintenance).
- It defines how the users and the operational and maintenance organizations will assess the acceptability of the finished product.
- All criteria are measurable.
- Each criterion is individually realistic.
- The criteria are realistic and consistent as a set. For example, high quality, early delivery and low cost may not go together.
- All criteria can be proven within the project life (for example, the maximum throughput of a water pump), or by proxy measures that provide reasonable indicators as to whether acceptance criteria will be achieved post-project (for example, a water pump that complies with reliability design and manufacturing standard).

  The quality expectations have considered:

- The characteristics of the key quality requirements (for example, fast/slow, large/small, national/global).
- The elements of the customer's Quality Management System that should be used.
- Any other standards that should be used.
- The level of customer/staff satisfaction that should be achieved if surveyed.

Quality Method

Review between the Project Manager and the Project Board.

A.26 QUALITY MANAGEMENT STRATEGY

Purpose

The purpose is to define how the supplier intends to deliver products that meet the customer's quality expectations and the agreed quality standards.

Composition

- Quality control and audit processes to be applied to project management.
- Quality control and audit process requirements for specialist work.
- Key product quality criteria.
- Quality Responsibility.
- Reference to any standards which need to be met.
- Change management procedures.
- Configuration Management Strategy.
- Any tools to be used to ensure quality.

Form(at)

The Quality Management Strategy is part of the Project Initiation Documentation.

Derivation

- Customer's quality expectations (project mandate and/or Project Brief).
- Corporate or programme Quality Management System (QMS).

Quality Criteria

- Does the plan clearly define ways to confirm that the customer's quality expectations will be met?
- Are the defined ways sufficient to achieve the required quality?
- Are responsibilities for quality defined up to a level which is independent of the project and Project Manager?
- Does the plan conform to corporate Quality Policy?

Quality Method

Review between the Project Manager and whoever is assuring the project on behalf of the customer.

A.27 QUALITY REGISTER

Purpose

- To issue a unique reference for each quality check or test planned.
- To act as a pointer to the quality check and test documentation for a product.
- To act as a summary of the number and type of quality checks and tests held.

The register summarizes all the quality checks and tests which are planned/ have taken place, and provides information for the End Stage and End Project Reports, as well as the Lessons Learned Report.

Composition

For each entry in the register:

- Quality check reference number.
- Product checked or tested.
- Planned date of the check.
- Actual date of the check.
- Result of the check.
- Number of action items found.
- Target sign-off date.
- Actual sign-off date.

Form(at)

Standard departmental form with the headings shown in 'Composition'.

Derivation

The first entries are made when a quality check or test is entered on a Stage Plan. The remaining information comes from the actual performance of the check. The sign-off date is when all corrective action items have been signed off.

Quality Criteria

- Is there a procedure in place which will ensure that every quality check is entered on the register?
- Has responsibility for the register been allocated?

Quality Method

Regular checking should be done by those with Project Assurance responsibility for the customer and provider. There may also be an inspection by an independent quality assurance function.

A.28 RISK MANAGEMENT STRATEGY

Purpose

The Risk Management Strategy describes the risk management procedure, techniques and standards to be applied and the responsibilities for risk management.

Composition

- *Introduction*: The purpose, objectives, scope and responsibility of the strategy.
- *The risk management procedure*: A description of (or reference to) the risk management procedure to be used. Any variance from corporate or programme management standards should be described, together with its justification.

The procedure should cover the risk activities of:

  - Identify.
  - Assess.
  - Plan.
  - Implement.
  - Communicate.

- *Risk tolerance*: The threshold levels of risk exposure, which, when exceeded, require the risk to be escalated to the next level of management. (For example, a project-level risk tolerance might be the threatened loss below a tolerance limit of certain workforce skills. Such risks would need to be escalated to corporate or programme management.) The risk tolerance should define the risk expectations of corporate or programme management and the Project Board.
- *Risk budget*: Describing if a risk budget is to be established and, if so, how it will be used.
- *Tools and techniques*: Any risk management systems or tools to be used, and any preference for techniques which may be used for each step in the risk management procedure.
- *Records*: Definition of the composition and format of the Risk Register and any other risk records to be used by the project.
- *Reporting*: Any risk management reports to be produced, their recipients, purpose and timing.
- *Timing of risk management activities*: When risk management activities are to be undertaken – for example, at end stage assessments and issue impact analysis.
- *Roles and responsibilities*: The roles and responsibilities for risk management activities.
- *Scales*: The scales to be used for estimating probability and impact of a risk – for example, to ensure that the scales for cost and time are relevant to the cost and timeframe of the project.
- *Proximity*: How the proximity of a risk is to be assessed. Typical proximity categories will be: imminent, within a month, within the stage, within the project, beyond the project.
- *Risk categories*: The risk categories to be used (if at all).
- *Risk response categories*: Definition of the risk response categories to be used.
- *Early-warning indicators*: Indicators to be used to track critical aspects of the project, so that if predefined levels are reached, corrective action will be triggered.

Form(at)

A Risk Management Strategy might be:

- A stand-alone document or a section of the Project Initiation Documentation
- Entry in a project management tool.

Derivation

- Any relevant corporate or programme management risk management process or strategy.
- Project Brief.
- Business Case.

Quality Criteria

- Responsibilities are clear and understood by both customer and supplier.
- The risk management procedure is clearly documented and can be understood by all parties.
- Scales, expected value and proximity definitions are clear and unambiguous.
- The chosen scales are appropriate for the level of control required.
- Risk reporting requirements are fully defined.

Quality Method

Assess against any risk standards used by the company. Formal quality review to include anyone with risk expertise and/or other project managers who have created successful risk strategies.

A.29 RISK REGISTER

Purpose

The purpose of the Risk Register is to:

- allocate a unique number to each risk;
- record the type of risk;
- summarize the risks, their analysis and status.

Composition

- Risk number.
- Risk type (business, project, stage).
- Author.
- Date risk identified.
- Date of last risk status update.
- Risk description.
- Likelihood.
- Severity.
- Countermeasure.
- Status.
- Responsibility.

Form(at)

Standard department form with the headings shown in 'Composition'.

Derivation

Business risks may have been identified in the Project Brief and should be sought during project initiation. There should be a check for any new risks every time the Risk Register is reviewed or a new plan made, minimally at each end stage assessment. The Project Board has the responsibility to constantly check external events for business risks.

Quality Criteria

- Does the status indicate whether action has been/is being taken or is in a contingency plan?
- Are the risks uniquely identified, including to which product they refer?
- Is access to the Risk Register controlled?
- Is the Risk Register kept in a safe place?
- Are activities to review the Risk Register in the Stage Plans?
- Has responsibility for monitoring the risk been identified and documented?

Quality Method

Regular review by the person who has business Project Assurance responsibility.

A.30 WORK PACKAGE

Purpose

A set of instructions to produce one or more required products given by the Project Manager to a Team Manager or team member.

Composition

Although the content may vary greatly according to the relationship between the Project Manager and the recipient of the Work Package, it should cover:

- A summary of the work to be done.
- Product Description of the products to be produced.
- Standards to be used.
- Product interfaces.
- Working interfaces and liaisons.
- Quality checking standards personnel to be involved.

Form(at)

This product will vary in content and in degree of formality, depending on circumstances. Where the work is being conducted by a single team working directly for the Project Manager, the Work Package may be a verbal instruction, although there are good reasons for putting it in writing, such as avoidance of misunderstanding and providing a link to performance assessment. Where a supplier under a contract is carrying out the work and the Project Manager is part of the customer organization, the Work Package should be a formal, written document.

Derivation

There could be many Work Packages authorized during each stage. The Project Manager creates a Work Package from the Stage Plan.

Quality Criteria

- Is the required Work Package clearly defined and understood by the assigned resource?
- Is there a Product Description for the required product with clearly identified and acceptable quality criteria?
- Does the Product Description match up with the other Work Package documentation?
- Are standards for the work agreed?
- Are the defined standards in line with those applied to similar products?
- Have all necessary interfaces been defined?
- Do the reporting arrangements include the provision for exception reporting?

Quality Method

Agreement between the Project Manager and recipient.

Appendix B

Project Management Team Roles

Here is a description for each role in the project management structure. These can be used as the basis for discussion of an individual's job and tailored to suit the project's circumstances. The tailored role description becomes that person's job description for the project. Two copies of an agreed job description should be signed by the individual, one for retention by the individual, the other to be filed in the project file.

B.1 PROJECT BOARD

General

The Project Board is appointed by corporate/programme management to provide overall direction and management of the project. The Project Board is accountable for the success of the project, and has responsibility and authority for the project within the limits set by corporate/programme management.

The Project Board is the project's 'voice' to the outside world and is responsible for any publicity or other dissemination of information about the project.

Specific Responsibilities

The Project Board approves all major plans and authorizes any major deviation from agreed Stage Plans. It is the authority that signs off the completion of each stage as well as authorizes the start of the next stage. It ensures that required resources are committed and arbitrates on any conflicts within the project or negotiates a solution to any problems between the project and external bodies. In addition, it approves the appointment and responsibility of the Project Manager and any delegation of its Project Assurance responsibility.

The Project Board has the following responsibilities. It is a general list and will need tailoring for a specific project.

At the beginning of the project:

- Assurance that the Project Initiation Documentation complies with relevant customer standards and policies, plus any associated contract with the supplier.
- Agreement with the Project Manager on that person's responsibility and objectives.
- Confirmation with corporate/programme management of project tolerances.
- Specification of external constraints on the project such as quality assurance.
- Approval of an accurate and satisfactory Project Initiation Documentation.
- Delegation of any Project Assurance roles.
- Commitment of project resources required by the next Stage Plan.

As the project progresses:

- Provision of overall guidance and direction to the project, ensuring it remains within any specified constraints.
- Review of each completed stage and approval of progress to the next.
- Review and approval of Stage Plans and any Exception Plans.
- 'Ownership' of one or more of the identified project risks as allocated at plan approval time, i.e. the responsibility to monitor the risk and advise the Project Manager of any change in its status and to take action, if appropriate, to ameliorate the risk.
- Approval of changes.
- Compliance with corporate/programme management directives.

At the end of the project:

- Assurance that all products have been delivered satisfactorily.
- Assurance that all acceptance criteria have been met.
- Approval of the End Project Report.
- Approval of the Lessons Report and the passage of this to the appropriate standards group to ensure action.
- Decisions on the recommendations for follow-on actions and the passage of these to the appropriate authorities.
- Arrangements, where appropriate, for one or more benefits reviews.
- Project closure notification to corporate/programme management.

The Project Board is ultimately responsible for the assurance of the project, that it remains on course to deliver the desired outcome of the required quality to meet the Business Case defined in the project contract. According to the size, complexity and risk of the project, the Project Board may decide to delegate some of this Project Assurance responsibility. Later in this appendix Project Assurance is defined in more detail.

One Project Board responsibility that should receive careful consideration is that of approving and funding changes. The chapter on change should be read before finalizing this responsibility of approving and funding changes.

The responsibilities of specific members of the Project Board are described in the respective sections below.

B.2 EXECUTIVE

General

The Executive is ultimately responsible for the project, supported by the Senior User and Senior Supplier. The Executive has to ensure that the project is value for money, ensuring a cost-conscious approach to the project, balancing the demands of business, user and supplier.

Throughout the project the Executive 'owns' the Business Case.

Specific Responsibilities

- Ensure that a tolerance is set for the project by corporate/programme management in the project mandate.
- Authorize customer expenditure and set stage tolerances.
- Approve the End Project Report and Lessons Report.
- Brief corporate/programme management about project progress.
- Organize and chair Project Board meetings.
- Recommend future action on the project to corporate/programme management if the project tolerance is exceeded.
- Approve the sending of the notification of project closure to corporate/programme management.

The Executive is responsible for overall business assurance of the project, i.e. that it remains on target to deliver products that will achieve the expected business benefits, and the project will be completed within its agreed tolerances for budget and schedule. Business Project Assurance covers the following:

- Validation and monitoring of the Business Case against external events and against project progress.
- Keeping the project in line with customer strategies.
- Monitoring project finance on behalf of the customer.
- Monitoring the business risks to ensure that these are kept under control.
- Monitoring any supplier and contractor payments.
- Monitoring changes to the Project Plan to see if there is any impact on the needs of the business or the project Business Case.
- Assessing the impact of potential changes on the Business Case and Project Plan.
- Constraining user and supplier excesses.
- Informing the project of any changes caused by a programme of which the project is part (this responsibility may be transferred if there is other programme representation on the project management team).
- Monitoring stage and project progress against the agreed tolerance.

If the project warrants it, the Executive may delegate some responsibility for the above business Project Assurance functions.

B.3 SENIOR USER

General

The Senior User is responsible for the specification of the needs of all those who will use the final product(s), user liaison with the project team and for monitoring that the solution will meet those needs within the constraints of the Business Case.

The role represents the interests of all those who will use the final product(s) of the project, those for whom the product will achieve an objective, or those who will use the product to deliver benefits. The Senior User role commits user resources and monitors products against requirements. This role may require more than one person to cover all the user interests. For the sake of effectiveness the role should not be split between too many people.

Specific Responsibilities

- Ensure the desired outcome of the project is specified.
- Make sure that progress towards the outcome required by the users remains consistent from the user perspective.
- Promote and maintain focus on the desired project outcome.
- Ensure that any user resources required for the project are made available.
- Approve product descriptions for those products which act as inputs or outputs (interim or final) from the supplier function, or will affect them directly, and that the products are signed off once completed.
- Prioritize and contribute user opinions on Project Board decisions on whether to implement recommendations on proposed changes.
- Resolve user requirements and priority conflicts.
- Provide the user view on recommended follow-up actions.
- Brief and advise user management on all matters concerning the project.

The Project Assurance responsibilities of the Senior User are the following:

- Ensure specification of the user's needs is accurate, complete and unambiguous.
- Monitor development of the solution at all stages to ensure that it will meet the user's needs and is progressing towards that target.
- Evaluate the impact of potential changes from the user point of view.
- Constantly monitor the risks to the users.
- Ensure testing of the product at all stages has the appropriate user representation.
- Ensure quality control procedures are used correctly so that products meet user requirements.
- Ensure user liaison is functioning effectively.

Where the project's size, complexity or importance warrants it, the Senior User may delegate the responsibility and authority for some of the Project Assurance responsibility.

B.4 SENIOR SUPPLIER

General

Represents the interests of those designing, developing, facilitating, procuring, implementing, operating and maintaining the project products. The Senior Supplier role must have the authority to commit or acquire supplier resources required.

If necessary, more than one person may be required to represent the suppliers.

Specific Responsibilities

- Agree objectives for specialist activities.
- Make sure that progress towards the outcome remains consistent from the supplier perspective.
- Promote and maintain focus on the desired project outcome from the point of view of supplier management.
- Ensure that the supplier resources required for the project are made available.
- Approve product descriptions for specialist products.
- Contribute supplier opinions on Project Board decisions on whether to implement recommendations on proposed changes.
- Resolve supplier requirements and priority conflicts.
- Arbitrate on, and ensure resolution of, any specialist priority or resource conflicts.
- Brief non-technical management on specialist aspects of the project.

The Senior Supplier is responsible for the specialist Project Assurance of the project. The specialist Project Assurance role responsibilities are the following:

- Advise on the selection of technical strategy, design and methods.
- Ensure that any specialist and operating standards defined for the project are met and used to good effect.
- Monitor potential changes and their impact on the correctness, completeness and assurance of products against their Product Description from a technical perspective.
- Monitor any risks in the specialist and production aspects of the project.
- Ensure quality control procedures are used correctly, so that products adhere to technical requirements.

If warranted, some of this Project Assurance responsibility may be delegated. Depending on the particular customer/supplier environment of a project, the customer may also wish to appoint people to specialist Project Assurance roles.

B.5 PROJECT MANAGER

General

The Project Manager has the authority to run the project on a day-to-day basis on behalf of the Project Board within the constraints laid down by the board. In a customer/supplier environment the Project Manager will normally come from the customer organization.

Responsibility

The Project Manager's prime responsibility is to ensure that the project produces the required products, to the required standard of quality and within the specified constraints of time and cost. The Project Manager is also responsible for the project producing a result that is capable of achieving the benefits defined in the Business Case.

Specific Responsibilities

- Manage the production of the required products.
- Direct and motivate the project team.
- Plan and monitor the project.
- Agree any delegation and use of Project Assurance roles required by the Project Board.
- Produce the project contract.
- Prepare Project, Stage and, if necessary, Exception Plans in conjunction with Team Managers and appointed Project Assurance roles, and agree them with the Project Board.
- Manage business and project risks, including the development of contingency plans.
- Liaise with programme management if the project is part of a programme.
- Liaise with programme management or related projects to ensure that work is neither overlooked nor duplicated.
- Take responsibility for overall progress and use of resources, and initiate corrective action where necessary.
- Be responsible for change control and any required configuration management.
- Report to the Project Board through Highlight Reports and end stage assessments.
- Liaise with the Project Board or its appointed Project Assurance roles to assure the overall direction and assurance of the project.
- Agree the technical and quality strategy with appropriate members of the Project Board.
- Prepare the Lessons Report.
- Prepare any follow-on action recommendations required.

- Prepare the End Project Report.
- Identify and obtain any support and advice required for the management, planning and control of the project.
- Be responsible for project administration.
- Liaise with any suppliers or account managers.

B.6 TEAM MANAGER

General

The allocation of this role to one or more people is optional. Where the project does not warrant the use of a Team Manager, the Project Manager takes the role.

The Project Manager may find that it is beneficial to delegate the authority and responsibility for planning the creation of certain products and managing a team of technicians to produce those products. There are many reasons why it may be decided to employ this role. Some of these are the size of the project, the particular specialist skills or knowledge needed for certain products, geographical location of some team members, and the preferences of the Project Board.

The Team Manager's prime responsibility is to ensure production of those products defined by the Project Manager to an appropriate quality, in a timescale and at a cost acceptable to the Project Board. The Team Manager reports to and takes direction from the Project Manager.

The use of this role should be discussed by the Project Manager with the Project Board and, if the role is required, planned at the outset of the project. This is discussed in the *Starting up a Project* and *Initiating a Project* processes.

Specific Responsibilities

- Prepare plans for the team's work and agree these with the Project Manager.
- Receive authorization from the Project Manager to create products (Work Package).
- Manage the team
- Direct, plan and monitor the team's work.
- Take responsibility for the progress of the team's work and use of team resources, and initiate corrective action where necessary within the constraints laid down by the Project Manager.
- Advise the Project Manager of any deviations from the plan, recommend corrective action, and help prepare any appropriate Exception Plans.
- Pass products which have been completed and approved in line with the agreed Work Package requirements back to the Project Manager.
- Ensure all Issue Reports are properly reported to the person maintaining the Issue Register.

- Ensure the evaluation of Issue Reports which arise within the team's work and recommend action to the Project Manager.
- Liaise with any Project Assurance roles.
- Attend any stage assessments as directed by the Project Manager.
- Arrange and lead team checkpoints.
- Ensure that quality controls of the team's work are planned and performed correctly.
- Maintain or ensure the maintenance of team files.
- Identify and advise the Project Manager of any risks associated with a Work Package.
- Ensure that such risks are entered on the Risk Register.
- Manage specific risks as directed by the Project Manager.

B.7 PROJECT ASSURANCE

General

The Project Board members do not work full-time on the project; therefore, they place a great deal of reliance on the Project Manager. Although they receive regular reports from the Project Manager, there may always be these questions at the back of their minds: 'Are things really going as well as we are being told?', 'Are any problems being hidden from us?', 'Is the solution going to be what we want?', 'Are we suddenly going to find that the project is over-budget or late?' There are other questions. The supplier may have a quality assurance function charged with the responsibility to check that all projects are adhering to the quality system.

All of these points mean that there is a need in the project organization for an independent monitoring of all aspects of the project's performance and products. This is the Project Assurance function.

To cater for a small project, we start by identifying these Project Assurance functions as part of the role of each Project Board member. According to the needs and desires of the Project Board, any of these Project Assurance responsibilities can be delegated, as long as the recipients are independent of the Project Manager and the rest of the project management team. Any appointed Project Assurance jobs assure the project on behalf of one or more members of the Project Board.

It is not mandatory that all Project Assurance roles be delegated. Each of the Project Assurance roles which is delegated may be assigned to one individual or shared. The Project Board decides when a Project Assurance role needs to be delegated. It may be for the entire project or only part of it. The person or persons filling a Project Assurance role may be changed during the project at the request of the Project Board. Any use of Project Assurance roles needs to be planned at the initiation stage, otherwise resource usage and costs for Project Assurance could easily get out of control.

There is no stipulation on how many Project Assurance roles there must be. Each Project Board role has Project Assurance responsibility. Again, each project should determine what support, if any, each Project Board role needs to achieve this Project Assurance.

For example, an international standards group, such as ISO, may certificate the supplier's work standards. A requirement of the certification is that there will be some form of quality assurance function that is required to monitor the supplier's work. Some of the Senior Supplier's Project Assurance responsibility may be delegated to this function. Note that they would only be delegated. The Project Board member retains accountability. Any delegation should be documented. The quality assurance could include verification by an external party that the Project Board is performing its functions correctly.

Assurance covers all interests of a project, including business, user and supplier.

Project Assurance has to be independent of the Project Manager; therefore, the Project Board cannot delegate any of its Project Assurance responsibility to the Project Manager.

Specific Responsibilities

The implementation of Project Assurance responsibility needs to answer the question: 'What is to be assured?' A list of possibilities would include the following:

- Maintenance of thorough liaison throughout the project between the supplier and the customer.
- Customer needs and expectations are being met or managed.
- Risks are being controlled.
- Adherence to the Business Case.
- Constant reassessment of the value-for-money solution.
- Fit with the overall programme or company strategy.
- The right people being involved in writing Product Descriptions, especially the quality criteria.
- The right people being planned to be involved in quality checking at the correct points in the product's development.
- Ensuring that staff are properly trained in the quality checking procedures.
- Ensuring that quality checking follow-up actions are dealt with correctly
- Ensuring that the quality checking procedures are being correctly followed.
- An acceptable solution is developed.
- Project remains viable.
- The scope of the project is not 'creeping up' unnoticed.
- Focus on the business need is maintained.
- Internal and external communications are working.
- Applicable standards are being used.
- Any legislative constraints are being observed.
- The needs of specialist interests, for example security, are being observed.
- Adherence to quality assurance standards.

It is not enough to believe that standards will be obeyed. It is not enough to ensure that a project is well set up and justified at the outset. All the aspects listed above need to be checked throughout the project as part of ensuring that it remains consistent with and continues to meet a business need and that no change to the external environment affects the validity of the project. This includes monitoring stage and team planning, Work Package and quality review preparation.

B.8 PROJECT SUPPORT

General

The provision of any Project Support on a formal basis is optional. It is driven by the needs of the individual project and Project Manager. Project Support could be in the form of advice on project management tools and administrative services, such as filing and the collection of actual data, to one or more related projects. Where set up as an official body, Project Support can act as a repository for lessons learned, and a central source of expertise in specialist support tools.

One support function that must be considered is that of configuration management. Depending on the project size and environment, there may be a need to formalize this, and it quickly becomes a task with which the Project Manager cannot cope without support. See the chapter on change for details of the work.

Specific Responsibilities

The following is a suggested list of tasks:

Administration

- Administer change control.
- Set up and maintain project files.
- Establish document control procedures.
- Compile, copy and distribute all project management products.
- Collect actual data and forecasts.
- Update plans.
- Administer the quality review process.
- Administer Project Board meetings.
- Assist with the compilation of reports.

Advice

- Specialist knowledge (for example, estimating, Management of Risk).
- Specialist tool expertise (for example, planning and control tools, risk analysis).
- Specialist techniques.
- Standards.

Appendix C

Product-based Planning

Product-based Planning is fundamental to PRINCE2 and I thoroughly recommend it. There are two reasons for this. First, a project delivers products, not activities, so why begin at a lower level? The second reason is about quality. We can measure the quality of a product. The quality of an activity can only be measured by the quality of its outcome (the product).

Product-based Planning has three components:

- Product Breakdown Structure.
- Product Description.
- Product Flow Diagram.

C.1 PRODUCT BREAKDOWN STRUCTURE

Most planning methods begin a plan by thinking of the activities to be undertaken, and listing these in a hierarchical structure called a Work Breakdown Structure (WBS). These activities, however, depend on what products are required to be produced by the project, so the correct start point for a plan is to list the products. In fact, by jumping straight to the lower level of detail of activities, it is possible to miss some vital products and hence vital activities from the plan.

A Product Breakdown Structure is a hierarchy of the products whose creation is to be planned (apart from creating products, there might be some that you purchase or obtain from other sources). At the top or core of the hierarchy is the final end product – for example, a computer system, a new yacht, or a department relocated to a new building. This is then broken down into its major constituents at the next level. Each constituent is then broken down into its parts, and this process continues until the planner has reached the level of detail required for the plan.

There are three types of 'product' that might appear in a Product Breakdown Structure: simple products, intermediate products and external products. Let's explain these terms.

Simple Products

Products at the lowest level of any branch of the hierarchy are 'simple products', so called because they are not broken down into more detail. Each of these requires a Product Description to be written for them.

The lowest level on a Product Breakdown Structure is not fixed. It depends on the level of detail required in the plan to allow the Project Board, Project Manager or Team Manager to exercise an appropriate level of control.

Intermediate Products

'Intermediate product' is a term used to describe a product that is broken down into further products, i.e. anything between the top level and the bottom level of the Product Breakdown Structure is called 'intermediate'.

An intermediate product may be a product itself where one or more activities, such as assembly or testing, will need to be applied to that product after its sub-products have been produced. These products should appear in the Product Flow Diagram and require a Product Description to be written for them. As with simple products, they should be represented in the diagram as a rectangle.

Another type of intermediate product is not a 'product' itself. It may simply be used as a trigger to further thoughts by the planner of what actual products are required. An example of this type of intermediate product might be 'training' – this is not a product in itself, but is used as a starting point to think of real products, such as lecture notes, student notes, exercises and case studies. This style of intermediate product may be used in the Product Breakdown Structure but should **not** be carried forward into the Product Flow Diagram.

Both types of intermediate product may appear in the Product Breakdown Structure. Figure C.1 is an example of a project whose objective is to purchase new equipment. There are many complications that can occur in purchasing, but for the sake of an example we shall keep this simple.

External Products

The Product Breakdown Structure should include not only the products to be delivered by the project, but also any products that already exist or are to be supplied from external sources. The Project Manager is not accountable for the creation of external products, but the project does need the product(s) in order to achieve its objectives. A plan must therefore include any external products required to achieve the plan's objectives, plus suitable dependencies on these external products.

A different symbol should be used to identify external products. An ellipse is used to indicate an external product in both the Product Breakdown Structure and the Product Flow Diagram. It should be noted that it is the product that is shown, not the source of the product. For example, if a plan needs the local train timetable, 'rail timetable' would be the external product, not the relevant train company.

There are two products in our example that will come from outside the project. 'Procurement process details' already exist in the company and the Project Manager has no control over whether the potential suppliers will actually submit a tender (Figure C.1).

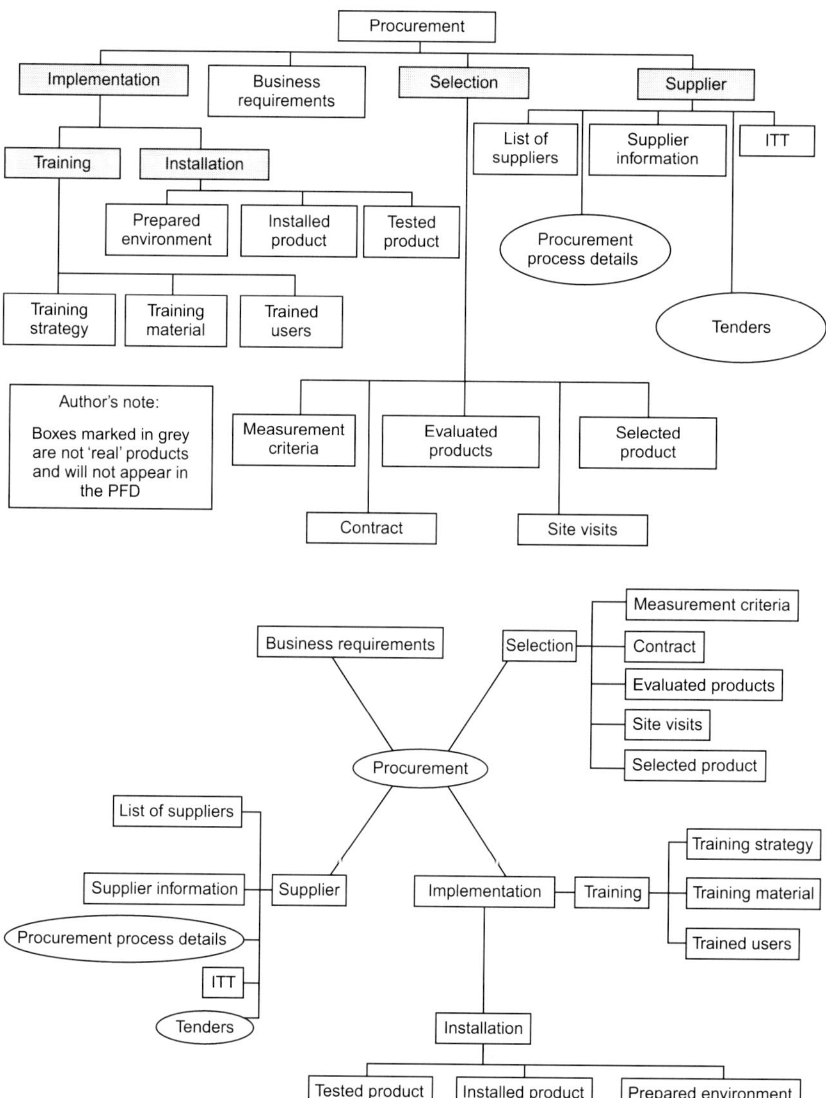

FIGURE C.1 Example Product Breakdown Structure for a purchasing project

C.2 PRODUCT DESCRIPTION

For each identified simple and integration product, a Product Description is produced. Its creation forces the planner to consider if sufficient is known about the product in order to plan its production. It is also the first time that the quality of the product is considered. The quality criteria should be measurable statements on the expected quality of the product and what type of quality checking will be required. As an example, 'faster' and 'better' are not measurable and would therefore not be useful quality criteria. 'Able to bear a weight of ten tonnes' and 'maximum response time of 3 seconds' are examples of measurable criteria.

The purposes of writing a Product Description are, therefore, to provide a guide:

- to the planner on how much effort will be required to create the product;
- to the author of the product on what is required;
- against which the finished product can be measured.

These descriptions are a vital checklist to be used at a quality check of the related products.

The description should contain:

- The purpose of the product.
- The composition of the product.
- The products from which it is derived.
- Any standards for format and presentation.
- The quality criteria to be applied to the product.
- The quality verification method to be used.

The Product Description is given to both the product's creator and those who will verify its quality.

Project Product Description

The first step in Product-based Planning is actually to write a Product Description of the final product. This helps establish if the customer actually understands and can describe the required final product and helps establish the customer's quality expectations (and therefore needs to be done during the *Starting up a Project* process).

C.3 PRODUCT FLOW DIAGRAM

The Product Flow Diagram is a diagram showing the sequence in which the products have to be produced and the dependencies between them. It is produced after the Product Breakdown Structure. Figure C.2 is a Product Flow Diagram for the purchasing example.

A

Garden Shed Product Description
Purpose: To house my garden tools.

B

Garden Shed Product Description
Purpose: To house my garden tools, including the sit-on lawnmower. To provide storage for plant pots, fertilizers, pesticide sprays and compost. With room for my old armchair when I wish to smoke my pipe in peace.

CARTOON C.1 (A) and (B) Product Description

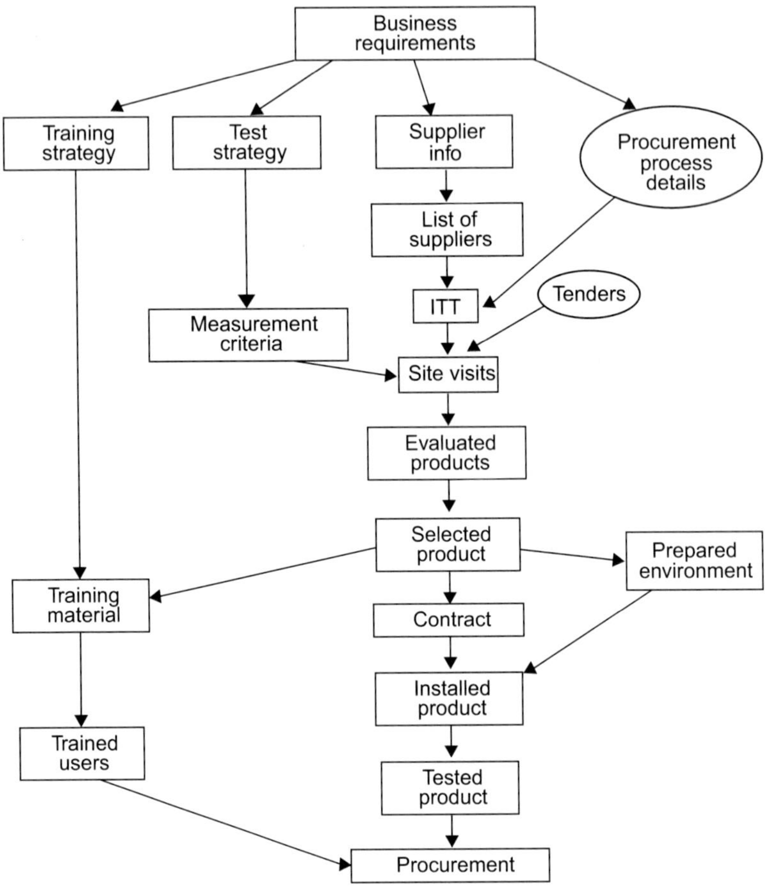

FIGURE C.2 Example Product Flow Diagram for a purchasing project

A Product Flow Diagram normally needs only the following symbols: a rectangle to contain the products, an ellipse to show any external products, and arrows to show the dependencies.

Basic example of the use of external products, product groupings and simple products

> 'From the scenario provided by the lecturer draw a Product Breakdown Structure and a Product Flow Diagram. When you have completed the Product Breakdown Structure the lecturer will give you an envelope containing the names of two products for which you then have to create Product Descriptions.'

The Product Breakdown Structure and Product Flow Diagram for this statement (not for whatever is the subject in the scenario) would look like those in Figures C.3 and C.4.

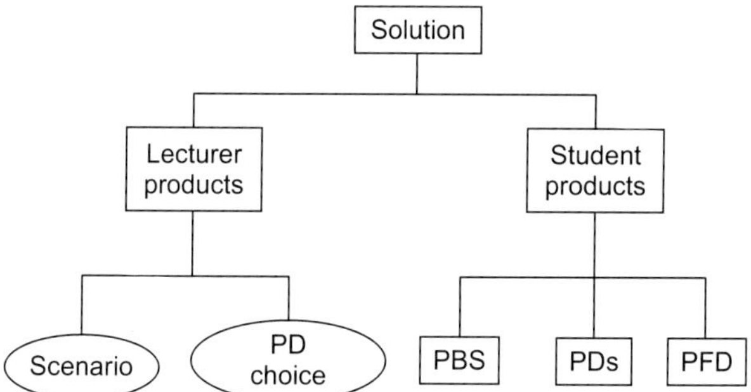

FIGURE C.3 Basic example Product Breakdown Structure

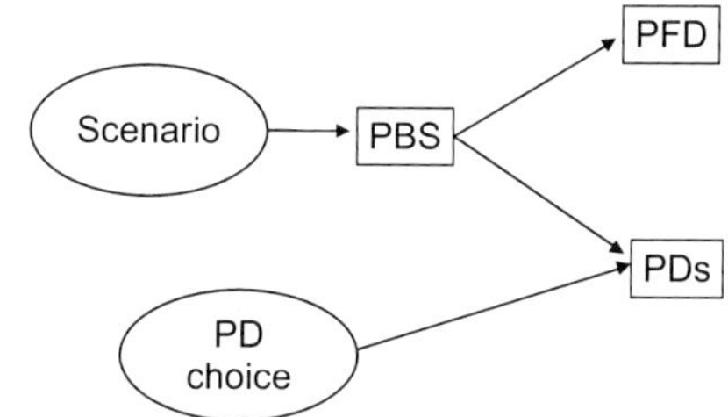

FIGURE C.4 Basic example Product Flow Diagram

Appendix D

Quality Review

This is a team method of checking a document's quality by a review process. The purpose of a quality review is to inspect a document for errors in a planned, independent, controlled and documented manner and ensure that any errors found are fixed.

The quality review technique is a structured way of reviewing documents to ensure that all aspects are properly covered. It needs to be used with common sense to avoid the dangers of an over-bureaucratic approach but with the intent to follow the procedures laid down (to ensure nothing is missed).

The major aim is to improve product quality. There are several subordinate objectives. These are to:

- trap errors as early as possible;
- encourage the concept of documents as team property rather than belonging to an individual;
- enhance product status data (i.e. not only has the creator declared it finished, but others have confirmed that it is of good quality);
- monitor the use of standards;
- spread knowledge of the document among those whose own products may interact with it (Cartoon D.1).

Quality review documentation, when filed in the quality file, provides, together with the Quality Register, a record that the document was inspected, that any errors found were corrected and that the corrections were themselves checked. Knowing that a document has been checked and declared error-free provides a more confident basis to move ahead and use that document as the basis of future work than simply taking the word of the creator.

D.1 ROLES AT THE QUALITY REVIEW

The roles involved in a quality review are the following:

- The presenter, who is the author of the document being reviewed. This role has to ensure that the reviewers have all the required information in order to perform their job. This means getting a copy of the document from the Configuration Librarian to them during the preparation phase, plus any documents needed to put it in context. Then the presenter has to answer questions about the document during the review until a decision can be reached on whether there is an error or not. Finally the presenter will do most, if not all, of the correcting work. The presenter must not be allowed to be defensive about the document.

- The chair: An open, objective attitude is needed. The chair has the following required attributes:
  - Sufficient authority to control the review.
  - Understands the quality review process thoroughly.
  - Chairmanship experience.

  The chair is responsible for ensuring that the quality review is properly organized and that it runs smoothly during all of its phases.

  For the preparation phase this includes checking that administrative procedures have been carried out and that the right people have been invited. This needs consultation with any appointed Project Assurance roles and reference to the Stage Plan.
- The reviewers, who must be competent to assess the product from their particular viewpoints.

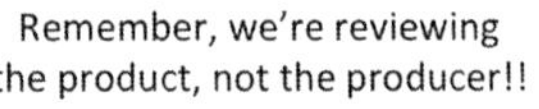

CARTOON D.1 Quality review

- The administrator – someone who will note down any required actions resulting from the review. This role may be taken by one of the other attendees, but if the review has several attendees it is sensible to give this role to someone other than the chair, so that the chair can concentrate on controlling the review.

It must be remembered that all these are roles. They must all be present at a quality review, but a person may take on more than one role.

People Involved

The interests of parties who should be considered when drawing up the list of attendees are:

- The product author.
- Those with Project Assurance responsibilities delegated by the Project Board.
- The customer.
- Staff who will use the document as a basis for further work.
- Other staff whose work will be affected by the product.
- Specialists in the relevant product area.
- Standards representatives.

D.2 PHASES

There are three distinct phases within the quality review procedure: preparation, review and follow-up.

Phase 1 – Preparation

The objective of this phase is to examine the document under review and to create a list of questions for the review.

The chair checks with the presenter that the document will be ready on time. If not, the Project Manager is advised. This will lead to an update of the Stage Plan and the Quality Register. The chair ensures that the team of reviewers is agreed, that they will all be available and that the venue for the review has been arranged. Project Assurance may wish to be involved in confirming that the team of reviewers is satisfactory to them.

An invitation is sent out, giving the time and place for the review with copies of the document, the relevant Product Description and any checklist available. This should be done with sufficient time before the review to allow the reviewers time to examine the document and to provide a question list to the presenter.

Each reviewer will study the document and supporting documents (including the quality criteria in the Product Description), annotate the document with any spelling or grammatical errors, and complete a question list.

A copy of the question lists will, wherever possible, be sent to the presenter before the review. The presenter and chair should review these to allow the chair to set up an agenda, prioritize the questions and roughly allocate time to each point. To save time at the review, the presenter can acknowledge questions that identify agreed errors.

Phase 2 – Review

The objective of the review is to agree a list of any actions needed to correct or complete the document. The chair and the presenter do not have to reconcile these actions at the meeting – it is sufficient for the chair and reviewers to agree that a particular area needs correction or at least re-examination. Provided that the action is logged the reviewers have an opportunity in the next phase to confirm that action has been taken.

The chair opens the meeting and, if necessary, introduces those present. Timing (suggested maximum of two hours) is announced.

The presenter then 'walks through' the questions in detail. This will be determined by the reviewers' question lists already sent to the presenter. If it is found that any part is understood and accepted, there is no point in walking through it.

The chair controls the discussion during the review, ensuring that no arguments or solutions are discussed (other than obvious and immediately accepted solutions!). The administrator notes actions on a follow-up action list. No other minutes are taken of the review.

At the conclusion of the walk-through, the chair asks the administrator to read back the actions and determines responsibility for correction of any points. A target date is set for each action, and the initials of the reviewer(s) who will sign-off each corrective action as it is completed and found acceptable are recorded on the follow-up action list by the administrator.

The chair, after seeking the reviewers' and presenter's opinions, will decide on the outcome of the review. There can be one of three outcomes:

- The document is error-free.
- The document will be acceptable on completion of the actions noted.
- There is so much corrective work to be done that the entire document needs to be re-reviewed.

In the last case, the chair will advise the Project Manager so that the Stage Plan can be updated. The Quality Register is updated. A result notification will be completed and the documents attached. These forms will be filed in the quality file.

The reviewers' question lists, copies of the document (probably containing the reviewer's annotations) and any other relevant documentation is collected by the chair and passed to the presenter to assist in the follow-up.

Phase 3 – Follow-up

The objective of the follow-up phase is to ensure that all actions identified on the follow-up action list are dealt with.

The presenter takes the follow-up action list away from the review and evaluates, discusses and corrects, if necessary, all the errors.

When an error has been fixed, the presenter will obtain sign-off from whoever is nominated on the follow-up action list. This person may be the reviewer who raised the initial query, but other reviewers have the option of checking the correction.

When all errors have been reconciled and sign-off obtained, the chair will confirm that the document is complete and sign off the follow-up action list. The documents will be filed in the Quality Register and the Stage Plan updated.

D.3 QUALITY REVIEW RESPONSIBILITIES

Chair's Responsibilities

Preparation Phase

- Check with the presenter that the product is ready for review.
- If the product is not ready for review, update the Stage Plan – for example, a revised completion date.
- Consult with the presenter and those performing Project Assurance roles to confirm appropriate reviewers.
- Agree the amount of preparation time required with the presenter (and reviewers, if this is appropriate).
- Arrange a time, location and duration for the review in consultation with the presenter and reviewers.
- Advise the Project Manager if there is to be any delay in holding the review.
- Arrange for copies of any relevant checklist or standard to be provided.
- Ensure the Configuration Librarian provides Product Descriptions and product copies for all reviewers.
- Send an invitation, Product Description, document copy, blank question list and product checklist (if there is one) to each reviewer.
- Send a copy of the invitation to the presenter.
- Decide if a short overview presentation of the document to the reviewers is required as part of the preparation, and arrange it if it is.
- Arrange with the reviewers for collection of their question lists prior to the review.
- Create an agenda for the review from the question lists in consultation with the presenter. Agree any obvious errors in the document with the presenter. Prioritize the questions and roughly allocate time.

- Confirm attendance with each reviewer shortly before the review. If a reviewer cannot attend, ensure that the reviewer's question list is made out and submitted. If too many reviewers cannot attend, reschedule the review and inform the Project Manager of the delay.
- If necessary, rehearse the review with the presenter.

Review

- Provide a copy of the agenda to all attendees.
- Open the review, stating objectives and apologizing for any non-attendees.
- Decide whether the reviewers present and the question lists from any unable to attend are adequate to review the document. If not, the review should be stopped, re-scheduled and the Project Manager advised.
- Identify any errors in the document already agreed by the presenter and ensure that these are documented on the follow-up action list.
- Step through the agenda, with the appropriate reviewer expanding where necessary on the question.
- Allow reasonable discussion on each question between presenter and reviewers to decide if action is required.
- Ensure that the administrator documents any agreed actions required on a follow-up action list.
- Prevent any discussion of possible solutions or matters of style.
- Ensure that reviewers are given a chance to voice their comments.
- Where agreement cannot be reached on a point in a reasonable timeframe, declare it an action point and note the reviewer(s) concerned.
- Where necessary, decide on the premature close of the review in the light of the comments made.
- If faults are identified in documents not under review, ensure that an issue is raised and sent to the Configuration Librarian.
- Collect any annotated documents detailing minor or typographical errors.
- Read back the follow-up action list and obtain confirmation from the presenter and reviewers that it is complete and correct.
- Identify who is to be involved in working on each action item. Obtain a target date for completion of the work.
- Agree with the reviewers who is to approve the work done on each action item and note this on the follow-up action list.
- Pass the follow-up action list and all copies of the annotated document to the presenter. Lodge a copy of the follow-up action list in the Quality Register.
- Decide with the reviewers what the status of the review is. It can be:
  - complete with no errors discovered;
  - complete with some re-work required;
  - in need of re-work and another review.

- If the review is incomplete, recommend a course of action to the Project Manager. There are five possible courses of action. The last two of these are not recommended:
  - The document should be re-worked prior to another review.
  - The review should be reconvened to finish with no interim need for re-work.
  - The review should be reconvened without re-work with a different set of reviewers.
  - The review should be declared complete, the errors found so far corrected and the rest of the document accepted as it is.
  - The review should be abandoned and the document used as it is, i.e. none of the errors corrected, but noted in an issue.

Follow-up

- Monitor the correction of errors and sign off the follow-up action list when all corrections have been approved.
- If an action cannot be taken within the time agreed, the chair and presenter may decide to transfer it to an issue as a possible error. This requires the agreement of the Project Manager. The follow-up action list is updated with the Issue Register number and those waiting to sign off the action item informed.
- On completion and sign-off of all action items, sign off the follow-up action list as complete and file it in the Quality Register with copies to all reviewers. Update the Quality Register.
- Supervise the passage of the error-free document to the Configuration Librarian.

Producer's Responsibilities

Preparation

- Ask the Project Manager to nominate a chair if none is identified in the Stage Plan.
- Confirm with the chair that the document is ready for review. This should occur several days prior to the planned review date to allow for preparation time.
- Confirm the attendees with the chair and those holding Project Assurance responsibilities.
- Agree with the chair and reviewers the length of preparation time needed and review location.
- Assess the question lists from the reviewers, identifying any errors in the document that can be agreed without further discussion.
- Agree the agenda with the chair in the light of the question lists.

Review

- Answer any questions about the document.
- Offer an opinion to the chair on whether a question has highlighted an error in the document.
- If the review is judged to be complete, collect from the chair the follow-up action list and any annotated copies of the document from the reviewers.

Follow-up

- Resolve all allocated action items.
- Obtain sign-off for each action item from the nominated reviewers.
- If an action item cannot be resolved within a reasonable timeframe, then decide with the chair to transfer it to an issue. An alternative is to agree new target dates.
- Pass the follow-up action list to the chair on resolution of all the action items.

Reviewer Responsibilities

Preparation

- Consult the Product Description and any pertinent checklists and standards against which the document should be judged.
- Allow sufficient time to prepare for the review.
- Consult any necessary source documents from which the document is derived.
- Annotate any spelling or typographical mistakes on the document copy, but do not add these to the question list.
- Check the document for completeness, defects, ambiguities, inconsistencies, lack of clarity or deviations from standards. Note any such items on the question list.
- Forward the question list to the chair in advance of the review. If possible, this should be done early enough to give the presenter time to digest the points and prepare an agenda with the chair.
- Forward a question list and the annotated document copy to the chair if unable to attend the review.

Review

- Ensure that the points noted on the question list are raised at the review.
- Restrict comments to faults in the document under review.
- Avoid attempting to redesign the document.
- Avoid 'improvement' comments if the document meets requirements and standards.

- Verify and approve the follow-up action list as complete and correct when read back by the chair.
- Agree to assist in the resolution of any action items if requested by the chair.
- Request to check and sign off any action items either raised personally or which impact the reviewer's area of expertise or interest.

Follow-up

- Work with the presenter to resolve any allocated action item.
- Check and sign off those action items where allocated as reviewer.
- Quality reviews can be either formal (i.e. a scheduled meeting conducted as described above) or informal (i.e. a 'get-together' between two people to informally walk through a document). A variation on a formal review is to have the reviewers forward their follow-up action lists, but only the chair and the presenter do the actual review.
- Informal quality reviews will follow a similar format to the formal quality review – the paperwork emerging from both meetings is similar. The main difference will be the informality of the proceedings during the three phases and the overall time required.
- For informal quality reviews two people can be given the task of checking each other's work on an ongoing basis. Alternatively, an experienced person can be asked to regularly hold reviews of an inexperienced person's work as it develops.

Factors in deciding whether a formal or informal review is needed are:

- The importance of the document.
- Whether it is a final deliverable.
- Whether it is the source for a number of other documents.
- The author's experience.
- Who the document's consumer is.
- Whether it is a review of a partial document.

Passing the PRINCE2 Foundation Exam

BACKGROUND

The Foundation exam was originally created for those who were to be part of a PRINCE2 project environment at a non-management level; for example, such roles as Project Support, Project Assurance, auditors, quality assurance and user or supplier staff who had to be aware of the PRINCE2 terms and structure of working. This purpose still exists, but the Foundation exam has now also become a prerequisite for those wishing to sit the Practitioner exam.

FOUNDATION EXAMINATION FORMAT

- 1 hour.
- 75 questions.
- Multiple choice.
- Closed book.

The candidate's score is based on answers to 75 of these questions. In order to pass, the candidate must answer 35 (of the 70 GENUINE questions) correctly. Each correct answer is worth 1 mark. There are no part marks. Each question has only one correct answer. There are no trick questions. 'Closed book' means that you can have no visible aids on your desk, on the walls or on your arm that contain information that might be helpful to you. It's you and your brain against the exam questions.

Trial Questions

Although the exam paper has 75 questions, you are only tested on 70. The other five questions are draft ones that are being trialled. An assessment of answers to the extra five questions is used by the examiners to see if they are fit to be used in future exams. The candidate's scores on the five trial questions are not used as part of the exam score. The candidate is not told which are the five trialled questions.

EXAM PURPOSE

Foundation level measures whether a candidate could act as an informed member of a PRINCE2 project management team. They need to show that they understand the following:

- The seven principles, the seven themes, the seven processes and the Product-based Planning and Quality Review techniques.
- Which management products are input to, output from and updated in the seven processes, and the activities.
- The purpose of all management products and the composition of the Business Case and Product Descriptions.
- The purpose and responsibilities of all roles.
- The relationship between principles, processes, themes, deliverables and roles within a PRINCE2 project.

The levels of ability required are defined by the terms knowledge and comprehension. These two terms are defined in the table below.

1. Knowledge	2. Comprehension/Understanding
Able to recall PRINCE2 facts, including terms, concepts, principles, themes, processes and responsibilities.	Understands the principles, processes, themes, the project's environment and roles and can explain how these are applied on a project.

It does not cover any assessment of a candidate's ability to apply the method or create any of the method's products.

How to Approach the Foundation Exam Paper

Exercise care. Remember that people frequently get a question wrong by:

- NOT READING THE QUESTION.
- NOT READING THE OPTIONS.

The brain is quite happy to 'interpret' the words on paper and give you what it thinks the eye has seen, so please read SLOWLY.

It is not a good generalization to say to yourself, '75 questions to be answered in 60 minutes gives me 0.8 of a minute per question (48 seconds).' The answer to some questions is going to be known immediately by you, and you should also leave about 10 minutes to look through your answers for any silly mistake or question (or page) that you have missed. Certainly do not waste time trying to guess which the trialled questions are.

I would recommend five passes through the question book to you.

Pass 1: Read each question in turn. If you definitely know the answer, tick the appropriate box and move on. Keep a count (five-barred gate) of the number that you have answered. At the end of the first pass, you know how many you are likely to have already answered correctly. Deduct the number that you have answered from 75, and the time taken from 50 minutes. You now have a much better idea of how many questions and how much time are left.

Pass 2: Re-read the unanswered questions and put a little cross against the text of the answers that you know are wrong (not in the answer box). If you are left with only one answer, then tick the appropriate answer box. If you still have several options possible, do not spend more time; move on. Again keep count of the new total of questions answered and check the remaining time.

Pass 3: You now have a better understanding of how much time you can afford to spend on each unanswered question. I would deduct 5 minutes from this figure and apportion a number of seconds to each unanswered question. (I am saving 5 minutes for Pass 4.) Let's say that you find that you have used 35 minutes so far. We are saving 10 minutes for a review plus another 5 minutes' safety margin. You have 20 answers to find, giving you 30 seconds per question. Spend that amount of time – no more – on each question, re-reading it and the remaining possible options. Ask yourself what the answer can be and what it can't be. This pass will free up some more answers. By the end of this pass you should be feeling comfortable that you now have far more answers than 35, with a good chance that most of them will be correct.

Pass 4: Use 5 minutes to go through looking for any questions still unanswered. Look at the options that you haven't been able to cross out and make a guess on which is the correct one.

Pass 5: Go through each question from the beginning and make sure that you have not missed a page, have an answer for each question and have ticked the right box.

Sample Foundation Exam Paper

Tick the relevant box.

1 Which is a PRINCE2 principle?

a) Learn from experience ☐
b) Plans ☐
c) Controls ☐
d) Define the quality ☐

2 Which theme discusses the importance of knowing why a project should be undertaken?

a) Risk ☐
b) Quality ☐
c) Business Case ☐
d) Plans ☐

3 Which of the following is NOT a PRINCE2 benefit?

a) Explicitly recognizes project responsibilities ☐
b) Ensures that participants focus on the viability of the project ☐
c) Defines a thorough but economical structure of reports ☐
d) Avoids involving stakeholders who are merely interested parties ☐

4 Which is NOT an aspect of project performance to be managed?

a) Costs ☐
b) Timescales ☐
c) Benefits ☐
d) Delegation ☐

5 Fill in the missing words in the following sentence.
'The PRINCE2 processes address the [?] of the project.'

a) shape and size ☐
b) chronological flow ☐
c) quality assurance ☐
d) formality ☐

6 Fill in the missing words in the following sentence.
'PRINCE2 defines a project as a [?] that is created for the purpose of delivering business products.'

a) specialist stage ☐
b) structure ☐
c) fixed set of resources ☐
d) set of mandatory techniques ☐

7 Which of the following are PRINCE2 plans?
1 Exception Plan
2 Stage Plan
3 Quality Plan
4 Benefits Review Plan

a) 1, 2, 3 ☐
b) 1, 2, 4 ☐
c) 1, 3, 4 ☐
d) 2, 3, 4 ☐

8 Which of the following are risk responses?
1 Avoid
2 Enhance
3 Fallback
4 Ignore

a) 1, 2, 3 ☐
b) 1, 2, 4 ☐
c) 1, 3, 4 ☐
d) 2, 3, 4 ☐

9 Before the Risk Register is created where will the Project Manager record any risks?

a) Quality Register ☐
b) Daily Log ☐
c) Issue Register ☐
d) Lessons Log ☐

10 What is the trigger for a project?

a) Project Initiation Documentation ☐
b) Project Brief ☐
c) Business Case ☐
d) Project mandate ☐

11 In which process is the request for project funding defined in detail?

a) Starting up a Project ☐
b) Initiating a Project ☐
c) Directing a Project ☐
d) Closing a Project ☐

12 Which activities are carried out by the role of the quality review chair?

1 Check that the product is ready for review.
2 Gather all question lists and set the review meeting agenda.
3 Lead the review team through the product section by section.
4 Ensure that all agreed errors are recorded on a follow-up action list.

a) 1, 2, 3 ☐
b) 1, 2, 4 ☐
c) 1, 3, 4 ☐
d) 2, 3, 4 ☐

13 Which does NOT involve the Project Board?

a) Exception assessment ☐
b) Highlight Reports ☐
c) Work Package authorization ☐
d) Project closure ☐

14 Identify the missing words in the following sentence.
'Effective risk management is a prerequisite of the [?] principle.'

a) focus on products ☐
b) continued business justification ☐
c) manage by exception ☐
d) manage by stages ☐

15 How are principles characterized?

a) Are capable of tailoring ☐
b) Justify the project ☐
c) Apply to every project ☐
d) Their use is optional ☐

16 Which is independent of the project management team?

a) Team Manager ☐
b) Project Assurance ☐
c) Project Support ☐
d) Quality assurance ☐

17 Which product defines the authorities for handling requests for change?

a) Communication Management Strategy ☐
b) Configuration Management Strategy ☐
c) Quality Management Strategy ☐
d) Risk Management Strategy ☐

18 Which are basic business options?

1 Do nothing
2 Do less
3 Do something
4 Do the minimum

a) 1, 2, 3 ☐
b) 1, 2, 4 ☐
c) 1, 3, 4 ☐
d) 2, 3, 4 ☐

19 Which part of the Business Case balances costs against benefits over a period of time?

a) Expected benefits ☐
b) Business options ☐
c) Investment appraisal ☐
d) Expected dis-benefits ☐

20 Which role is responsible for realizing post-project benefits?

a) Executive ☐
b) Senior User ☐
c) Senior Supplier ☐
d) Project Manager ☐

21 Which of the following statements is FALSE?

a) A company's quality management system becomes part of PRINCE2. ☐
b) The customer's quality expectations should be discovered in the Starting up a Project process. ☐
c) PRINCE2 may form part of a company's quality management system. ☐
d) The use of Team Plans is optional. ☐

22 Which is NOT one of the four tasks of the Product-based Planning technique?

a) Identifying dependencies ☐
b) Producing a Product Breakdown Structure ☐
c) Creating a Product Checklist ☐
d) Writing Product Descriptions of each significant product ☐

23 Which of the following reviews the benefits achieved by the project?

a) End Project Report ☐
b) Lessons Report ☐
c) Post-project review ☐
d) Quality review ☐

24 Who is responsible for assessing and updating the Business Case at the end of a stage?

a) Senior User ☐
b) Executive ☐
c) Project Manager ☐
d) Project Assurance ☐

25 Whose role is it to ensure that planned communications actually occur?

- **a)** Project Board ☐
- **b)** Project Manager ☐
- **c)** Project Assurance ☐
- **d)** Corporate management ☐

26 In which process is the Quality Management Strategy created?

- **a)** Starting up a Project ☐
- **b)** Initiating a Project ☐
- **c)** Directing a Project ☐
- **d)** Managing a Stage Boundary ☐

27 Which theme is central to the approach to quality?

- **a)** Manage by exception ☐
- **b)** Continued business justification ☐
- **c)** Focus on products ☐
- **d)** Defined roles and responsibilities ☐

28 Which product relates planned quality activities to those actually performed?

- **a)** Quality Register ☐
- **b)** Project Approach ☐
- **c)** Quality Management Strategy ☐
- **d)** Lessons Log ☐

29 Which action is NOT part of Accept a Work Package?

- **a)** Agree tolerance margins ☐
- **b)** Understand the reporting requirements ☐
- **c)** Produce a Team Plan ☐
- **d)** Monitor and control any Work Package risks ☐

30 Comparing a product against defined criteria is an objective of what?

- **a)** Work Package ☐
- **b)** Investment appraisal ☐
- **c)** Quality review ☐
- **d)** Quality Register ☐

31 Which process defines quality responsibilities?

- **a)** Starting up a Project ☐
- **b)** Initiating a Project ☐
- **c)** Directing a Project ☐
- **d)** Managing a Stage Boundary ☐

32 Who checks that a product is ready for its quality review?

- **a)** Chair ☐
- **b)** Administrator ☐
- **c)** Presenter ☐
- **d)** Reviewer ☐

33 Whose task is it to produce products consistent with their Product Descriptions?

a) Senior User ☐
b) Project Manager ☐
c) Team Manager ☐
d) Senior Supplier ☐

34 What provides the Business Case with planned costs?

a) Project Brief ☐
b) Project Plan ☐
c) Initiation Stage Plan ☐
d) Project Approach ☐

35 What is identified first in the planning philosophy?

a) Dependencies ☐
b) Activities ☐
c) Products ☐
d) Resources ☐

36 In which process is the means of reviewing benefits developed?

a) Closing a Project ☐
b) Initiating a Project ☐
c) Managing a Stage Boundary ☐
d) Starting up a Project ☐

37 In which process are previous lessons captured?

a) Starting up a Project ☐
b) Initiating a Project ☐
c) Managing a Stage Boundary ☐
d) Closing a Project ☐

38 Which product defines whether the solution will be developed in house?

a) Project mandate ☐
b) Project Approach ☐
c) Business Case ☐
d) Project Plan ☐

39 Which process ensures that there is an interface with corporate management throughout the project?

a) Starting up a Project ☐
b) Managing a Stage Boundary ☐
c) Directing a Project ☐
d) Initiating a Project ☐

40 Which statement is NOT a purpose of the Closing a Project process?

a) Confirm acceptance by the customer of the project's products. ☐

b) Recognize that approved changes to the objectives in the Project Initiation Documentation have been achieved. ☐

c) Recognize that the project has nothing more to contribute. ☐

d) Place formal requirements on accepting and delivering project work. ☐

41 Which is NOT a Project Board activity?

a) Authorize initiation ☐

b) Give ad hoc direction ☐

c) Authorize a Work Package ☐

d) Authorize the project ☐

42 What information is input to the Starting up a Project process?

a) Project mandate ☐

b) Project Initiation Documentation ☐

c) An appointed Executive ☐

d) Outline Business Case ☐

43 Which of the following is NOT input to the Project Board?

a) Informal request for advice ☐

b) Escalated Issue Report ☐

c) Project authorization notification ☐

d) Highlight Report ☐

44 Which document contains any follow-on action recommendations?

a) Lessons Report ☐

b) End Stage Report ☐

c) End Project Report ☐

d) Benefits Review Plan ☐

45 Which product captures user quality expectations and acceptance criteria?

a) Project Product Description ☐

b) Quality Management Strategy ☐

c) Project Brief ☐

d) Daily Log ☐

46 Which of the following are done in the Starting up a Project process?

1 Set up the project management team.
2 Develop the project mandate into the Project Brief.
3 Create the Issue Register.
4 Devise the Project Approach.

a) 1, 2, 3 ☐

b) 1, 2, 4 ☐

c) 1, 3, 4 ☐

d) 2, 3, 4 ☐

47 An example of Work Package [?] might be: 'I need this by Thursday close of work, but by Friday lunchtime at the latest.'

a) approval requirements ☐
b) constraint ☐
c) tolerance ☐
d) reporting and problem handling ☐

48 The need for configuration management is described in which theme?

a) Quality ☐
b) Plans ☐
c) Progress ☐
d) Change ☐

49 Which are purposes of a summary risk profile?

1 Shows the risk owners
2 Snapshot of the risk environment
3 Shows risk trends
4 Identifies risks beyond the risk appetite

a) 1, 2, 3 ☐
b) 1, 2, 4 ☐
c) 1, 3, 4 ☐
d) 2, 3, 4 ☐

50 In which process is the Business Case reviewed and updated?

a) Controlling a Stage ☐
b) Managing Product Delivery ☐
c) Managing a Stage Boundary ☐
d) Directing a Project ☐

51 Which is NOT part of an unambiguous expression of a risk?

a) Probability ☐
b) Cause ☐
c) Effect ☐
d) Event ☐

52 What does an early-warning indicator provide?

a) Proximity of a risk ☐
b) A project objective could be at risk ☐
c) An opportunity is about to present itself ☐
d) Date of a stage end approaching ☐

53 What does a risk budget cover?

a) Cost of risks carried over to follow-on action recommendations ☐
b) Off-specification costs ☐
c) Costs of administering risk management ☐
d) Cost of fallback plans ☐

54 Which document contains the Change Control procedure?

- **a)** Quality Management Strategy ☐
- **b)** Configuration Management Strategy ☐
- **c)** Risk Management Strategy ☐
- **d)** Communication Management Strategy ☐

55 What is product status accounting?

- **a)** Recording Work Package progress from a review of timesheets and the Team Plan. ☐
- **b)** An audit comparing actual product status with that shown in the Configuration Item Records. ☐
- **c)** Reporting on the current and historical state of products. ☐
- **d)** A summary of the state of the Quality Register at the end of a stage. ☐

56 What is the second step in an Issue and Change Control procedure?

- **a)** Decide ☐
- **b)** Capture ☐
- **c)** Propose ☐
- **d)** Examine ☐

57 Which principle is NOT supported by the Progress theme?

- **a)** Manage by exception ☐
- **b)** Continued business justification ☐
- **c)** Tailoring PRINCE2 ☐
- **d)** Manage by stages ☐

58 Who sets project tolerances?

- **a)** Corporate management ☐
- **b)** Project Board ☐
- **c)** Project Manager ☐
- **d)** Executive ☐

59 Why might dividing a project into a small number of lengthy stages be a problem?

- **a)** Makes project planning more difficult ☐
- **b)** Increases project management administration costs ☐
- **c)** Reduces the level of Project Board control ☐
- **d)** Reduces the amount of risk monitoring ☐

60 Which is an event-driven control?

- **a)** Highlight Report ☐
- **b)** Checkpoint Report ☐
- **c)** End Stage Report ☐
- **d)** Review Work Package Status ☐

61 Which product is NOT reviewed when reviewing Work Package status?

a) Checkpoint Report ☐
b) Project Plan ☐
c) Team Plan ☐
d) Quality Register ☐

62 Where are suitable reviewers first identified for a quality review?

a) Quality Management Strategy ☐
b) Project Plan ☐
c) Quality review preparation step ☐
d) Stage Plan ☐

63 Which of the following statements are TRUE?

1 The Executive role is responsible for the business interests of the customer and supplier.
2 There will always be two Business Cases in customer/supplier situations.
3 The customer and supplier may be part of the same corporate body or may be independent of each other.
4 A project's Business Case means the customer's Business Case.

a) 1, 2, 3 ☐
b) 1, 2, 4 ☐
c) 1, 3, 4 ☐
d) 2, 3, 4 ☐

64 Which product reviews a project's actual achievements against the Project Initiation Documentation?

a) Lessons Report ☐
b) Follow-on action recommendations ☐
c) End Project Report ☐
d) Benefits Review Plan ☐

65 Which product records a forecast failure to meet a requirement?

a) Risk Register ☐
b) Concession ☐
c) Highlight Report ☐
d) Off-specification ☐

66 What product would the Project Manager call for when reviewing stage status to check on a phased handover of products?

a) Stage Plan ☐
b) Quality Register ☐
c) Product Status Account ☐
d) Risk Register ☐

67 Who should prepare the outline Business Case?

a) Senior User ☐
b) Executive ☐
c) Project Manager ☐
d) Corporate management ☐

68 If an issue can be dealt with informally, where should a note of it be made?

a) Issue Register ☐
b) Daily Log ☐
c) Lessons Log ☐
d) Risk Register ☐

69 Which of these statements is FALSE?

a) The Project Board approves Team Plans. ☐
b) The Project Board approves a stage Exception Plan. ☐
c) A Stage Plan is required for each stage in the Project Plan. ☐
d) The Project Plan is an overview of the total project. ☐

70 When would an Exception Report be required?

a) Whenever a new risk is identified ☐
b) When a stakeholder raises a complaint ☐
c) When a request for change or off-specification is received ☐
d) When a stage is forecast to deviate outside its tolerance bounds ☐

71 What is the final step in risk management?

a) Appoint a risk owner ☐
b) Decide ☐
c) Communicate ☐
d) Implement ☐

72 When tailoring PRINCE2 for a project, which principles can be omitted?

a) None ☐
b) All except continued business justification ☐
c) Manage by stages ☐
d) Manage by exception ☐

73 In tailoring a project within a programme environment, why might responsibility for the Benefits Review Plan be removed from the Executive's role?

a) Given to the Senior User ☐
b) No project benefits to be reviewed ☐
c) Moved to Project Assurance ☐
d) A programme responsibility ☐

74 Which project role would sit on the programme board?

a) None ☐

b) Senior User ☐

c) Executive ☐

d) Quality assurance ☐

75 Which theme is most affected when used in simple projects?

a) Business Case ☐

b) Organization ☐

c) Risk ☐

d) Change ☐

Sample Foundation Exam Paper Answer Sheet

Question	Answer	R/W	Question	Answer	R/W	Question	Answer	R/W
1			26			51		
2			27			52		
3			28			53		
4			29			54		
5			30			55		
6			31			56		
7			32			57		
8			33			58		
9			34			59		
10			35			60		
11			36			61		
12			37			62		
13			38			63		
14			39			64		
15			40			65		
16			41			66		
17			42			67		
18			43			68		
19			44			69		
20			45			70		
21			46			71		
22			47			72		
23			48			73		
24			49			74		
25			50			75		

Sample Foundation Exam Paper Rationale

1	Which is a PRINCE2 principle?	Correct Answer:
	a) Learn from experience	✓
	b) Plans	
	c) Controls	
	d) Define the quality	
	Where to find the answer:	*2.4*
	a) Rationale	Correct. This is the second PRINCE2 principle, leading to a review of previous projects' Lessons Reports when starting up a project. Any useful lessons are documented in the current project's Lessons Log, which is checked for relevant lessons when creating the products in Starting up a Project and Initiating a Project.
	b) Rationale	No. Every project needs plans, so it is not a unique PRINCE2 principle. It is a theme.
	c) Rationale	Not a principle. Principles are unique to PRINCE2, whereas control is required with any method. Control needs are described in the Progress theme.
	d) Rationale	This is just a statement, not a principle. Quality comes under the 'focus on products' principle. Quality is a theme.

2	Which theme discusses the importance of knowing why a project should be undertaken?	Correct Answer:
	a) Risk	
	b) Quality	
	c) Business Case	✓
	d) Plans	

Where to find the answer:	*10*
a) Rationale	Risk is to control uncertainty in the execution of a project. The Business Case summarizes the major risks, but this is separate from the reasons for undertaking the project.
b) Rationale	Quality is not interested in why, just the quality of what is produced.
c) Rationale	Correct. The Business Case must contain the reasons for undertaking the project.
d) Rationale	No. Plans define how and when you will do something, not why you are doing it.

3 Which of the following is NOT a PRINCE2 benefit?	Correct Answer:
a) Clearly identifies project responsibilities	
b) Ensures that participants focus on the viability of the project	
c) Defines a thorough but economical structure of reports	
d) Avoids involving stakeholders who are merely interested parties	✓
Where to find the answer:	*1.1*
a) Rationale	The Organization theme explains role responsibilities.
b) Rationale	The Business Case contains the driving force of a project and its justification.
c) Rationale	PRINCE2 offers a good set of reports without unnecessary progress meetings.
d) Rationale	Correct. PRINCE2 ensures that all stakeholders are involved. See the Communication Management Strategy (4.6).

4 Which is NOT an aspect of project performance to be managed?	Correct Answer:
a) Costs	
b) Timescales	
c) Benefits	
d) Delegation	✓
Where to find the answer:	*2.3*

a) Rationale	Costs have to be managed, hence the update of Stage and Project Plans on a regular basis.
b) Rationale	Timescales have to be managed, hence the update of Stage and Project Plans on a regular basis and the agreement on target dates for Team Plans and quality checks.
c) Rationale	The Business Case is reviewed at the end of each stage to ensure that the project is still viable and that the benefits are still achievable.
d) Rationale	Correct. Delegation is not one of the six areas of tolerance to be managed.

5 Fill in the missing words in the following sentence. 'The PRINCE2 processes address the [?] of the project.'	Correct Answer:
a) shape and size	
b) chronological flow	✓
c) quality assurance	
d) formality	
Where to find the answer:	*2.7*
a) Rationale	No. The processes do not address the shape or size of a project. Any merging of processes or how many times a process needs to be used are considered as part of tailoring the method for a project.
b) Rationale	Correct. The processes address the flow from starting to closing a project.
c) Rationale	No. Quality assurance sits outside a project. The Organization theme addresses how to involve QA in a project.
d) Rationale	No. The formality will be mainly in how reports are made and the organization of the project management team. Processes look at what needs to be done and when.

6 Fill in the missing words in the following sentence. 'PRINCE2 defines a project as a [?] that is created for the purpose of delivering business products.'	Correct Answer:
a) specialist stage	
b) temporary structure	✓
c) fixed set of resources	
d) set of mandatory techniques	
Where to find the answer:	*2.2*
a) Rationale	No. For example, initiation is a stage in every PRINCE2 project, but is not a specialist stage.

b) Rationale	Correct. A project's team is assembled just for that project and is disbanded at the project close.
c) Rationale	No. The resources required may vary from stage to stage.
d) Rationale	No. PRINCE2 techniques are not mandatory. A company may already have, for example, a quality checking technique, which it wishes to use in preference to the PRINCE2 quality review.
7 Which of the following are PRINCE2 plans? 1 Exception Plan 2 Stage Plan 3 Quality Plan 4 Benefits Review Plan	Correct Answer:
a) 1, 2, 3	
b) 1, 2, 4	✓
c) 1, 3, 4	
d) 2, 3, 4	
Where to find the answer:	*12.2*
a) Rationale	(4) There is a Benefits Review Plan that describes how benefit achievement will be checked.
b) Rationale	Correct. (3) Although PRINCE2 discusses quality planning, there is no separate Quality Plan. Quality planning consists of understanding the customer's quality expectations and acceptance criteria, creating a Project Product Description, a Quality Management Strategy and a Quality Register.
c) Rationale	(2) Every PRINCE2 stage has a plan.
d) Rationale	(1) An Exception Plan replaces a plan that is forecast to deviate outside its tolerances.
8 Which of the following are risk responses? 1 Avoid 2 Enhance 3 Fallback 4 Ignore	Correct Answer:
a) 1, 2, 3	✓
b) 1, 2, 4	
c) 1, 3, 4	
d) 2, 3, 4	
Where to find the answer:	*Table 15.6.1*
a) Rationale	Correct. (4) Risks are never ignored.
b) Rationale	(3) Fallback is a response prepared in case a known risk does occur. The risk may have been considered unlikely to occur or too expensive to avoid or reduce.

c) Rationale	(2) A risk may be a threat or an opportunity. It may be sensible to enhance the chance of an opportunity occurring.
d) Rationale	(1) Risk avoidance is a sensible response.

9 Before the Risk Register is created where will the Project Manager record any risks?	Correct Answer:
a) Quality Register	
b) Daily Log	✓
c) Issue Register	
d) Lessons Log	
Where to find the answer:	*3.5.4*
a) Rationale	The Quality Register records all planned quality checks, attendees and results.
b) Rationale	Correct. Risks are recorded here during Starting up a Project until the Risk Register is created during initiation.
c) Rationale	On analysis some issues may be recognized as risks, but if originally recognized as a risk, they would not be entered here.
d) Rationale	Lessons may come from how risks were dealt with, but new risks are not added to the Lessons Log.

10 What is the trigger for a project?	Correct Answer:
a) Project Initiation Documentation	
b) Project Brief	
c) Business Case	
d) Project mandate	✓
Where to find the answer:	*3.1*
a) Rationale	The Project Initiation Documentation is not created until initiation and contains all the information required by the Project Board for it to decide if a project should be authorized.
b) Rationale	The Project Brief is used by the Project Board to decide if a project should be initiated and is based on the project mandate.
c) Rationale	The project mandate may or may not include some Business Case information.
d) Rationale	Correct. The project mandate is provided by the responsible authority that is commissioning the project, and is the basis for the Project Brief.

11 In which process is the request for project funding defined in detail?	Correct Answer:
a) Starting up a Project	
b) Initiating a Project	✓

c) Directing a Project	
d) Closing a Project	
Where to find the answer:	*4.9*
a) Rationale	Only an outline Business Case is completed during Starting up a Project.
b) Rationale	Correct. The Project Plan and full Business Case are created here.
c) Rationale	Directing a Project covers the decision-making activities of the Project Board. Information such as the request for funding has to be prepared in other processes for presentation to the Project Board.
d) Rationale	A request for project funding has to be created before major resources are committed by the Project Board. When closing a project, there is a review to see whether the money was well spent.

12 Which activities are carried out by the role of the quality review chair? 1 Check that the product is ready for review. 2 Gather all question lists and set the review meeting agenda. 3 Lead the review team through the product section by section. 4 Ensure that all agreed errors are recorded on a follow-up action list.	Correct Answer:
a) 1, 2, 3	
b) 1, 2, 4	✓
c) 1, 3, 4	
d) 2, 3, 4	
Where to find the answer:	*D.2*
a) Rationale	(4) The chair ensures that all agreed actions are recorded.
b) Rationale	Correct. (3) The presenter leads the reviewers through the product.
c) Rationale	(2) The chair is responsible for creating the agenda from the question lists.
d) Rationale	(1) The chair is responsible for checking that the product is ready for review, even if the task is delegated to the administrator.

13 Which does NOT involve the Project Board?	Correct Answer:
a) Exception assessment	
b) Highlight Reports	

c) Work Package authorization	✓
d) Project closure	
Where to find the answer:	*6.3*
a) Rationale	The Project Board reviews an Exception Plan during an exception assessment.
b) Rationale	The Project Board receives Highlight Reports from the Project Manager.
c) Rationale	Correct. Work Packages are authorized by the Project Manager after discussion with a Team Manager.
d) Rationale	Project closure must be approved by the Project Board.

14 Identify the missing words in the following sentence. 'Effective risk management is a prerequisite of the [?] principle.'	Correct Answer:
a) focus on products	
b) continued business justification	✓
c) manage by exception	
d) manage by stages	
Where to find the answer:	*15.5.2.2*
a) Rationale	The focus on products relates mainly to quality and planning.
b) Rationale	Correct. Without effective risk management there will be no confidence that the project will meet its objectives.
c) Rationale	Manage by exception relates mainly to the use of tolerances.
d) Rationale	Manage by stages relates to controls and planning.

15 How are principles characterized?	Correct Answer:
a) Are capable of tailoring	
b) Justify the project	
c) Apply to every project	✓
d) Their use is optional	
Where to find the answer:	*2.4*
a) Rationale	Processes and themes may be tailored, but not the principles.
b) Rationale	A project is justified by its Business Case.
c) Rationale	Correct. PRINCE2 principles are universal and can be applied to every project, no matter how small.
d) Rationale	Principles are not optional. They provide a framework of good practice.

16 Which is independent of the project management team?	Correct Answer:
a) Team Manager	
b) Project Assurance	
c) Project Support	
d) Quality assurance	✓
Where to find the answer:	*11.4 and 4.3.4*
a) Rationale	The Team Manager is part of the project management team.
b) Rationale	Project Assurance is part of a Project Board member's work, which may be delegated.
c) Rationale	Project Support is a project role.
d) Rationale	Correct. Quality assurance is a company-wide function responsible for all standards.

17 Which product defines the authorities for handling requests for change?	Correct Answer:
a) Communication Management Strategy	
b) Configuration Management Strategy	✓
c) Quality Management Strategy	
d) Risk Management Strategy	
Where to find the answer:	*16.2*
a) Rationale	This defines the content, frequency and medium of all project communications.
b) Rationale	Correct. This defines configuration management and change control procedures.
c) Rationale	Whilst quality can be affected by poor handling of requests for change, the Quality Management Strategy does not describe how to handle them.
d) Rationale	This only contains procedures for handling risks.

18 Which are basic business options? 1 Do nothing 2 Do less 3 Do something 4 Do the minimum	Correct Answer:
a) 1, 2, 3	
b) 1, 2, 4	
c) 1, 3, 4	✓
d) 2, 3, 4	
Where to find the answer:	*10.2.1*

a) Rationale	(4) 'Do the minimum' may be a business option.
b) Rationale	(3) 'Do something' includes all the positive business options.
c) Rationale	Correct. (2) 'Do less' is not a business option.
d) Rationale	(1) 'Do nothing' is always a business option that should be considered.

19 Which part of the Business Case balances costs against benefits over a period of time?	Correct Answer:
a) Expected benefits	
b) Business options	
c) Investment appraisal	✓
d) Expected dis-benefits	
Where to find the answer:	*10.2.4*
a) Rationale	This looks only at the benefits and does not include how much it will cost to obtain them.
b) Rationale	This lists the considered options on how to solve the business problem.
c) Rationale	Correct. This compares the project and maintenance costs against the benefit and savings value.
d) Rationale	This looks at the negative side of what the impact of the chosen option will bring.

20 Which role is responsible for realizing post-project benefits?	Correct Answer:
a) Executive	
b) Senior User	✓
c) Senior Supplier	
d) Project Manager	
Where to find the answer:	*10.2.6*
a) Rationale	The Executive is responsible for the Benefits Review Plan during the project, but not for checking how well the benefits have been achieved. Corporate management will manage post-project benefit reviews and expect the Senior User(s) to provide the evidence of realization.
b) Rationale	Correct. As the Senior User will be closest to those using the final product, this role is charged with checking on the achievement of the benefits.
c) Rationale	The Senior Supplier may be responsible for the supplier's Business Case, but not for the project's (customer's) Business Case.
d) Rationale	The Project Manager is responsible for reviewing any changes to the Business Case during the project and advising the Executive.

21 Which of the following statements is FALSE?	Correct Answer:
a) A company's quality management system becomes part of PRINCE2.	✓
b) The customer's quality expectations should be discovered in the Starting up a Project process.	
c) PRINCE2 may form part of a company's quality management system.	
d) The use of Team Plans is optional.	
Where to find the answer:	*14.3.1, 14.5.2 and 12.2.3*
a) Rationale	Correct. A company's quality management system should cover standards for all its work, not just those for project work.
b) Rationale	The customer's quality expectations are discovered as part of the activity of preparing the outline Business Case.
c) Rationale	PRINCE2 may form that part of a company's quality management system that covers project work.
d) Rationale	A project may not need Team Plans, but the Project and Stage Plans are mandatory.

22 Which is NOT one of the four tasks of the Product-based Planning technique?	Correct Answer:
a) Identifying dependencies	
b) Producing a Product Breakdown Structure	
c) Creating a Product Checklist	✓
d) Writing Product Descriptions of each significant product	
Where to find the answer:	*Appendix C*
a) Rationale	Dependencies are identified when creating a Product Flow Diagram, part of Product-based Planning.
b) Rationale	A Product Breakdown Structure is a hierarchical structure. Its creation is a task of Product-based Planning.
c) Rationale	Correct. Product Checklists are an optional, tabular presentation of a plan; part of planning, but not of Product-based Planning.
d) Rationale	Writing Product Descriptions is an integral part of Product-based Planning.

23 Which of the following reviews the benefits achieved by the project?	Correct Answer:
a) End Project Report	
b) Lessons Report	
c) Post-project review	✓
d) Quality review	
Where to find the answer:	*10.2.6*
a) Rationale	The End Project Report will identify any benefits achieved during the project cycle, but not those benefits that will be gained after the project closes.
b) Rationale	The Lessons Report does not cover benefit achievement and does not extend beyond the project cycle.
c) Rationale	Correct. The Benefits Review Plan sets out when and how the achievement of benefits is to be checked. The check is done in one or more post-project benefits reviews.
d) Rationale	A quality review only looks at the quality of a single product. There may be a quality review of the Benefits Review Plan, but it does not review benefit achievement.

24 Who is responsible for assessing and updating the Business Case at the end of a stage?	Correct Answer:
a) Senior User	
b) Executive	
c) Project Manager	✓
d) Project Assurance	
Where to find the answer:	*8.5*
a) Rationale	The Senior User, as a member of the Project Board, will review the updated Business Case as part of the decision on whether to authorize the next stage, but does not update it.
b) Rationale	The Executive is responsible for the Business Case during the project, but does not update it – only reviews it when presented by the Project Manager.
c) Rationale	Correct. The Project Manager does this as part of Managing a Stage Boundary for presentation to the Project Board.
d) Rationale	Project Assurance will verify any Business Case update by the Project Manager before its presentation to the Project Board.

25	Whose role is it to ensure that planned communications actually occur?	Correct Answer:
	a) Project Board	
	b) Project Manager	
	c) Project Assurance	✓
	d) Corporate management	
	Where to find the answer:	*B.7*
	a) Rationale	The Project Board has input into its own communication needs and those of stakeholders, but checking that these are met is part of Project Assurance.
	b) Rationale	The Project Manager is responsible for creating most of the communications, but not for ensuring that they occur.
	c) Rationale	Correct. Part of the Project Assurance role is to verify that what is planned in the Communication Management Strategy actually occurs.
	d) Rationale	Corporate management will have an input of their communication needs, but monitoring that they receive communications is part of Project Assurance.
26	In which process is the Quality Management Strategy created?	Correct Answer:
	a) Starting up a Project	
	b) Initiating a Project	✓
	c) Directing a Project	
	d) Managing a Stage Boundary	
	Where to find the answer:	*4.3.8*
	a) Rationale	No. The customer's quality expectations and acceptance criteria are established here, but they feed into initiation.
	b) Rationale	Correct. As part of the Project Initiation Documentation, the Quality Management Strategy (QMS) is created during initiation.
	c) Rationale	No. Directing a Project does not cover the creation of any of the strategies, but covers the review of the Project Initiation Documentation in which they are held.
	d) Rationale	No. The QMS is required to be in place before any stages are complete.
27	Which theme is central to the approach to quality?	Correct Answer:
	a) Manage by exception	
	b) Continued business justification	

c) Focus on products	✓
d) Defined roles and responsibilities	
Where to find the answer:	*14.1*
a) Rationale	No. An exception may be triggered by a threat to exceed quality tolerances, but this is only one of several reasons for an exception.
b) Rationale	No. This focuses on business justification for the project.
c) Rationale	Correct. Quality in PRINCE2 focuses on defining the quality of products in such things as writing Product Descriptions.
d) Rationale	No. Roles will have some quality responsibilities, but this theme covers all project responsibilities, not just quality.

28 Which product relates planned quality activities to those actually performed?	Correct Answer:
a) Quality Register	✓
b) Project Approach	
c) Quality Management Strategy	
d) Lessons Log	
Where to find the answer:	*14.3.8*
a) Rationale	Correct. The Quality Register contains an entry for every planned quality action, and is updated with the results of the inspection.
b) Rationale	No. The Project Approach describes how the provision of the selected business option will be done, and does not contain quality activities.
c) Rationale	No. The QMS defines the standards to be used and quality responsibilities, but not the detailed quality actions, which are not planned until planning each stage.
d) Rationale	No. The Lessons Log contains details of good or bad lessons found, and is not a record of planned quality actions.

29 Which action is NOT part of Accept a Work Package?	Correct Answer:
a) Agree tolerance margins	
b) Understand the reporting requirements	
c) Produce a Team Plan	
d) Monitor and control any Work Package risks	✓

Where to find the answer:	*7.3*
a) Rationale	This is part of the Team Manager's job when accepting a Work Package.
b) Rationale	This is part of the Team Manager's job when accepting a Work Package.
c) Rationale	This is part of the Team Manager's job before accepting a Work Package.
d) Rationale	Correct. Monitoring and control comes during the execution of a Work Package, after accepting it.

30 Comparing a product against defined criteria is an objective of what?	Correct Answer:
a) Work Package	
b) Investment appraisal	
c) Quality review	✓
d) Quality Register	
Where to find the answer:	*14.1*
a) Rationale	No. A Work Package is an agreement between the Project Manager and Team Manager, but the Product Description contains the quality method and criteria.
b) Rationale	No. This compares the cost of developing and maintaining a product against its expected benefit and savings value.
c) Rationale	Correct. In a quality review, the reviewers compare a product against the quality criteria held in the Product Description.
d) Rationale	No. The Quality Register contains a summary of the result of such a check.

31 Which process defines quality responsibilities?	Correct Answer:
a) Starting up a Project	
b) Initiating a Project	✓
c) Directing a Project	
d) Managing a Stage Boundary	
Where to find the answer:	*4.1*
a) Rationale	No. The customer's quality expectations are discovered here, but quality responsibilities are defined during initiation.
b) Rationale	Correct. The Quality Management Strategy is created during initiation.
c) Rationale	No. Directing a Project covers approval of the QMS as part of the Project Initiation Documentation, but not its creation.
d) Rationale	No. Quality responsibilities have to be known before any specialist stages are undertaken.

32 Who checks that a product is ready for its quality review?	Correct Answer:
a) Chair	✓
b) Administrator	
c) Presenter	
d) Reviewer	
Where to find the answer:	*Appendix D*
a) Rationale	Correct. Part of the role of quality review chair is to check that a product is ready when planned.
b) Rationale	No. The administrator may be delegated to do this by the chair, but it remains the chair's responsibility.
c) Rationale	No. The presenter is normally the person who has developed the product and therefore would not need to check whether it is ready for review.
d) Rationale	No. There may be a number of reviewers, whose job is to look at the draft product. They do not carry out the check to see if the product is ready.

33 Whose task is it to produce products consistent with their Product Descriptions?	Correct Answer:
a) Senior User	
b) Project Manager	
c) Team Manager	✓
d) Senior Supplier	
Where to find the answer:	*11.4.6*
a) Rationale	No. The Senior User should approve the Product Descriptions.
b) Rationale	No. The Project Manager has responsibility for all project work, but delegates the production of products to Team Managers.
c) Rationale	Correct. Products are created during the *Managing Product Delivery* process, which covers the Team Manager's work.
d) Rationale	No. The Senior Supplier is responsible for providing supplier resources and is accountable for the quality of all products delivered by supplier resources, but not at the detailed level of the actual production of them.

34 What provides the Business Case with planned costs?	Correct Answer:
a) Project Brief	
b) Project Plan	✓
c) Initiation Stage Plan	
d) Project Approach	
Where to find the answer:	*10.2*

a) Rationale	No. The Project Brief may not contain any costs. If it does, these are likely to be from an earlier feasibility study and too old or too vague to be used in the Business Case.
b) Rationale	Correct. The Project Plan contains the overall timeframe and the total cost of the project, which is why it must precede refinement of the Business Case.
c) Rationale	No. The initiation Stage Plan only contains the cost of initiation.
d) Rationale	No. The Project Approach does not contain costs, just a description of the way in which the selected business option will be provided.

---

35 What is identified first in the planning philosophy?	Correct Answer:
a) Dependencies	
b) Activities	
c) Products	✓
d) Resources	
Where to find the answer:	*12.3.2*
a) Rationale	No. Dependencies cannot be identified until there are products or activities that may have dependencies between them.
b) Rationale	No. In PRINCE2, activities are based on the products they are to produce or obtain.
c) Rationale	Correct. PRINCE2 planning is product based. After identifying the required products, their dependencies and then the activities required to produce the products are identified.
d) Rationale	No. Resources are not considered until the products, their activities, dependencies and effort required are known.

---

36 In which process is the means of reviewing benefits developed?	Correct Answer:
a) Closing a Project	
b) Initiating a Project	✓
c) Managing a Stage Boundary	
d) Starting up a Project	
Where to find the answer:	*4.9.2*
a) Rationale	No. The Benefits Review Plan is reviewed and possibly updated here, but it is created at the beginning of the project.

b) Rationale	Correct. The Quality Review Plan is created during initiation.
c) Rationale	No. The means of reviewing benefits may be reviewed here for any changes, but it is created during initiation.
d) Rationale	No. Work on this will not be done until the Project Board has authorized initiation.

37 In which process are previous lessons captured?	Correct Answer:
a) Starting up a Project	✓
b) Initiating a Project	
c) Managing a Stage Boundary	
d) Closing a Project	
Where to find the answer:	*3.2*
a) Rationale	Correct. The Lessons Reports of earlier projects are reviewed here and any that may apply to the current project copied to the Lessons Log.
b) Rationale	No. When creating all initiation products the Lessons Log is checked for any earlier lessons that may apply to them.
c) Rationale	No. There may be lessons from the current project that make it worthwhile to create a Lessons Report during this process, but lessons from earlier projects will have been captured during start-up.
d) Rationale	No. Lessons from the current project are written up in a Lessons Report for future projects.

38 Which product defines whether the solution will be developed in house?	Correct Answer:
a) Project mandate	
b) Project Approach	✓
c) Business Case	
d) Project Plan	
Where to find the answer:	*3.7*
a) Rationale	No. If the project is part of a programme, there may be information in the project mandate that makes it clear what the Project Approach has to be, but it is formally defined in the Project Approach.
b) Rationale	Correct. The purpose of the Project Approach is to identify the type of solution to the chosen business option, where an in-house development is one of the possibilities.
c) Rationale	No. The Business Case contains the selected option to resolve the business problem, such as falling sales, but does not say how that option is to be delivered.
d) Rationale	No. The Project Plan is based on the Project Approach.

39	Which process ensures that there is an interface with corporate management throughout the project?	Correct Answer:
	a) Starting up a Project	
	b) Managing a Stage Boundary	
	c) Directing a Project	✓
	d) Initiating a Project	
	Where to find the answer:	*5.5.4*
	a) Rationale	No. Corporate management will perform some of the work of starting up, such as appointing the Executive, but the process only covers pre-project work.
	b) Rationale	No. This will simply follow any requirements laid down in the Communication Management Strategy.
	c) Rationale	Correct. It is a responsibility of the Project Board to maintain communication links with corporate management. How and when this is done will be described in the Communication Management Strategy.
	d) Rationale	No. The Communication Management Strategy is created here, but the initiation process does not run throughout the project.
40	Which statement is NOT a purpose of the Closing a Project process?	Correct Answer:
	a) Confirm acceptance by the customer of the project's products.	
	b) Recognize that approved changes to the objectives in the Project Initiation Documentation have been achieved.	
	c) Recognize that the project has nothing more to contribute.	
	d) Place formal requirements on accepting and delivering project work.	✓
	Where to find the answer:	*9*
	a) Rationale	Acceptance of the project's products is formally done as part of Closing a Project.
	b) Rationale	Whether the project is being closed normally or prematurely, the Closing a Project process has to confirm to the Project Board that the project has nothing more to contribute and should therefore be closed.

c) Rationale	A major part of Closing a Project is to compare how the project performed in meeting the Project Initiation Documentation. Any changes made to the Project Initiation Documentation during the project must be included to make this comparison meaningful.
d) Rationale	Correct. This is far too late to define acceptance of project work. This must be done before delivery of any specialist products occurs.

41 Which is NOT a Project Board activity?	Correct Answer:
a) Authorize initiation	
b) Give ad hoc direction	
c) Authorize a Work Package	✓
d) Authorize the project	
Where to find the answer:	*6.3*
a) Rationale	This is the first decision made by the Project Board after Starting up a Project.
b) Rationale	This is an ongoing Project Board activity, reviewing Highlight Reports and any Exception Reports, and passing external information to the Project Manager.
c) Rationale	Correct. This is a Project Manager activity.
d) Rationale	This is the second decision of the Project Board after initiation.

42 What information is input to the Starting up a Project process?	Correct Answer:
a) Project mandate	✓
b) Project Initiation Documentation	
c) An appointed Executive	
d) Outline Business Case	
Where to find the answer:	*3*
a) Rationale	Correct. The project mandate is the trigger for this process.
b) Rationale	No. The Project Initiation Documentation is not created until the initiation stage.
c) Rationale	No. The Executive is appointed during Starting up a Project.
d) Rationale	No. The outline Business Case is created during Starting up a Project.

43 Which of the following is NOT input to the Project Board?	Correct Answer:
a) Informal request for advice	
b) Escalated Issue Report	

c) Project authorization notification	✓
d) Highlight Report	
Where to find the answer:	*Figure 5.3*
a) Rationale	Informal requests for advice from the Project Board can be made at any time by the Project Manager.
b) Rationale	This can be input to the Project Board for an opinion before the Project Manager raises an Exception Report.
c) Rationale	Correct. This is sent by the Project Board to corporate management as part of authorizing the project to tell them that the project has been started.
d) Rationale	This is sent to the Project Board by the Project Manager on a regular frequency.

44 Which document contains any follow-on action recommendations?	Correct Answer:
a) Lessons Report	
b) End Stage Report	
c) End Project Report	✓
d) Benefits Review Plan	
Where to find the answer:	*9.3.4*
a) Rationale	No. This forms a part of the End Project Report together with the follow-on action recommendations.
b) Rationale	No. Follow-on action recommendations are only assembled at project closure time.
c) Rationale	Correct. Follow-on action recommendations form part of the End Project Report, and are then separated and sent on to the team that will maintain the product.
d) Rationale	No. This is only a plan of when and how to measure benefit realization.

45 Which product captures user quality expectations and acceptance criteria?	Correct Answer:
a) Project Product Description	✓
b) Quality Management Strategy	
c) Project Brief	
d) Daily Log	
Where to find the answer:	*3.6.4*
a) Rationale	Correct. This documents the expectations and describes the standards and processes that will be needed in order to achieve that quality.

b) Rationale	No. This describes the standards and techniques that will be used, i.e. it follows on from the Project Product Description's statement of quality needs and says what the project has found to match those quality checking needs.
c) Rationale	No. This describes what the project needs to achieve, objectives, scope and constraints, but not the quality expectations.
d) Rationale	No. This is a diary of recorded events, actions and notes for the Project Manager or Team Manager.

---

46 Which of the following are done in the Starting up a Project process? 1 Set up the project management team. 2 Develop the project mandate into the Project Brief. 3 Create the Issue Register. 4 Devise the Project Approach.	Correct Answer:
a) 1, 2, 3	
b) 1, 2, 4	✓
c) 1, 3, 4	
d) 2, 3, 4	
Where to find the answer:	*3 and 4.3.4*
a) Rationale	(4) The Project Approach is devised during Starting up a Project.
b) Rationale	Correct. (3) The Issue Register is not created until the initiation process.
c) Rationale	(2) The project mandate is enhanced to become the Project Brief during the Starting up a Project process.
d) Rationale	(1) The project management team is devised and appointed during Starting up a Project.

---

47 An example of Work Package [?] might be: 'I need this by Thursday close of work, but by Friday lunchtime at the latest.'	Correct Answer:
a) approval requirements	
b) constraints	
c) tolerance	✓
d) reporting and problem handling	
Where to find the answer:	*6.3.1*
a) Rationale	No. Approval requirements say who has to approve the completed products of the Work Package and how.

b) Rationale	No. These are constraints on the work, such as people to be involved or rules to be followed.
c) Rationale	Correct. Tolerance gives a range, in this case of time, within which the delivery is acceptable.
d) Rationale	No. This covers any need for Checkpoint Reports or what the Team Manager has to do if a problem occurs, e.g. raise an issue to the Project Manager.

---

48 The need for configuration management is described in which theme?	Correct Answer:
a) Quality	
b) Plans	
c) Progress	
d) Change	✓
Where to find the answer:	*16*
a) Rationale	No. Quality will suffer without configuration management, but it is not described here.
b) Rationale	No. Plans need to be configuration managed, but how this is to be done is not described here.
c) Rationale	No. Progress covers tolerances, monitoring and reporting.
d) Rationale	Correct. This theme covers configuration management and change control.

---

49 Which are purposes of a summary risk profile? 1 Shows the risk owners 2 Snapshot of the risk environment 3 Shows risk trends 4 Identifies risks beyond the risk appetite	Correct Answer:
a) 1, 2, 3	
b) 1, 2, 4	
c) 1, 3, 4	
d) 2, 3, 4	✓
Where to find the answer:	*15.9*
a) Rationale	(4) The risk tolerance line can be drawn on the profile to identify risks that would be beyond it.
b) Rationale	(3) A combination of several snapshots of the risk profile over a period of time would reveal any risk trends.
c) Rationale	(2) A summary risk profile is a snapshot of risk probability and impact at one moment in time.
d) Rationale	Correct. (1) A summary risk profile does not show risk owners.

50 In which process is the Business Case reviewed and updated? — Correct Answer:

a) Controlling a Stage
b) Managing Product Delivery
c) Managing a Stage Boundary ✓
d) Directing a Project

Where to find the answer: *8.5*

a) Rationale — Controlling a Stage checks the Business Case for impact of new risks or issues, but does not update it.

b) Rationale — The Managing Product Delivery process has nothing to do with the Business Case.

c) Rationale — Correct. The Business Case is updated against the Project Plan updated with actuals from the current stage and the next Stage Plan, plus any issues or risks that may affect it.

d) Rationale — Directing a Project will be shown the updated Business Case, but does not cover its updating.

51 Which is NOT part of an unambiguous expression of a risk? — Correct Answer:

a) Probability ✓
b) Cause
c) Effect
d) Event

Where to find the answer: *15.5.1*

a) Rationale — Correct. Probability is part of the analysis of a risk, once it has been identified.

b) Rationale — Cause is part of a risk statement, e.g. 'because of the heavy rain ...'.

c) Rationale — Effect is the impact of the risk, e.g. 'leading to closure of the golf course'.

d) Rationale — Event is the actual risk, e.g. 'the greens may be under water'.

52 What does an early-warning indicator provide? — Correct Answer:

a) Proximity of a risk
b) A project objective could be at risk ✓
c) An opportunity is about to present itself
d) Date of a stage end approaching

Where to find the answer: *15.5.1 and A.28*

a) Rationale	No. Proximity is an assessment of how soon a risk might occur – if it is going to occur. Early-warning indicators would be monitored to give an estimate of proximity.
b) Rationale	Correct. An early-warning indicator is a piece of information that is monitored because it may reveal that one or more of the project's objectives could be at risk. For example, if you are worried that you might catch a cold, your temperature would be an early-warning indicator.
c) Rationale	No. It is concerned with risks, not tolerances.
d) Rationale	No. Early-warning indicators are like barometers, and are not dates.

53 What does a risk budget cover?	Correct Answer:
a) Cost of risks carried over to follow-on action recommendations	
b) Off-specification costs	
c) Costs of administering risk management	
d) Cost of fallback plans	✓
Where to find the answer:	*15.10*
a) Rationale	No. A risk budget is for use within a project, not post-project.
b) Rationale	No. An off-specification is not a risk – it is a known failure to meet some part of the specification or plan.
c) Rationale	No. The cost of risk administration should be built into a plan, whereas a risk budget is only spent if a fallback plan has to be used.
d) Rationale	Correct. Fallback plans are prepared in case a known risk occurs, and they require a risk budget.

54 Which document contains the Change Control procedure?	Correct Answer:
a) Quality Management Strategy	
b) Configuration Management Strategy	✓
c) Risk Management Strategy	
d) Communication Management Strategy	
Where to find the answer:	*16.4*
a) Rationale	No. The QMS has nothing to do with change control or configuration management.
b) Rationale	Correct. Configuration management is closely linked with change control and both are covered in the Configuration Management Strategy.

c) Rationale	No. Risk management has nothing to do with change control or configuration.
d) Rationale	No. The Communication Management Strategy defines who needs what information at what frequency and who should supply it. It does not cover change control.

55 What is product status accounting?	Correct Answer:
a) Recording Work Package progress from a review of timesheets and the Team Plan.	
b) An audit comparing actual product status with that shown in the Configuration Item Records.	
c) Reporting on the current and historical state of products.	✓
d) A summary of the state of the Quality Register at the end of a stage.	
Where to find the answer:	*16.5.5*
a) Rationale	This is done in the activity Review the Work Package Status and looks at information from the Team Manager, not from the configuration library.
b) Rationale	This is a configuration audit, not a Product Status Account.
c) Rationale	Correct. The Project Manager can call for a Product Status Account at any time to view the current state of products or their history.
d) Rationale	This would form part of the End Stage Report, not a Product Status Account.

56 What is the second step in an Issue and Change Control procedure?	Correct Answer:
a) Decide	
b) Capture	
c) Propose	
d) Examine	✓
Where to find the answer:	*16.4 and 16.4.2*
a) Rationale	This follows the proposal step.
b) Rationale	This is the first step.
c) Rationale	This step follows the examination.
d) Rationale	Correct. This is the second step following capture.

57 Which principle is NOT supported by the Progress theme?	Correct Answer:
a) Manage by exception	
b) Continued business justification	
c) Tailoring PRINCE2	✓
d) Manage by stages	
Where to find the answer:	*13.1*
a) Rationale	Management by exception forms a key part of the Progress theme, being linked to the use of tolerances.
b) Rationale	Part of Progress is monitoring, and one of the things monitored is the Business Case at such progress points as end stage assessments.
c) Rationale	Correct. The Progress theme does not describe how controls can be modified for different implementations of the PRINCE2 method.
d) Rationale	The breakdown of a project into stages is a central part of Progress, where the Project Board reviews the continued business justification.

58 Who sets project tolerances?	Correct Answer:
a) Corporate management	✓
b) Project Board	
c) Project Manager	
d) Executive	
Where to find the answer:	*13.3.2*
a) Rationale	Correct. This should be part of a project mandate, but the Executive may have to find out what they are by questioning the Project Board during Starting up a Project.
b) Rationale	No. The Project Board sets stage tolerances within the project tolerances given to them by corporate management.
c) Rationale	No. The Project Manager receives stage tolerances from the Project Board and sets Work Package tolerances for a Team Manager.
d) Rationale	No. The Executive has to find out from corporate management what the project tolerances are.

59 Why might dividing a project into a small number of lengthy stages be a problem?	Correct Answer:
a) Makes project planning more difficult	
b) Increases project management administration costs	

c) Reduces the level of Project Board control	✓
d) Reduces the amount of risk monitoring	
Where to find the answer:	*13.2.3 and 13.2.4*
a) Rationale	The Project Plan may show where the stage boundaries occur, but they do not affect the difficulty of preparing it.
b) Rationale	A smaller number of controls for the Project Board may mean problems are seen later than with more stage breaks, but having fewer stages does not automatically increase administration costs. In fact, fewer stage ends may mean lower administration costs.
c) Rationale	Correct. A major Project Board control is end stage assessment, so longer but fewer stages would mean fewer control points for it.
d) Rationale	Risks are monitored throughout the stages, not just at end stage assessment times.

60 Which is an event-driven control?	Correct Answer:
a) Highlight Report	
b) Checkpoint Report	
c) End Stage Report	✓
d) Review Work Package Status	
Where to find the answer:	*13.5*
a) Rationale	Highlight Reports are produced at a regular frequency, so is time-driven.
b) Rationale	Checkpoint Reports are produced at a frequency defined in a Work Package, so is another time-driven control.
c) Rationale	Correct. The end of a stage triggers this.
d) Rationale	No actual frequency is laid down for this activity, but it is a regular review, normally done weekly, and is not triggered by a specific event.

61 Which product is NOT reviewed when reviewing Work Package status?	Correct Answer:
a) Checkpoint Report	
b) Project Plan	✓
c) Team Plan	
d) Quality Register	
Where to find the answer:	*6.4*

a) Rationale	This is reviewed.
b) Rationale	Correct. The activity looks at Checkpoint Reports, Team Plans, the registers and the Configuration Item Records for the products involved.
c) Rationale	This is reviewed.
d) Rationale	This is reviewed.

---

62 Where are suitable reviewers first identified for a quality review?	Correct Answer:
a) Quality Management Strategy	
b) Project Plan	
c) Quality review preparation step	
d) Stage Plan	✓
Where to find the answer:	*8.3.4*
a) Rationale	The QMS identifies standards, quality techniques and quality responsibilities at a high level, but not for individual quality checks.
b) Rationale	The Project Plan does not go down to the level of detail where individual quality checks are identified.
c) Rationale	The quality review preparation step is where reviewers are given the product to prepare their question lists.
d) Rationale	Correct. The Project Manager should identify at least the chair of each quality review and possibly some reviewers when planning a stage.

---

63 Which of the following statements are TRUE? 1 The Executive role is responsible for the business interests of the customer and supplier. 2 There will always be two Business Cases in customer/supplier situations. 3 The customer and supplier may be part of the same corporate body or may be independent of each other. 4 A project's Business Case means the customer's Business Case.	Correct Answer:
a) 1, 2, 3	
b) 1, 2, 4	
c) 1, 3, 4	
d) 2, 3, 4	✓

Where to find the answer:	*10.1 and 10.3*
a) Rationale	(4) A project concentrates on the customer's Business Case.
b) Rationale	(3) Supplier resources may come from the customer's company or be from third party suppliers.
c) Rationale	(2) The customer has a Business Case to define if the project will bring sufficient benefits to warrant the costs. The supplier has a Business Case to see if the commitment of resources will bring a profit.
d) Rationale	Correct. (1) The Executive is only responsible for the customer's Business Case.

---

64 Which product reviews a project's actual achievements against the Project Initiation Documentation?	Correct Answer:
a) Lessons Report	
b) Follow-on action recommendations	
c) End Project Report	✓
d) Benefits Review Plan	
Where to find the answer:	*9.6*
a) Rationale	The Lessons Report provides any useful information on what went well and what went badly in terms of such things as the project management method and the techniques used.
b) Rationale	Follow-on action recommendations are items that are still outstanding at the close of the project and need to be passed to those who will maintain the product.
c) Rationale	Correct. The End Project Report describes how well the project met the requirements of the Project Initiation Documentation, not how successful the final product is at achieving its expected benefits.
d) Rationale	The Benefits Review Plan describes when and how achievement of the expected benefits can be measured.

---

65 Which product records a forecast failure to meet a requirement?	Correct Answer:
a) Risk Register	
b) Concession	
c) Highlight Report	
d) Off-specification	✓
Where to find the answer:	*16.4.1*
a) Rationale	A risk is something that might happen. A forecast failure that it appears will happen and needs action now.

b) Rationale — A concession is an acceptance by the Project Board of an off-specification.

c) Rationale — A Highlight Report is a regular progress report from the Project Manager to the Project Board.

d) Rationale — Correct. This records some failure or forecast failure to meet either part of the product's specification or part of the Project Initiation Documentation, such as the Project Plan.

---

66 What product would the Project Manager call for when reviewing stage status to check on a phased handover of products?

Correct Answer:

a) Stage Plan
b) Quality Register
c) Product Status Account ✓
d) Risk Register

Where to find the answer: *6.6.4*

a) Rationale — This would give a general indication that work on the products involved has been completed, but more precise information is needed.

b) Rationale — The Quality Register would show that any checks on the products have been completed, but there may be other work to assemble the package that would not be shown here.

c) Rationale — Correct. A Product Status Account would confirm whether the relevant products have been tested and accepted.

d) Rationale — The Risk Register might show whether there is a risk open about a product that is to be part of the phased handover, but the fact that it is complete and has been accepted is more significant.

---

67 Who should prepare the outline Business Case?

Correct Answer:

a) Senior User
b) Executive ✓
c) Project Manager
d) Corporate management

Where to find the answer: *3.6.4*

a) Rationale — The Senior User will be asked to contribute and will be responsible after the project to verify that the benefits were achieved, but he/she does not produce the outline.

b) Rationale — Correct. The Executive checks to see if information for the outline Business Case was included in the project mandate, otherwise he/she has to produce it during Starting up a Project.

c) Rationale	The Project Manager may be consulted for advice on what is required, but is not responsible.
d) Rationale	Corporate management may have included the relevant information in the project mandate, but often do not.

68 If an issue can be dealt with informally, where should a note of it be made?	Correct Answer:
a) Issue Register	
b) Daily Log	✓
c) Lessons Log	
d) Risk Register	
Where to find the answer:	*16.4.1*
a) Rationale	Entry here means that the issue is being dealt with formally.
b) Rationale	Correct. This avoids the need for document completion and administrative work, whilst ensuring that a record is kept.
c) Rationale	This records after the event anything that might be useful in future, but is not used to trigger any action to resolve that particular issue.
d) Rationale	An entry here would mean that the issue was not only being dealt with formally, but had been assessed to be a risk.

69 Which of these statements is FALSE?	Correct Answer:
a) The Project Board approves Team Plans.	✓
b) The Project Board approves a stage Exception Plan.	
c) A Stage Plan is required for each stage in the Project Plan.	
d) The Project Plan is an overview of the total project.	
Where to find the answer:	*6.3.4*
a) Rationale	Correct. The Project Manager approves Team Plans.
b) Rationale	Only the Project Board can approve a stage Exception Plan.
c) Rationale	True. You need a Stage Plan, however simple, for initiation. In small projects it may be possible to physically add the content of, say, the single specialist stage to the Project Plan, but they are still separate plans.
d) Rationale	The Project Plan should not have too much detail to prevent the Project Board seeing the major product deliveries and timings.

70 When would an Exception Report be required?	Correct Answer:
a) Whenever a new risk is identified	
b) When a stakeholder raises a complaint	
c) When a request for change or off-specification is received	
d) When a stage is forecast to deviate outside its tolerance bounds	✓
Where to find the answer:	*16.4.4*
a) Rationale	The Project Board should not be involved in every small detail. The risk may be unlikely to occur or a response can be found to take care of it without asking for a Project Board decision.
b) Rationale	A complaint may be many things that are not connected with a deviation beyond tolerances and can be dealt with in other ways.
c) Rationale	It is too early to know. Without analysis it is not known on receipt of an issue whether it will cause an exception situation.
d) Rationale	Correct. The Project Board must be informed and an Exception Report defines the information it needs.

71 What is the final step in risk management?	Correct Answer:
a) Appoint a risk owner	
b) Decide	
c) Communicate	✓
d) Implement	
Where to find the answer:	*Figure 15.1 and 15.8*
a) Rationale	This is part of the implementation.
b) Rationale	The decision has to be followed by implementation.
c) Rationale	Correct. Having reviewed the risk and decided what action to take, it is necessary to inform the relevant people.
d) Rationale	You implement the decision and then communicate what has been done.

72 When tailoring PRINCE2 for a project, which principles can be omitted?	Correct Answer:
a) None	✓
b) All except continued business justification	

c) Manage by stages
d) Manage by exception

Where to find the answer:	*17.1.1*
a) Rationale	Correct. The principles are universal in that they apply to every project.
b) Rationale	Every project should be justified.
c) Rationale	Every PRINCE2 project has at least two stages, the first being initiation, however short.
d) Rationale	Any project should have tolerances set, and therefore the principle of manage by exception is always required.

---

73 In tailoring a project within a programme environment, why might responsibility for the Benefits Review Plan be removed from the Executive's role? — Correct Answer:

a) Given to the Senior User
b) No project benefits to be reviewed
c) Moved to Project Assurance
d) A programme responsibility ✓

Where to find the answer:	*10.2.6*
a) Rationale	The Senior User is responsible for the work of checking benefit achievement, but the Executive is responsible for the plan.
b) Rationale	Without offering any benefits the project should not have started.
c) Rationale	Project Assurance only monitors on behalf of the Project Board, but does not have responsibility for producing any product other than, possibly, a configuration audit.
d) Rationale	Correct. The project may simply be contributing to the programme's benefits and may not have its own Benefits Review Plan.

---

74 Which project role would sit on the programme board? — Correct Answer:

a) None
b) Senior User
c) Executive ✓
d) Quality assurance

Where to find the answer:	*17.1.3*
a) Rationale	Communication and decisions at programme level affect the projects and should have representation.

b) Rationale	The Executive is the person ultimately responsible for a project and will be a single person, whereas the Senior User role may be shared, resulting in an over-large group at programme level.
c) Rationale	Correct. The Executives of the various projects of a programme would sit on the programme board to ensure they all contribute to the same objectives and strategy.
d) Rationale	Quality assurance has a company-wide role, but is not a programme or project decision-maker.

75 Which theme is most affected when used in simple projects?	Correct Answer:
a) Business Case	
b) Organization	✓
c) Risk	
d) Change	
Where to find the answer:	*17.1.3*
a) Rationale	The Business Case may be simpler, but will not be greatly affected.
b) Rationale	Correct. Several roles may be combined in simple projects.
c) Rationale	Risk will still be present in simple projects.
d) Rationale	Even the simplest of projects may be subject to change. Failure to control changes will result in loss of control of the project.

Index